God Uses Cracked Pots

Patsy Clairmont

Guideposts®

CARMEL • NEW YORK 10512

GOD USES CRACKED POTS

Editor: Janet Kobobel

Designer: Timothy Jones

Cover illustrator: Greg MacNair

Printed in the United States of America

To the men in my life

My husband

Les, without your constant nudging and your willingness to help me carve out time in my jammed schedule and your vigilance to guard that time, this book would not have been completed. Your confidence in this project was a constant source of encouragement. Thank you, too, for adding your spunky and mischievous humor to my life, our marriage and our home.

Our sons

Marty and Jason, I take delight in both of you. Thank you for all the ways you lace my life with laughter and fill my heart with joy.

Contents

Acknowledgments

Thanks to all of you who supported this effort through your friendship and words of encouragement. I feel fortunate to have so many cheerleaders in my life.

I have often been aware of my mom's (Rebecca McEuen) prayers and am grateful for her love for Him and for me.

A big thank you to the Pauls for the loan of paradise during the countdown on my manuscript.

Thank you, Bob and Sarah, for helping to "prop" me up.

Mary-Lou, thanks for your willingness to put the manuscript into the computer. What a tedious task, which you did with such grace.

Ginny, your calls and notes of love and confidence were often the gentle nudge I needed.

I had tried to write previous to this book without success. I believe the key that unlocked my words was two-fold: the Lord's timing and my gifted editor, Janet Kobobel.

Janet, your expertise and wonderful gift of encouragement helped me to realize a lifetime dream. Thank you for being both firm and funny and knowing when to do which. Thank you for your editorial nurturing, for laughing at my stories and at times being my counselor as well as my friend.

For the past ten years, I have had the life- and ministry-expanding opportunity to work and travel with Florence Littauer on her C.L.A.S.S. staff. I would be amiss if I did not say a neon-sign thank-you to Florence for believing in me and for years of guidance.

Thanks also to Edith, Lana, Barbara, Jan, Lauren, Betty, Nancy, Joyce, Will, Rose, Jo Ann and Carol for listening and laughing.

All We, Like Cracked Pots

Would you say you are a person given to bursts of babble? Do you just *love* to talk?

Imagine your family's reaction if you suddenly became a quiet person. Perhaps they would say, "Praise the Lord; He lives!" Because they know it would take the power of God to make that adjustment in your personality.

Likewise those of you who are quiet and sweet...oh, so *sweet*. If you were to speak up loud and clear, your family might say, "Praise the Lord; He lives, and so does she!" They have been waiting to hear from you.

Such changes are examples of God working in our cracked lives. Picture an empty pitcher with a network of cracks down the front. Now imagine that pitcher filled with light and a lid put on the top. Where does the light shine through? The cracks.

That is the same way the Lord's light shines through our lives. Not so much by what we do well naturally, but by what He must do in us supernaturally for it to be so. Like going from talkative to tranquil and from cringing to courageous.

The stories in this book will validate that I am a cracked pot in need of divine repair. My prayer for myself is that His light shines through my cracks. And my prayer for you is that within these pages you will find reprieve from life's pressures, which add stress to your "pot," and that you might continue to shine brightly for Him.

Lookin' Good

I remember the day well. It was one of those times when everything goes right. I took a shower and fixed my hair. It went just the way I wanted it to, as it so seldom does. I pulled on my new pink sweater, giving me added color, since I need all the help I can get. I pulled on my gray slacks and my taupe heels.

I checked the mirror and thought, *Lookin' good!*

Since it was a cool Michigan day, I slipped on my gray trench coat with pink on the lapels. I was color-coded from head to toe.

When I arrived in downtown Brighton, where I intended to take care of some errands, I was surprised to find heavy traffic. Brighton is a small town, but it has a large health food store. Usually, I can park right in front and run in.

But today business was so brisk I had to park two blocks away. When your attitude is right, and it's a great day, however, inconveniences and interruptions are no big deal.

I thought, *I'll just bounce down the street in time to the sunshine.*

3

I got out of the car, bounced down the street, crossed the road and entered the store.

As I headed toward the back of the store, I caught my reflection in the glass doors of the refrigeration system. It reaffirmed I was lookin' good. While enjoying my mirrored self, I noticed something was following me. I turned and realized it was my panty hose!

I remembered the night before when I had done a little Wonder Woman act and taken panty hose and slacks off in one fell swoop. This morning I put on new panty hose and must have pushed the old hose through when I pulled on my slacks.

I believe they made their emergence as I bounced down the street in time to the sunshine. I remembered the truck driver who stopped his truck to let me cross. As I looked up, he was laughing, and I thought, *Oh, look! The whole world is happy today.*

So I waved. Little did I realize how much I was waving.

I assumed I had reached some amount of maturity by this time in my life, but I can honestly say that when I looked back and saw that . . . that . . . dangling participle, the thought that crossed my mind was *I am going to die!*

I knew they were my panty hose because the right foot was securely wrapped around my right ankle. I knew it was secure because I tried to shake the thing off and pretend I had picked it up in the street.

It's amazing to me that we gals buy these things in flat little packages, we wear them once, and they grow. Now I had a mammoth handful of panty hose and no place to pitch them. The shelves were crowded with groceries, and my purse was too small and full, so I stuffed them in my coat pocket. They became a protruding hump on my right hip.

I decided to never leave that store. I knew all the store owners in town, and I figured that by now they would have all their employees at the windows waiting for a return parade.

I glanced cautiously around the store and noticed it was Senior Citizens' Day. They were having their blood pressures read, so I got in line to avoid having to leave the store.

The bad news was no one noticed I didn't belong in line. The good news was I had an elevated blood pressure reading. Usually nurses take mine and say, "I'm sorry but you died two days ago." Today I registered well up the scale.

Finally I realized I'd have to leave. I slipped out the door, down the street, into my car and off for home.

All the way home I said, "I'll never tell anyone I did this, I'll never tell anyone I did this, I'LL NEVER TELL ANYONE I DID THIS!"

I made it home and got out of the car. My husband was in the yard raking.

I screamed, "Do you know what I did?!"

He was so proud to know his wife had gone through town dragging her underwear. I told him I thought we should move—to another state— in the night. He thought that was extreme and suggested instead that for a while I could walk ten feet behind him. After thinking that through, we decided it should be ten feet in front of him so he could check me out.

If you have ever done anything to embarrass yourself, you know that the more you try not to think about it, the more it comes to you in living color. As I walked through my house, the replay of what I did came to me again and again.

At last I cried out to the Lord, "You take ashes and create beauty, but can You do anything with panty hose?"

Almost immediately I realized that I had dragged a lot worse things through my life than panty hose. I dragged guilt, anger, fear and shame. I was reminded by the Lord that those were far more unattractive and distracting than my hose, for they prevented others from seeing His presence and His power in my life. I needed to resolve the pain in my past that I might live more fully today and look forward to my tomorrows.

Excuse me, but what is that you're dragging?

Guest Appearance

I had just finished doing a seminar with speaker Florence Littauer in Texas. She had made a special point of reminding the audience, "Be alert to the people the Lord places around you, especially on airplanes."

This was a new thought for me. When I get on an airplane, I have two people in mind—the pilot and me. I am in deep prayer for both of us.

As I headed for the airport, I reminded myself to be alert.

The first leg of my flight was uneventful. Then we changed planes in Chicago, and I noticed an airline attendant helping to board an older woman in a wheelchair.

When my row was called, I found I was seated in front of the older woman. We each had an empty seat next to us. A few minutes later a young couple came down the aisle. They stopped at the row of the older woman.

The young woman looked at her ticket, looked at the number on the overhead panel, then leaned into the woman and said with contempt,

"You're in my seat."

I turned around at this abruptness and saw the older lady shake her head and shrug her shoulders in an attempt to say, "I don't understand." When the woman shrugged, the younger gal announced for all to hear, "You're in my seat!"

I tried to defuse the situation by saying, "Excuse me, but I don't think she speaks English."

The young woman turned on me and hissed, "I don't care what she speaks, I want her out of my seat." With that she called, "Stewardess."

Good, let the airlines handle her, I thought. I didn't want to deal with this traveling time bomb.

Usually flight personnel are trained to handle people problems. I think this attendant missed that class. She was almost as crude as the tactless traveler.

She looked down at the confused woman and demanded, "Let me see your tickets."

The older passenger realized this must be serious when she saw the attendant's uniform. Not understanding what they wanted, she gave her entire purse to the stewardess.

After rifling through her belongings, the flight gal found the ticket that verified the woman was in the wrong seat.

"Excuse me," I called to the attendant, "did you realize they boarded her in a wheelchair?"

"Really?" she whined, obviously annoyed. "This is going to make it harder to move her."

"Listen, why don't I move back there with her, and this ... this ... this couple can sit here," I said, pointing to my seat and the empty one beside me.

As I changed rows and took my new seat, I wanted this woman to know that all was well. I looked at her and smiled. She didn't respond.

Then I noticed she didn't have her seat belt on. I decided to help. It was a bigger job than I thought. I extended that belt as far as it would go, and it was prayer that closed it.

With that accomplished, I put on my belt, leaned back and closed my eyes. As the plane was taxiing for takeoff, I felt a hand on my hand. I turned and looked.

The older woman leaned over to me and slowly spoke the first words she had said, "You . . . first . . . Amer-i-can . . . be nice . . . to me."

Then taking her bracelet off her wrist, she pressed it into my hand and said, "I give you, you keep . . . okay?"

For a moment I couldn't respond. Then I swallowed the growing lump in my throat, slipped on the friendship bracelet and patted her hand. Her eyes filled with tears. My heart filled with gratitude.

Any room in your schedule for an unexpected guest?

Wiped Out

Mom, Mom, come quick! You've got to see what's on TV," Jason insisted.

Certain it would be something to make housework easier, I raced to the living room. Much to my surprise, the young girl on the screen leaned forward and announced, "I've got a zit right here," pointing to her nose. "But it's okay," she encouraged, "because I have a stick of Erase."

Confused (and unamused) I stared at Jason, who sheepishly confessed, "Well, I just thought maybe you could use it on those . . . those . . . wrinkles." He gestured toward my well-deserved grooves of maturity.

"These are not wrinkles," I stated clearly.

Jason surveyed my face again, as if he was reading a well-worn map. "They look just like wrin—" he stammered, losing confidence as I moved toward him.

"Jason," I interrupted, "this is depth! The good Lord has just entrusted some of us with more depth than others."

I marched off, feeling insulted or at least slightly defaced. I thought about the girl on TV and remembered her remedy. I began to picture a stick of Erase, in fact a great big stick. Then I mentally erased Jason.

That was such fun I began to think of others who had said or done something I didn't appreciate. I thought of our eldest son, Marty.

Each day I would meet him at the door with a melodic greeting as he returned from work. His typical response was to grunt. I erased him.

Then my husband came to mind. Now he never actually says it, but at times his attitude seems to shout, "Is this all you've done today?" Erase.

I was really getting into this game. I thought of other family members, neighbors, checkout clerks, co-workers, bank tellers, beauticians . . .

Now, the only drawback to this mental game was that everyone at one time or another had said or done something I didn't appreciate. By the time I erased them, it left me all alone. Somehow I didn't like the company.

I began to think of some things I've said or done I wished I could erase—like the last hasty word I felt "led" to say, or my unloving attitude with the clerk who was too slow, or the years I lost to agoraphobia, house-bound in fear. This game wasn't much fun after all.

Then I remembered that God provided a stick of Erase—a permanent eraser, the shed blood of Jesus. Our sins and iniquities He remembers no more—erase!

What a relief. What a release.

Pardon me, is that a stick of erase in your ha—

Hair-Raising

I can hardly believe that French braids are popular again. I was certain that type of braiding was leftover torture tactics from World War II and had worn out its welcome.

I certainly didn't welcome the times when Mom would call me into the living room where she had the weapons of warfare laid out before her: a brush and comb, a glass of water to help catch any stray ends, rubber bands and some ribbons. Sounds harmless enough . . . unless you're on the receiving end.

When Mom would plait my hair, it stayed in for a week. Those braids would not have dared move once she had placed them, nor did I while the braiding procedure was taking place.

I knew, from past experience, that the brush had a duo purpose of smoothing or rapping. She used quick staccato raps as reminders not to move. It worked.

The constant surprised look on my face in childhood pictures was actually caused by my coiffure. To implement this technique, Mom would first firmly grip three hanks of hair at the top of my head. It was imperative at this point to place one's knee in the middle of the braidee's back to secure one's hair hold, then pull until the victim's eyebrows arc and touch the first notch in the design of the braid. Come to think of it, I saw Hulk Hogan use that same tactic on one of his opponents . . . and win!

My mom always won, too. When she finished, my hair and I were enmeshed. Once Mom secured the lacing of hair and scalp with a rubber band, she then finished off the end with a ribbon, disguising this maiming updo with an innocent look.

People always commented on what a high forehead I had as a child. Actually that was my neck. It had been pulled up over my face in Mother's zeal to make the braids stay in. Had I continued to wear them that might not have mattered, but when the braids were finally released, my neck slid back down to my shoulders, leaving my face looking like a venetian blind.

The braiding did keep me from falling asleep in school. My lids were pulled so taut there wasn't enough skin left to cover my eyes.

Braids gave the boys a definite advantage, serving as handles to tug and jerk. Any girl with French braids would become hostile with the behind-the-back attack. Not only was it disconcerting, but we also knew if one of those braids was dislodged, our moms would redo the process.

Les and I have sons, but I've always wondered if we had had a daughter, would I have passed on this part of my heritage?

What painful part of your past are you passing on?

Forget It

I am the type of person who can walk from one room to another and not know why I've gone there. I know I had a reason when I began my trek, but I lost it on the way. Sometimes I try backing up in hopes it might come to me.

My family can usually tell this is the problem by the bewildered look on my face. Walking in reverse also seems to be a giveaway. Sometimes they try to help and other times they just let me wander aimlessly, figuring I'll wise up or wear out.

I try to blame this forgetfulness on age. But those who have known me for years remind me that my wires have never all been touching, although turning forty has seemed to loosen a few more.

I read in an article that after we turn forty, one thousand brain cells die each day. But according to the writer, it doesn't matter because we have millions . . . or was that billions, anyway lots of them. My problem is the cells I've been losing were filled with valuable information I meant to retain—like where I'm going, how old I am, the names of family members, etc.

Names. Isn't it embarrassing when you know you know but you draw a blank? I realize that our names are important to us, and we don't want to be forgotten. That's why I think name tags should be mandatory. They should be pinned on us at birth and removed after the funeral. Think of all the awkward moments that could alleviate.

The guy, oh, what's his name, who sang "I Left My Heart in San Francisco" doesn't know how lucky he is. I left my bifocals in Indiana, my alarm clock in Ohio, my Bible on an airplane heading for Texas, my slip in Colorado, and heaven only knows where my watch is . . . probably with my sunglasses and keys.

Have you ever been digging through a drawer when all of a sudden you realize you don't know what you're looking for? If anyone is watching me, I just keep digging. I've found a lot of lost items that way.

It's disconcerting for me to dial the phone, and by the time the call connects, to find my mind has disconnected—I've forgotten whom I'm calling. Sometimes I hang up until I remember. Other times I listen in hopes I'll recognize the voice. Occasionally I've been brave and confessed to the anonymous party that I can't remember whom I dialed and hope they'll claim me.

The point I'm trying to make is . . . is . . .

Get the Kid

Mommy, Mommy, Mommy, Mommy, Mommy, Mommy." Marty's persistence matched his rhythmic tugging on my blouse's hem.

I felt like screaming. In fact, I did.

To a little guy my response was probably similar to the release of Mt. St. Helens as I erupted, "What?!"

Why a mother waits so long to respond and allows the repetition to light her lava is beyond me. I only know that after spewing all over him I felt terrible . . . and so did he.

Where did all this volcanic anger come from? I seemed to always be upset at something or someone. Often my reactions were greater than the situation called for. I realized that Marty's little-child ways didn't deserve such strong responses.

Have you ever tried making things right when you know you're wrong but don't know how to admit it or quit it? That was often my frustration with Marty.

I'd send him to his room, leaving me with the realization that his punishment was greater than his crime. Then I'd try to make up by slipping him a Twinkie or playing a game with him. I soon found that Twinkies don't build good bridges of communication—too squishy.

During a prayer time, as I cried out to the Lord for help with my temper, especially with my son, an idea formed I believe was heaven-sent because it made a difference.

I was to pray with Marty before I administered any form of discipline. Sometimes those prayers sounded strange and strained as I almost shouted, "Dear Lord, help this miserable little boy and help his miserable mommy who wants so desperately to raise him in a way that would honor You."

By the time I said "amen," I was almost a reasonable person. I was able to see past my emotions and do what was in Marty's best interest.

Sometimes he needed a firm hand, but he was dealt with in love instead of anger, and the moment drew us together instead of tearing us apart. Many times all he needed was time and a mother's tender touch.

But one day that boy really ticked me off! I remember heading across the room for him like a high-speed locomotive, steam coming out all sides. I had one goal and intent—get the kid, get the kid, get the kid!

Just as I loomed over him, his eyes the size of saucers, he held up one hand and yelled, "Let's pray!"

Marty had learned a valuable lesson in life: "When Mommy talks to Jesus, we're all a lot better off."

Who lights your lava?

Half-Pint

My dad was a milkman when I was growing up, which might explain his nickname for me, "Half-Pint." His route was in the area where I attended school. I would sometimes see his truck from the window of my classroom as he delivered to his customers. One delivery stands out in my mind . . .

The girls' gym class was playing baseball on one end of the school field, and the boys were playing at the farthest opposite point. I guess that was supposed to help us stay focused on the game and not the guys. Actually, the boys were so far from us we didn't know they were there until . . . The Big Spill.

I was playing shortstop. I think I was given that spot because I was five feet tall (maybe that was why Dad called me Half-Pint).

I certainly wasn't put in the infield because I was good at catching the ball. Any hopes of that skill developing came to an abrupt halt when I stopped a line drive with my throat. That game forever drove home the term "hard ball." Ever since, when a baseball would head in my direction, I'd sidestep it or duck.

This particular day, my team was heading for our field positions after I had made the third out. I turned to face home plate when I spotted my dad's milk truck coming down a side road toward the field.

"Dad, Dad, hi Dad!" I shouted enthusiastically and repeatedly, while jumping up and down, waving my baseball mitt.

My dad spotted me and leaned out his truck's open door to return my greeting. His truck was the kind you drive standing up. As he waved, he veered too close to the edge of an incline, and the truck slid and tipped sideways. As the truck fell to the right, my dad jumped out the door to the left just as the load of milk shifted to the front. In those days most of the milk was in glass bottles, which we could hear shattering as the cases collided.

I couldn't move. I realized my dad was safe and unhurt, but there was still the ditched truck and damaged cargo. Tears began to run down my face. I felt responsible because I had distracted him.

As I stood staring at my dad while he surveyed his "milk shake," something else began to shake. It was the earth beneath my feet. I turned to see the boys' gym class stampeding across the field toward the girls' now halted game. They ran through and around us, out to the road, and over to my dad's dairy disaster. With the strength of young men motivated by the squeals of the girls, they were able to upright the milk "cart."

My dad was so relieved he didn't have to call a tow and the inside damage sounded worse than it was, he rewarded the boys by throwing boxes of ice cream bars into their midst.

The boys, equally thrilled with themselves, began to run down the road (now affectionately called the Milky Way) with their reward, laughing, with the rest of the group in hot pursuit. The poor coach was winded from blowing his whistle in attempts to regroup his "milk men."

I still had not moved. I was peeking through the webbing of my mitt. My gym suit was wet with tears.

Which just goes to prove . . .

It's not worth crying over spilled milk.

Kin

From my earliest years Aunt Pearl was my favorite kinfolk. Her Southern-country upbringing spiced her conversation with unexpected surprises that delighted the heart and often startled you into laughter.

Her wit was quick, but so was her temper. Even though she was my favorite, I knew better than to sass her. When I stayed at her house, which was every chance I could, you can bet your shoofly pie I obeyed her.

She was short and round and twirled her long brown hair into a tight little circle on the top of her head, capped by a hairnet. She moved fast, worked hard and relaxed fully. Aunt Pearl deeply loved the Lord, her family and a good meal, especially if it was served with laughter.

On one of her visits to Michigan, I remember her sitting at my kitchen table sharing life lessons with me.

She looked up and said, "Child, there ain't nothin' worse than a whuppin' from the Lord."

"A whuppin' from the Lord?" I puzzled.

"Yes, child, ain't you never had no whuppin'?" she questioned.

"I guess I have. My mom used to send me out to get a switch off the tree. The worst part of that whuppin' was picking the weapon to be used on you."

"That ain't nothin' like a whuppin' from the Lord," she insisted.

"I was at this here hospital a-waitin' in the hall to visit my friend," she continued, "when they come abringin' a woman down the hall on a gurney. The Spirit of the Lord said to me, 'Take that woman's hand.'"

She resisted, "Lord, I can't be a-takin' that woman's hand. I don't know her."

Again she heard Him state, "Take that woman's hand."

Aunt Pearl said at this point she began to "ar-gee" with the Lord, "afeard" someone "would be a-lockin' her up if she wusta be takin' that woman's hand."

The woman was rolled passed her, and for one moment their eyes met. Then she was gone down that long hall and through the double doors. Word came out a short time later that the woman had died.

With tears in her eyes, Aunt Pearl said, "Child, there ain't nothin' worse than a whuppin' from the Lord."

She believed the Lord had given her the opportunity to be the last person on this earth to touch that woman with His love, and she had failed to respond.

Then, with new determination in her voice, she announced, "Now when the Lord tells me to take someone's hand, I take her hand, her arm, I hug her neck, and I don't wanna let her go. 'Cause I don't want no more whoopin's from the Lord."

Have you been to the woodshed lately?

Leaning

Why, oh why did I ever say I would do this?

Fear was bobsledding through my body, creating havoc in my breathing apparatus and digestive tract. My tummy was gurgling so loud people were turning around, trying to decide who was guilty of such distracting sounds. When they looked in my direction, I'd roll my eyes toward the lady on my right, then I'd give a slight smile, as if we shared a secret about her noisy anatomy.

I was speaking for a ladies' retreat day to 250 women. I was only doing the book reviews, but I knew I was incompetent and would probably be incoherent by the time I crawled my way up on stage. I wasn't sure of my name much less what was in the six books I was to review.

I had notes, but they seemed so small now. My eyes didn't seem capable of focusing.

Maybe I needed a doctor. Yes, that's it . . . a doctor. I was way overdue for a physical. This seemed like a good time, so I stood to leave.

My friend Joyce had been observing my twitchy behavior and sensed I was bolting to run. She grabbed my arm, stuck a postcard in my face and said with authority, "Read this."

I wasn't in a reading mood, but something in her voice made me do it anyway. Still struggling with my eyes and concentration, the only thing I could make out was the title of what appeared to be a poem. It was called, "Lean Hard on Me."

The title was enough. I made an about-face and headed for the platform.

I kept repeating, "Lean hard on Him, lean hard on Him."

And I was. Had you been standing in the back watching me walk to the front, I'm sure I would have been at a thirty-degree angle I was leaning so hard.

I was now at the front row, and my friend Rose was announcing the book reviews. She introduced me as Klutzy Paramount. Well, the audience got almost hysterical over the slip.

Being inexperienced on stage, I didn't know what one should do when the audience was in gales of laughter at your name. I walked up the steps and started across the stage.

When they saw me they laughed harder. I'm not sure if they were agreeing the name fit my appearance or what.

As the hilarity began to subside, I leaned into the microphone and said, "My name is—" but before I could set the record straight, they were off in riotous laughter once again.

When they took a breath, I rattled off my reviews and retreated . . . relieved and rejoicing.

Are you leaving or leaning?

11

Main Attraction

I have a theory about why opposites attract. I think it's because we have a deep desire to get on each other's nerves.

My husband loves TV nature specials. I personally have never been that interested in the brain cells of a bumblebee or the anatomy of an anteater. He, in turn, does not understand my elation as I watch my video collection of "Winnie the Pooh" cartoons.

Les believes to be on time means to arrive a half hour early. I believe to enter as the big hand strikes the appointed hour is soon enough. Besides, if you arrive too early, you end up as part of the work crew.

Les loves his air conditioner . . . on high . . . while I have been accused of having a fixation for my electric blanket (which I wouldn't need so often if he'd turn off his air).

My husband longs to travel, but his job keeps him home. I enjoy being home, but my job keeps me on the road.

Country-and-western music is what Les sings along with, while I can lose myself in classical.

Les is your basic get-it-over-with shopper, while I'm a detailed investigative researcher.

I love books. Les looks forward to the newspaper.

My husband is a trivia buff. The only thing I retain is water.

He is a meat-and-potatoes man. I am a salad-and-veggie-plate gal.

Sometimes I think Les likes things just the opposite of me to agitate me, but then I remember . . . these are the things that drew me to him in the first place.

Do you let differences divide or define your relationships?

Hungry Heart

As a child, my favorite pastime was a board game covered with colorful pictures of scrumptious sweets. Today, as an adult, I'm still following a tantalizing trail of tempting treats.

I've noticed that thin people don't have to work as hard as us hefties to make it down the trail. After all, we have to hold in our tummies. Tummy tucking (T.T.) takes stamina. I discovered a rich source of stamina can be found in French silk pie covered in mounds of shaved chocolate and also in goblets of tapioca smothered with dollops of fresh whipped cream.

Did you ever notice what happens to your anatomy when you hold in your tummy? First, T.T. punches your stomach into your diaphragm, which then catapults your esophagus into your tonsils. Your propelled tonsils, in turn, spiral your sinuses into your brain, causing you to blow your top!

If you release your tummy tuck position too quickly, because of the acceleration of gravity, you could bottom out. No wonder weight is such a heavy issue.

Speaking of heavy issues, try this appet-teaser test. It will help you weigh your eating choices. You might want to grab an eclair before beginning; tests can be strenuous.

Check appropriate boxes:

I eat because,
- ☐ I'm mad
- ☐ I'm glad
- ☐ I'm sad
- ☐ I've been bad
- ☐ I'm bored
- ☐ It's there
- ☐ Everyone else is eating
- ☐ I need it to sustain life

Depending on the results of your test, you, like me, may want to go on a diet . . . again.

I've learned from experience at times it is best not to diet. For instance, if you are on a business trip, vacation, expecting guests, eating out, holidays, stressful times, when you're moving, potlucks, picnics, in the evening or during daylight.

Sometimes I get miffed with a modified menu life-style. Tonight I rebelled and ate two pieces of homemade pumpkin pie and filled up—with regret. Usually I can bury my guilt, temporarily, under an avalanche of chocolate chip cookie crumbs. I have no room left this time, not even for Jell-O.

I wonder which weighs more: my groceries or my guilt? One makes my scale heavy, the other my heart.

Are you eating because you're hungry . . . or hurting?

Viewpoint

When your full stature measures five foot, you find yourself drawn to Scripture like "You shall say to this mountain, 'Move from here to there,' and it shall move" (Matt. 17:20, NAS).

I, believe it or not, was captain of a girls' basketball team in high school. I loved this position because I enjoy telling other people what to do.

But I had this problem, for me a mountainous problem, that I kept running into. Her name was Mount Kathy. She stood five feet eleven inches.

In those days, when giants walked the land, girls played half-court basketball. That meant you either shot the baskets or you guarded your opponents. I was a guard by choice. First, because I did not want to purposely embarrass myself attempting to get that big heavy ball into that exceedingly high hoop.

Second, I enjoyed being a guard and was pretty good at it. My height, or lack thereof, was at times to my advantage since I could move quickly around the half court. I was aggressive and as aggravating as a swarm of mosquitoes to the opposing forwards.

Then into my life lumbered Mount Kathy, who began to rob me of my reputation and my confidence. I just couldn't seem to get past her. I certainly couldn't go over her. The best I could do was get us into a jump ball situation.

Now that was a joke. I would jump my little heart out, and she didn't even have to move to her tiptoes. She'd stand flat-footed, looming over me, smiling down, braces and all, and then with a flick of her wrist direct the ball anywhere she wanted it to go. She certainly had no interference from me. Try as I might, I could not attain her altitude.

Probably just as well. I understand the higher you go, the harder it is to breathe.

I don't think Kathy read the same Bible verses I did, because no matter how often I said, "Move from here to there," she didn't budge.

Gratefully the basketball season ended, and now volleyball season was upon us. I once again was captain.

At our first game, after my serve I rotated to the front. I crouched, ready for serious play when I realized I was staring into a familiar pair of knee caps. Sure enough, it was Kathy.

I wonder if there are some mountains
He doesn't move . . . to keep us humble?

14

Musical Pews

I love to sing. I have yet to find anyone who loves to hear me. I don't sound that bad to myself, but I've had a number of people who have encouraged me in the art of humming.

I remember in junior high school my music teacher turned pale when she realized I had taken her class again. That semester she put me in the bass section with the boys. Her strategy worked; I was so embarrassed I switched to Home Ec.

Evidently voices don't improve with age. I remember singing a favorite of mine, "He Touched Me," at church one Sunday morning.

My friend Shirley was in the pew in front of me. I was really projecting on the chorus when she turned around, motioned me toward her, and whispered, "Trust me on this; He hasn't touched you yet, Patsy. Just mouth the words."

One good thing about a person's bathtub, there's no pew in front of you. Besides, I enjoy the acoustical benefit of the tiles when I shower.

I was into the bouncing chorus of "Zippity Doodah," as I lathered up, when my husband's panicked voice yelled through the door, "What's the matter?"

"Nothing, I was just singing," I called out melodically.

"Singing?" he asked incredulously. "I thought you were in pain!"

Even the shower isn't sacred anymore.

Invariably when I speak for a retreat, they seat me beside the soloist. That used to make me uncomfortable.

Sometimes I try what Shirley suggested: I mouth the words and hope people nearby think the singer's voice is coming out of me.

Why is it that those of us who can't sing marry those who can? Punishment maybe, for some past crime we forgot to confess.

Les has a delightful voice and knows a thousand songs. Except, I notice when I try to join him, he changes the words.

I've asked to join the church choir several times; but our director, Bill, always walks away laughing.

"That's a good one, Patsy," he says. "That's a good one."

Do the people around you seem uncomfortable with your
singing? Take my advice—change pews.

15

Imprints

Isn't it funny what we remember about people?

In elementary school, my friend Diane had us call her Fred. Her hero was Fred Mertz of "I Love Lucy," and she wanted to grow up to be just like him.

I thought this was an unusual goal.

She called me Fatsy instead of Patsy.

Diane made us laugh a lot.

When I was in high school, a girl named Eva was in my gym class. She was the only girl I knew who shaved off her eyebrows and drew in new ones—very artistic, long, curved, full brows that were coal black.

When we had swimming class, her carefully applied artwork would wash away. I had never seen naked eyebrows before. I was fascinated. I tried not to stare, but sometimes I just couldn't help it.

Another unique feature about Eva was her honesty. When she found out I had a private scoop on a mutual friend, she said, "Well, whatever you do, don't tell me! I can't keep a secret."

I had never heard anyone admit that aloud, especially before she even heard the tantalizing tidbit. Eva impressed me with her bare brows and her heroic honesty.

I was from a good-sized high school, but when we got a new shorthand teacher, the school was abuzz. One reason was her unusual appearance. She must have been a trendsetter, because she was back-combing her hair long before anyone else. She had it so voluminous you could have hid a basketball in there, and no one would have known.

When I saw her I was certain I wouldn't like her. Who could like someone who looked like her hair had been inflated with a tire pump? She ended up being the best teacher I ever had.

For a while, as a young married couple, Les and I lived in a mobile home. Next door to us was a lot that was used for short-term travel trailers.

A couple in their thirties from Texas pulled into that spot on April 3, 1966. I remember the date because it was my twenty-first birthday. That was significant for two reasons: one, in that era it meant you had attained maturity; two, not one member in my family remembered this was my day!

To prove my grown-up status, I had been pouting all evening.

When I spotted our new neighbors backing into the lot, I invited them in for coffee in an attempt to cheer myself up.

The woman was unique-looking. She wore her hair in braids that were in a circle on the side of her head, and she had filled the circle with hibiscus. I hadn't seen anything like that since the movie *South Pacific*.

As we were getting acquainted, I mentioned it was my (sniff) birthday, and Les almost fell off the couch. He went from realization to repentance. He knew he had goofed.

Our guests, feeling the awkwardness of the situation, quickly departed. I felt they feared a family feud might follow, so they fled.

About an hour later there was a knock at our door. I opened it to find my new neighbor holding up a cake. She had gone home, baked, decorated and even swirled my name and all-important age in frosting on this creation.

Even though they were next door for only a couple of days, I've never forgotten her.

What kind of imprint are you leaving?

16

Night Life

When my parents called in the middle of the night because their furnace broke, Les went to help them. I felt a little pang of discomfort at being left alone. Well, to say I was alone isn't accurate—both our young boys were upstairs asleep. Also, our fearless cockapoo, Tuesday, was snoozing outside.

Tuesday was a lovable dog, but she had no discernment. She greeted beggar and thief, as well as doctor and chief, with sloppy enthusiasm.

She also had what I thought was a strange defect for a dog. Her barker was broken. Seldom if ever did she gr-r-r or arf. That was until . . . The Night of the Broken Furnace.

Les was gone about an hour when the barking began. I was startled at the unfamiliar sound and thought it must be a stray. I peeked out cautiously. Tuesday was on our porch, arfing in the direction of the woods.

Oh, yes, did I mention we were living on a Boy Scout reservation containing six hundred acres of woods, swamps, lakes and assorted monsters? The latter was my immediate concern.

Stop and think about it. What else would cause a bow-wow's broken barker to suddenly kick in?

Tuesday began to run from the front door, to the back door, to the front again. I knew what this meant. Whatever was out there was closing in.

I crept out of bed and began to look for a weapon. I had always believed investing in the Kirby vacuum cleaner would one day pay off. This was the day.

I took the long nozzled tube section to bed with me for protection. I placed the telephone beside me with the phone book open to emergency numbers. My heart was thumping as I strained to hear sounds of the approaching monster.

With Kirby in hand, I rotated my vision from watching the window to the door, to the window to the door, when suddenly I turned my head too far and caught my reflection in the mirror.

You want to talk about frightening . . . no . . . make that ridiculous.

I said to myself, "What's wrong with this picture?"

I've known the Lord well enough and long enough to realize He wants to be my refuge and hiding place. Here I was, trying in my anemic strength to handle this imagined invasion.

I laid down my Kirby sword and picked up the sword of the Spirit, which is the Word of God. I reviewed every peace and power promise I'd ever read. I'm not sure how long I'd been reading when fear started to drain out and quietness began to seep in, and I nodded off.

Soon I was sound asleep. I never heard my husband when he pulled up in front. I didn't hear him when he came in the door. I didn't even hear him when he entered our room. I didn't hear him until he shook my foot and asked, "What's the vacuum cleaner doing in bed with you?"

Caught with my sword down.

Are you armed or alarmed?

Feathered Friends

I f anyone had told me I would become a bird-watcher, I would never have believed it . . . nor would anyone else. Did you know that the different species have unique personalities?

Ms. Hummingbird is our flitter. She has so much nervous energy her wings seem to hum her theme song, "Much to do, much to do, much to do."

She actually could conserve a lot of her strength if she didn't worry about what the other hummingbirds were doing. We have three feeders for them, but let even one of her own kind get near the feeders, and she gets herself in an uproar. Ms. Flit dive-bombs anyone who attempts to drink the sweet water, preventing others from getting the nurturing they need.

Then there's Mr. Woodpecker. What a guy—seems to always be beating his head against a dead tree. He's a handsome bird—a classy dresser with every feather in place. He taps his message repeatedly, "Picky, Picky, Picky." It seems kind of sad to see him knock himself out over the tiniest matter.

Watch out, here come the Jays. Boy, what squawkers. When they fly in, everybody knows it. A flash of blue, and then they start bossing. They think they should be in charge of the whole seed scene. The Jay family has a lot to offer, if they just weren't so pushy and demanding.

Mr. and Mrs. Cardinal are a real study. She's a dear and is content to share the feeder with all who are hungry. But that husband of hers is so brazen. Many times he won't even allow her to eat until he's done. A real chauvinist, if you ask me. They make such a good-looking couple. I just wish he were more thoughtful of her.

My friend Margret raises peacocks—beautiful but obviously arrogant birds that strut around so everyone can see their newest attire. With beaks in the air, they ruffle and fan, and if they don't get enough attention, they repeatedly cry, "Help! Help!" I guess they've done it too many times though, because no one seems to take them seriously anymore.

Let's see now, is this a list of our fowl . . . or our friends?

18

Oba. . .Who?

I'm not into heights, closed places, or riding in vehicles where I can't make suggestions on the maneuvering of it. Therefore, flying has never interested me—until I received an invitation I couldn't resist.

My friend Florence Littauer invited me to a leadership seminar in California. I was excited about everything except the flight. I made plans, purchased my tickets and packed my suitcase.

Flight day arrived, and my husband escorted me through the airport toward my gate. Actually, he was shoving me as my resistance grew. I remember passing a large plate glass window and seeing the ominous aircraft with a big AA tattooed on its side.

Fear can do funny things. This time, it grew feet and scampered up my arm, jumped onto my shoulder, leaned into my ear and screamed, "Run!"

My husband, using a linebacker's lunge, prevented my escape. Reluctantly, I trudged onto the plane.

My friend Rose, who was also attending the seminar, was my seat partner. That should have helped, but several minutes after we took our seats she reached into her bag and came up with a camera.

Puzzled, I asked, "Why are you taking that out now?"

"I want to capture fear in color when they start the engines," she informed me, aiming the camera in my direction.

"Oh, great, I'm shaking in my seat belt, and I've got Ms. Candid Camera sitting next to me," I fumed as the flash illuminated our row.

The day was cold, slushy and gray. I still remember the contrast as we moved up through the murky clouds and into the brilliant sunlight. As I watched out the window, there, arched in the heavens, from one cloud to another, was a rainbow.

I knew it was mine. It was a telegram from the Lord that read, "You're going to make it."

The lady beside me responded with, "Oh, look, a rainbow!"

"It's mine," I stated too abruptly. Realizing my overreaction, I softened it with, "Excuse me," and then under my breath whispered, "but it is mine." I needed that rainbow-gram too bad to share it with her.

After reaching our cruising altitude, the ride was smooth and uneventful.

Then the pilot, a man who obviously needed counseling, began to share information he should have kept to himself. "Strong Santa Ana winds are being reported ahead. We are running lower on fuel than we had anticipated. We'd like everyone to stay in their seats for the remainder of the flight."

His voice was unemotional. He didn't need to have any emotions because I had enough for both of us. I began to scan the heavens for another rainbow of promise.

Rose was reading her Bible. I think she thought it was the yellow pages as she let her fingers do the walking. She would let her Bible fall open, read a passage and then move to another.

On one portion she nudged me and said with a giggle, "Look."

I nervously glanced down and began to read. "Give that to me!" I said. "It's my other rainbow."

Listen to what it says in Obadiah (who really reads Obadiah?): " . . . Who says in his heart, Who can bring me down to the ground? Though you mount on high as the eagle, and though you set your nest among the stars, I will bring you down from there, says the Lord."

Thank You, Lord, and thank you, Obadiah! Now, I know Obadiah didn't pen that one with me in mind, but it sure helped this trembling traveler until we touched down.

After sharing this story at a retreat, a lady came up and said, "My version reads differently than yours. Where yours says, ' "I will bring you down," declares the Lord,' mine reads, ' "I will plummet you to the earth," saith the Lord.' "

Somehow I wasn't interested in her version. One plummet, and it would have been all over for me.

That plane flight gave me a new appreciation for terms like "land-lubber," "westward ho," and "good old terra firma." Nevertheless, there is an upcoming flight I don't want to miss. I understand flight time is minimal, ". . . in the twinkling of an eye." We won't even have a chance to buckle our seat belt, although in-flight music will be provided—trumpets, I believe.

Yes, one glad morning with fearless abandon, I'll fly away.

Are you booked?

Messages

When our big twenty-fifth anniversary arrived, Les bought me nothing. Of course that's what I had asked for, but what does that have to do with anything? Mates are supposed to be able to decipher mixed messages. Les is supposed to discern when I mean "absolutely no" from when I mean "sort of no."

Here's the thing. Wives don't want to shoulder the responsibility of giving husbands permission to be extravagant. It frees us from guilt if we say no and our husbands don't listen to us, which of course is what we're hoping will happen. That way we can say to others, "I told him not to do this, but he did it anyway."

Les and I agreed to take a trip south as a shared gift, but I was hoping for something a little more personal. I must have been too convincing when I said, "If you get me anything I'll be mad." Maybe I should have said, "If you get me anything I might, in a minute way, be temporarily displeased."

Most of us gals secretly hope for a good "show and tell" kind of gift, especially for our twenty-fifth. It's difficult to flaunt—I mean show—a trip to your friends.

I decided to subtly retract my giftless declaration at the first appropriate moment.

A week later Les dropped me off for a speaking engagement and announced he was going to the area mall for his morning coffee. The word "mall" flashed like a neon opportunity.

With more zeal and clarity than I meant to display, I blurted out, "Why don't you buy me something!"

Oops, I probably confused him by being that . . . that . . . honest. Not that I'm not always honest . . . sort of.

When Les came back to pick me up, he had heard the message, for there, on the front seat, was a beautifully wrapped gift. I admired it for a moment and then began to remove the floral paper. Inside were layers of soft white tissue secured with a gold seal that read "lingerie."

Well, this was proof that honesty did pay; I was getting what I deserved. So what if it was a week late.

I gently pulled back the last layer of tissue and lifted out my . . . my . . . prehistoric gift. What unfolded was a long white cotton nightshirt sporting a gregarious dinosaur, which wore a lopsided hat.

This truth thing, girls, . . . you'll need to be more specific!

Pricey

I have always wanted to play an instrument. Well, not any instrument. Mostly I dreamed of playing a piano. I pictured myself moving my fingers across the ivories without looking, as I threw back my head and sang with throaty gusto. It didn't take me long to find out I couldn't sing. But piano . . . that took a little longer.

I was in my thirties when my friend Rose grew tired of hearing me whine about being deprived of piano lessons. She announced she would teach me. I was thrilled.

My husband lovingly, although somewhat reluctantly, moved an old upright into our living room. Those things weigh a ton. I could tell by the purple arteries that had inched their way out on his neck.

Not wanting his effort to be in vain, I began my serious study of the piano, certain I would soon be in concert. But I ran into an immediate problem.

It was my teacher. She quite honestly was . . . boring. This surprised me because Rose has a lot of verve. She usually was full of fun but not so as a piano instructor.

She kept insisting I do scale exercises. Either of those words I avoid regularly; combined, they were depressing. Dull, repetitious pinging sounded childish.

I explained to her that this was not what I had in mind, so she agreed to teach me some real songs.

Now, when she said real, I didn't know she was talking about "Old MacDonald Had a Farm."

How do you think it looks and sounds to have a woman in her thirties e-i-e-i-o-ing? After a few weeks of musical farming, I'd had it, and so had my family. I could tell they were stressed when the veins on their temples seemed to pulsate in time to my barnyard plunking.

"I don't want to play 'Old MacDonald.' I want to play 'How Great Thou Art,'" I stated with artistic fervor to Rose.

"You cannot play 'How Great Thou Art' until you first learn to play 'Old MacDonald,' " Rose replied through tight teeth.

"How boring, how unimaginative," I complained.

"Patsy, you don't want to learn how to play the piano. You just want to play the piano," she accused.

Boy, did she hit a chord. No way was I willing to put in the time and effort necessary to become a pianist.

I gave up my musical illusions. Les and the boys joyfully, gratefully and quickly removed the piano. Rose once again became her entertaining self.

What price is your dream?

21

Perks

Eve . . . what a perk-y lady! She definitely had advantages.

Stop and think about it. When she and Adam met, she didn't have to wonder, *Is this the right man for me?* She didn't have any immediate concerns if some sweet young thing was vying for her man's attention.

When they were wed, she didn't have to worry about forgetting someone from the invitation list or deciding who the attendants would be. No decisions were necessary on which photographer, caterer or florist. Talk about simplifying life . . .

Guess what? No mother-in-law or father-in-law conflicts. Never once did she have to hear, "Sure wish you could make applesauce like my mom." They never squabbled over whose family they would spend the holidays with.

She never had to worry about ironing Adam's dress shirts or getting the crease straight in his suit pants. There was no friction about Adam not picking up his dirty clothes, at least not in their garden home. Nor did she have to take any ribbing about where she put Adam's lost snakeskin sandals.

Eve was unique. She's the only gal who didn't have to go through puberty, peer pressure or pimples. She didn't go through the agony of handing her parents a bad report card or the knee-knocking experience of trying to explain why she was late getting home. She never once had to hear her parents say, "Why aren't you more like your sister Ethel?"

When she and Adam talked, it wasn't filled with endless tales of the good ol' days and the good ol' boys. Nor did she have to compete with the World Series or the six o'clock Eden news report.

They had a romance, marriage, honeymoon and home life that was made in paradise.

Eve had it all . . . well, almost all.

Why is it we always seem to want what we don't have?

Quiet Noise

Even when I'm still I'm not quiet. My mind is busy embroidering life, one thread at a time, according to the events of a day. Therefore, when I sit down for my quiet time, I have to battle against my mental cross-stitching.

"Sh-h-h," I tell my brain, in an attempt to focus on my prayers. I start to pray for my sons, and my mind somehow switches gears. I'm making a mental grocery list instead.

I've learned to pray with my eyes open and not to get too comfortable. Far more times than I'd like to confess, I've nodded off right in the middle of "and God bless . . ."

Now I pray wide-eyed, sitting in a straight-back chair, which has some drawbacks. I was praying for a family member the other morning when I noticed a build-up of dust under the chair in my living area.

The next thing I knew I had the vacuum out, running it around the room. Then I remembered I was supposed to be praying. I sat back down and resumed talking with the Lord.

Before long I was at the freezer taking meat out for dinner, even though I still hadn't finished my prayer time.

My mind is far too active, and my concentration span is about the length of a commercial.

I tried walking around the house and praying aloud. But then I put things in unusual places, without realizing it, keeping my family confused and frustrated.

One day I found Les looking in the refrigerator for his electric razor. When I raised my eyebrows in surprise, he simply said, "With your filing system, I just had to check."

Kneeling is a proper spiritual position, but for me it is physically defeating. I get leg cramps, go numb and limp pitifully the rest of the day. It seems like poor advertising to tell people I've been debilitated by my prayer time.

What seems to work best is writing my prayers. It helps me focus and finish before I flit off. As I write out my noisy thoughts to free my mind, it untangles the threads of my day for directed prayer. I keep my printed petitions in a notebook. I could add your name if you'd like.

Let's see now . . .
where did I put that book?

23

Gotcha

I loved the idea of my two-hundred-pound husband wearing short pants and a whistle. Les had taken a job as Associate Ranger for the Boy Scouts; we would be living on their six-hundred-acre reservation.

Raised as a northern woodsman, Les was more than qualified for his position. Now me, I was a city slicker. But I loved the country atmosphere.

I was determined to adapt to my new life-style. In fact, I began to daydream I would become a world-famous outdoors woman, making valuable contributions to our environment. These were rather high hopes for someone whose past experience included occasional childhood family picnics. Still, I might have fulfilled my dream except . . .

On a beautiful spring day, new life was budding all through our heavily wooded grounds. The birds were singing and so was I, as I strolled around admiring God's handiwork. The daffodils and lilacs were bursting with color and fragrance.

As I approached them, I noticed my nose was running. Within minutes I was having little fits of sneezing. Then I started itching. First my arms, next my face, then my ears. My eyes began to water and feel sandpapery.

Determined not to give in to these unpleasant reactions, I decided to get involved with a project.

I spotted a forsythia bush. Covered in brilliant yellow flowers, it was lovely except for some straggly limbs I thought should be cut off. I didn't realize there is a time to prune and a time to refrain from pruning.

As I looked for a pair of shears, I noticed my head was blocking up, and I seemed to be developing a cough, but I forged on. Finding the tools to my new trade, I began to snip and clip, feeling like quite the botanist.

I leaned down to get an unruly spray, when out of the ground came a stream of yellow jackets. They seemed to be deeply offended that I was pruning out of season and filed their grievance down my scoop-neck top.

I ran through the yard, beating on my shirt like an old Tarzan movie. My sister, who was in the yard a safe distance from me, caught a glimpse of the invasion and began to chase me.

My mom was indoors visiting with her friend Edith when she heard me yelling. She looked out the window as I ran by, quickly followed by my sister, and commented to her friend, "Oh, look, they're playing."

One good thing about living in the country is if you need to disrobe you can. So I did. The remaining attackers had to be plucked from my bod. I then took refuge in my home.

I had spots and dots, was sneezing and wheezing, itching and twitching, and I was riddled with stings. My daydream of becoming Environmentalist Extraordinaire faded with the intrusion of reality.

I had Les screen in our front porch, and that's where I enjoyed the out-of-doors.

Any intruders dive-bomb your dreams lately?

24

Real Estate

My mom was a mover and a shaker. She loved moving from one home to another, and it would always shake me up!

I think moving was a hobby for her. She'd buy a house, fix it up and sell it. Then she would start all over again. It always meant a different school and establishing new friendships. I made friends easily enough, but I hated leaving the old ones.

I decided when I grew up I would live in one house for the rest of my life. Then I married Leslie "The Mover" Clairmont.

Somehow my mom's mobility genes had bypassed me and entered Les. I didn't even realize that was possible.

I had felt safe marrying a man who had only lived in two homes from birth until marriage. But I counted recently, and in twenty-eight years we have moved twenty-three times.

At about house number seventeen, I decided I had moveaphobia, and I wasn't going to pack one more time.

I cried out, "Lord, it isn't fair! You know a woman gets a lot of her security and identity from where she lives."

I tried to validate my opinion with Scripture. If I could do that, I figured the next time Les made me move, I could send him on a guilt trip.

The problem was I couldn't find any Scripture that suggested we should depend on a place, position, possession or even person (other than Jesus) for our security and identity. I had to re-think my house "hold" and learn not to hang on so tightly.

I did feel encouraged when I read, "I go to prepare a place for you."

Notice place is singular. I don't have to take my Samsonite or rent one more U-Haul, y'all. I get to live in one place forever and ever. Amen.

The thought crossed my mind that when the Lord builds my husband's place, He should add on a room for my mom. Then He could put their mansion on rollers, and they could move all through eternity.

When they rolled by, I could lean out of my immovable place and wave. That would be heaven for us all!

Our home here is meant to be a haven . . .
heaven comes later.

25

Atmospheric Pressure

I don't feel well when I have to say "I'm sorry." I get strong, flu-like symptoms. I become nauseated. My knees get weak, my hands shake, and I get facial ticks.

If I have to say "I'm sorry and I was wrong," it's much worse. Then, along with the jerky behavior, my vision blurs, and my speech patterns slur.

I have noticed, though, that once I've said what needs to be said I make an amazing recovery.

One day Les was feeling frustrated with our eldest son over a work situation and needed to release a flurry of words. He came into my home office and spewed his displeasure about Marty onto me. Once Les said how he felt, he was ready to move past his aggravation.

After he left, I began to process their conflict and decided I could make the whole thing better. I envisioned myself as a Goodwill Angel (not to be confused with the Goodyear Blimp).

I fluttered into Marty's room and announced what he needed to do and when he needed to do it. For some reason Marty was not impressed with this angelic visitation.

In fact, he told me, "If Dad has a problem with me that's job-related, then he can talk to me."

Well, Marty might be twenty-five years old, but how dare he insinuate I was butting in? Setting aside my helping halo, in my loudest mother's voice I trumpeted my heated annoyance. I finally ended my tirade by stomping up the steps. Marty placed his exclamation point on our meeting by slamming out of the house.

I packed away my singed raiment and was still sizzling when I heard Les come in. I went down to make a pronouncement on his son's poor behavior. By the look on Les's face it was obvious he had already encountered Marty.

"If I had wanted you to go to Marty, I would have asked you," he stated through clenched teeth. "Patsy, this was none of your business."

"None of my business!" I bellowed. A cloudburst of tears followed as I ran to my room, tripping several times on my lopsided wings.

"I was only trying to help," I kept consoling myself.

When the tears and excuses stopped, I began to wonder if maybe I could have been wrong. Flu-like symptoms intensified when I realized I needed to apologize to both of them for interfering.

By the time I made my way out to Les and Marty, my vision had blurred. My head was pounding (probably from that heavy halo) as I stammered the dreaded words, "I-I was wr-wrong for interfering, I'm s-sorry, will you f-forgive me?"

Within moments we were all hugging.

As I walked back to the house, I noticed my headache and vexed vision had vanished, and it was almost . . . as if my feet weren't touching the ground.

Hey Angel Face, anyone in your sphere deserve an apology?

26

Amazing Grace

I was so familiar with our five-mile stretch of country road into town that I developed a rhythm to my driving. Sometimes my rhythm was faster than the posted pace. After following me into town on several occasions, Les mentioned I needed to lighten up on my footwork.

At times when I drove to town, I wouldn't remember the ride in because I was on autopilot. I knew every curve and turn by heart, and my mind tended to wander.

Often I would sing my way to town, and if the song happened to be a bouncy one, without realizing it, I would drive to the beat. This wasn't a problem if I was singing "How Great Thou Art." However, when I got into the rousing chorus of "I'll Fly Away," my little wagon seemed to be doing that very thing. Les warned me more than once to pay closer attention to my selections.

On one particularly beautiful autumn day, I was on my way to speak for an area women's retreat. My six-year-old, Jason, was in the back seat, looking forward to seeing his friends at the child-care room. I was into the rhythm of the road while I rehearsed my opening thoughts with great enthusiasm.

I glanced in my rearview mirror as something beckoned for my attention. There I spotted someone else who seemed to be quite enthusiastic in his desire to share some thoughts with me. A colorful character. I could tell by the red and blue circular lights on his car.

As he approached my car, I couldn't help chuckling as I pictured Les doing the "I told you so" nod.

Jason questioned, "Mom, why are you laughing?"

"Oh, honey, it's just Daddy told me this would happen one day."

The nice officer was not laughing. He leaned down and boomed with a voice that instantly reduced me to a teeny person, "And where are we going in such a hurry?"

I meekly looked into his convicting face and whispered, "Church."

"You're kidding!" he bellowed.

"I'm the speaker," I confessed. "My topic is 'Renewed Living.' I guess I'm not doing too well . . . with it," I trailed off, wishing I could disappear.

He asked me a series of intelligent questions that I could not answer with any degree of accuracy—things like "Where is your car registration?" and "Where is your title?"

I was totally in the wrong, which was obvious to all of us.

So I was amazed when he announced, "I'm going to let you go without a ticket, but you must slow down and place the proper papers in your car."

That day the officer was like Jesus. He extended mercy when I didn't deserve it.

Need another chance?

Bag It

Men and women, generally speaking, approach shopping quite differently. Men see it as a nuisance and yet a necessity. Women, however, see it as a challenge and a calling. Men tend to buy willy-nilly, while a woman investigates, evaluates and meditates her purchases . . . Unless of course it's a once in a lifetime opportunity, and she must buy immediately or lose her chance. It's amazing how many of those "once" chances a woman can find.

It drives my husband wild when I find something I like, but I take several hours looking around at other stores only to circle back and purchase that first item. Recently I resisted this urge and bought the first pair of shoes that appealed to me, only to find out later (after I wore them) that another store in the mall had them for twenty dollars less. To make matters worse, my friend had bought the same shoes—at the sale price.

This would be like a man entering a fishing contest and thinking he had won, only to have his best friend arrive with a catch twice as big and walk off with the trophy.

Sales tags are like trophies for a dedicated shopper. We would have them mounted and displayed if it weren't considered tacky. We've learned to weave our savings in our salutations.

"Nice hat; new?"

"Yes, $15.95 at Kerwin's."

"Really?"

"Yeah. Why?"

"I saw it at Lem's for $9.94."

"No!"

"Yep."

"See you."

"Bye."

You can always spot the devoted ones. They have their own language, called "Shop Talk." Words like "bargain," "grand opening," "clearance," "closeout," "refund," "coupons," "discount" and others decorate their discourse.

For me, shopping can be motivational. At times when I've felt too exhausted to clean up the kitchen, I've been able to make several loops around the two-mile mall to find the right shade of socks to go with my jeans and sweatshirt. To really raise my energy level, announce a five-minute special and watch me become almost aerobic.

Here are a couple of health warnings for shopaholics: If you browse daily, you could get Shopper's Stare from looking at one too many price tags. To prevent this, every couple hundred tags or so, take a brownie break.

Also many avid shoppers are bothered with Blue Light Bursitis from nudging their way to sales tables. They should try taking a friend and sending her through the crowd first, opening up a path.

Worst of all is the dreaded Grip. That's where the buyer and her bags have bonded, and she can't let go of her bargains. If this happens to you, train a loved one to say, "Tomorrow is another day, you can go shopping then," as they gently part you from your parcels.

Oh, yes, one more warning . . . this one from the surgeon general: "It has been proven that shopping is hazardous to your wealth."

> *Of course, girls, we have to take into consideration*
> *the general who said that is a man.*

28

Mouth Peace

I received a small catalog in the mail from an area home improvement store. I can honestly say I'm not interested in hardware, but the lettering across the front page won my attention.

In bold red print was every shopper's favorite word, "Sale." Above "sale" appeared the word "security." I need security, and I hunt for sales, so I opened their booklet to see what they had to offer.

The first page showed pictures and prices on a line of doors. The one that caught my eye was a steel door. The past week I had released several thoughts to loved ones that I should have kept to myself. If I had a steel door hinged on the side of my mouth, perhaps the next time I felt tempted to say something stinging I could slam that door shut.

The next page offered dead-bolt locks, which seemed like a good investment. Knowing myself as I do, even with the steel door closed I might kick it open to get in the last steamy word. The dead bolt could at least slow down that process.

As I scanned through the pamphlet a second time, I noticed I could purchase a door viewer for a small price. This promised to give me a 160-degree field of vision. I wonder, if I had a clearer view or a different perspective on the individual with whom I was frustrated, would I still want to sound off?

Then I came across coupons for smoke alarms. This could be the ultimate answer. If I had one installed on the roof of my mouth, when my words started heating up, the detector would go off. That would drown out all the sizzling sentences. Then, when my conversation cooled down, the siren would automatically cease and reset.

Steel doors, viewers, dead-bolt locks and smoke alarms, what a security system!

Are you wired for sound?

29

Pollution Solution

'm told two types of people exist—those who proclaim, "Good morning, Lord," when they wake up, and those who exclaim, "Good Lord, it's morning."

Early has never been one of my day's highlights, and the morning mirror has certainly not helped to cheer me on. But I did find Scripture that helped me understand my a.m. reflection: It was "formless and void and darkness was upon the surface of the deep . . ."

I was encouraged to read that things did eventually lighten and brighten up, when God proclaimed: "Let there be light."

For me that's after I apply my blush, mascara and lipstick.

I'm married to the kind of guy who leaps out of bed in the morning, skips down the hall and sings in the shower. For years that got on my nerves.

Plus I didn't think anyone should move that quickly; he could injure something he might need in the future.

Les told people, "Patsy runs around the block every morning and then kicks the block back under the bed."

I limited my exercise to jumping to conclusions, stretching the truth and dodging my reflection.

But slowly I began to realize that Les was a living example, and I would do well to learn from him. I needed a "Good morning, Lord" injection.

If this change was to take place, I'd need a plan. No, make that a miracle!

I began by memorizing, "This is the day which the Lord hath made; we will rejoice and be glad in it" (Ps. 118:24, KJV).

As soon as my brain received the jolt that a new day had begun, I would start to recite my verse—first silently, then in a whisper and finally in a shout.

My recitation started out more like a question, "This is the day . . . ?" As I continued my sunrise salute, it became a proclamation.

Gradually my new routine began to make a difference in my m.o. (morning outlook).

I honestly can't say I leap from the bed now, but I do get up. I don't skip down the hall; it's more like a crawl. I still don't sing in the shower, but I hum, and for me that's progress. No, make that a miracle!

What pollutes your sunrise salute?

30

Good-Bye

What do you mean join the Air Force?" I heard myself trumpeting at my firstborn son, Marty.

"Mom," he calmly responded, "when I graduate, I'm going to sign up. I might even make a career of it."

"Sure, sure, after you finish school and work for a few years then you can join, . . . say when you're forty," I suggested.

If anyone would have told me how difficult it is to release children I would not have believed it. In fact, I had observed families struggling with good-byes and thought they must be overly protective. Now that it was my turn, I was giving the word "possessive" new glue.

I tried reasoning with Marty; when that didn't work I threatened, I pleaded, I cajoled, I bribed, and then I cried. I delayed but did not divert him from finally signing Uncle Sam's dotted line.

I tried to be grown-up in my responses during our remaining weeks, but then I would see Marty, and grief would run down my face and splash off his high tops. Marty did his best to wade through my overwrought behavior. That wasn't easy because when he was home I flooded his every move with my presence, realizing he would soon be gone.

When I would pass him in the hall, I would ask him if I could hug him. He'd say, "All right, go ahead; hurry up."

I'd quickly squeeze him and then sniff off into another room.

"Patsy, when are you going to grow up?" my husband questioned in disbelief at my Velcro behavior. "Why do you think we had this boy?" Before I could respond, he would answer, "So that one day we could send him out into the grand adventure of life."

He made this announcement dry-eyed and slightly irritated with his weeping woman.

By the time the day came to say good-bye, I had released my emotions and was actually feeling pretty good about Marty's departure. In fact, I marched to the door like a brave soldier, gave him a kiss and even saluted him as he drove off.

I headed back to the house, grinning ear to ear with my new-found freedom. Then I bumped into Les, who was standing in a pool of anguish.

"Don't you have a heart?" he said haltingly. "That's our son leaving. We might . . . never see him again."

Being a woman of deep sensitivity, I realized Les had just gotten in touch with his grief, and so I tried to encourage him.

"When are you going to grow up? Why do you think we had this boy? So that one day we could send him out into the grand adventure of life," I echoed sweetly.

How many of your good-byes have brought you grief . . .
how many relief?

31

Hello

Our son Marty was about to return home from the Air Force. He had been stationed in Guam, and we hadn't seen him for eighteen months.

The night before his flight was to arrive, Les and I were at the mall, and I headed for the Party Center Store. I found cone-shaped hats with gala fringe spewing out the top, horns arrayed in sparkling glitter and multi-colored confetti shaped like stars.

This is going to be one fun reunion, I thought, as I headed for the checkout counter.

"What are you doing?" I heard a voice ask behind me. I turned; Les was standing there with his eyebrows bumping together in puzzlement.

It seemed obvious to me what I was doing, but I humored him. "I'm getting supplies for our celebration."

"Just where do you think you're going to use them?" The words sounded more like a threat than a question.

"At the airport tomorrow, of course," I responded uneasily.

"What airport?" he questioned. "Not the same airport I'm going to. If you're taking that stuff, you'll have to go to a different airport by yourself."

I couldn't believe my ears. But I decided at such a happy time we shouldn't be hassling over horns and hats, so I put the party favors back.

When we arrived at Marty's gate, two of his friends were already waiting. We sat chatting excitedly; then I mentioned that ol' Mr. Party Pooper wouldn't let me buy the delightful hats, horns and confetti.

In unison the two young men turned to my husband and said, "Thank you!"

Before I could respond, an airline representative announced the plane had touched down.

I learned that day that mothers don't need party paraphernalia to celebrate. I didn't need hats or horns because I had hands and a mouth. I started leaping in the air, trying to get a glimpse of Marty deplaning. My hands came together like clanging cymbals, over and over sounding out my joy. I began to laugh and whoop out words for the world to hear, "My son is home, my son is home!"

Then I was in his arms baptizing his uniform in a mother's relief.

At this point I'm not sure where Les and Marty's friends were . . . hmmm, now that I think about it, they seemed to have faded back in the crowd.

How about you? Do you welcome loved ones as
a loud greeter or a silent meeter?

32

Bird Brain

It started off as a Sunday afternoon stroll in the woods. I had the bright idea that Les and I should go on a bird-watching walk. Because we live on property surrounded by thousands of acres of state land, which has many miles of trails, it's the perfect setting for a leisurely outing.

First the equipment was found and organized: thirty-six ounces of diet pop, two pairs of binoculars, one bird book for ID, a pen to list all sightings and our sanguine Shih Tzu, Pumpkin.

As we headed out the door, Les asked, "Have you ever been on the trails across the road?"

By the look of the trails when we arrived, Crockett was the last one on them. The path didn't seem well defined to me, and I mentioned that to Les. He mumbled something about being a northern woodsman.

As we followed the winding path, it seemed to be closing in on us. In fact, I was thigh-high in weeds. The branches of sinister-shaped bushes and threatening trees began to smack me across the face.

"Les, get me out of here," I whined.

"You're all right. Just keep walking," he instructed, disappearing around a bend.

For a moment I was distracted from my weedy world by the sound of what I thought must be a herd of hummingbirds. It turned out to be militant mosquitoes. They motivated me to move quickly, and soon I caught up with Les. He didn't seem bothered by the mosquitoes. I think it was because of the horse flies that were devouring chunks of his hide.

My resourceful woodsman pulled off two low-hanging branches, and we took turns beating off each others' attackers.

We'd been in the woods forty minutes, and I wanted to leave—now. All I desired was to see some birds. Instead, I was branch-bruised and bug-bitten. This was no fun.

"The closest way out," Les informed me, "is the way we came in."

"No way! I'm not going back there," I stated, forging forward.

Because I had underestimated the heat, the ice cubes in the pop had long since melted. We now had Laodicean lukewarm liquid—not very refreshing but helpful when sloshed through the teeth to loosen the bugs from between our bicuspids. I learned that in certain circumstances it is appropriate for a woman to spit.

I was watching my feet as I moved through the thick undergrowth when something caught my eye. It was the rotting carcass of a mouse being eaten by gigantic black-and-yellow beetles. If I had had any lunch, I'm sure I would have lost it. I increased my pace to something close to a gallop.

We had not seen one bird. Not one!

Sweat began to drip down our branch-whipped faces, when up ahead we spotted sunlight. The woods opened up and deposited us on a dirt road at the bottom of a large hill.

As we stepped from our treacherous trail, three unsuspecting victims passed us to enter the forbidden forest. One of them had her dog on a leash. Our dog took one look at that mutt, turned around and hightailed it right back into the thickets.

Les went running after Pumpkin, making clear reference to her intelligence and her uncertain life expectancy. A short time later he came stumbling out with a repentant pooch.

Now we had to face the hill. To say we limped up it would put us in a better light than we deserve. Les had to carry Pumpkin because she was panting so hard from her run-away escapade that we were concerned she would have cardiac arrest. I was hanging on to Les's elbow for support and motivation.

Halfway up, we sat down on the edge of the road. When we started to discuss our will, I realized this had not been a positive experience for us.

Finally we stumbled into our living room. As I headed for our recliner, something caught my peripheral attention. I turned and six birds were . . . in my front yard.

Isn't that funny?
I went looking for something I already had.

33

Color Bind

When Les picked me up from the airport, he was dangling the house keys with obvious excitement. He had been out of work following heart surgery, and we felt grateful not only for a job but also that a house was provided for our family. He was to be the director of a Christian conference center, and we would live on the grounds.

But I had not anticipated how quickly my gratitude could seep out.

My first glance of the house left me speechless. Even the cover of night was not enough to disguise the color wheel environment of our "new" dwelling.

My friend Mary Ann summed it up when she stepped in the front door, gasped, screamed and then proclaimed, "This is ghastly!"

Truly it was. Living here would be like trying to live in a kaleidoscope that some child kept twirling. The colors collided so loudly that the place was noisy.

Come take a tour. First, picture the color orange. Got it? Now brighten it. Now intensify that. You now have my kitchen cupboards.

These reflect in interesting patterns off my luscious lime green coun-tertops. The wallpaper in the kitchen is bursting with giant coffee pots in red, rust and orange.

The kitchen is open to the dining area, where the walls are painted powder blue. The carpeting is green and yellow shag, highlighted with oval-shaped animal stains . . . memoirs of Fido and Felix, I presume.

The dining room is also open to the living room. Both the living room and dining area have large plate glass windows with smaller windows above those. The smaller ones are painted deep royal blue with a full moon in the center of each pane (which truly is a pain). Eight full moons gave us a real orbital addition.

Someone must have read that wood adds to the decor. So, that person added a half-wall of gray barn wood, a full wall of red-stained plywood and a high but narrow wall of brown lumber.

Did I mention these walls are all in the same rooms with the moons, stains and colors? Just checking. I didn't want you to miss any of the ambience.

That evening I left there with an attitude. I didn't realize anyone had noticed until just before we moved.

Marty, our eldest, was sitting on the couch when I came downstairs. Like his mother, Marty does not care for early a.m. chatter. We don't usually get into meaningful conversations till noonish. So it was a surprise when I heard words coming from his lips.

"I can't believe it," he stated while staring at the floor.

"What can't you believe?" I inquired, amazed he was talking.

"I just can't believe it!" he repeated with greater conviction, still staring floor-ward.

This short but vague conversation was already getting on my nerves. "Why don't you tell me what you can't believe so I can't believe it with you," I insisted.

Slowly lifting and shaking his head, he gently stated, "I can't believe your attitude."

"My attitude?!" I responded defensively, elevating to my full, intimidating five-foot stature.

"Yes," he went on to clarify, "your attitude about our new home. Here you've been praying for a job for Dad and a home for our family. When it's provided, you allow something as surface as paint to distract you and rob us all of joy."

I turned and headed for the kitchen, feeling unable to defend myself. As I walked away I thought, *Who raised that kid anyway?*

I stood in the kitchen and decided I needed to talk with a woman. I prayed and immediately a name came to my mind.

"No, Lord, that's not it; try again." It didn't seem like the right name. She was a gracious and loving woman but not someone I had ever called for help. Yet the name seemed to stay pressed firmly in the forefront of my mind, so I dialed the phone.

Eleanor was home and took the time to listen to my dilemma. When I got all done with my colorful tale of woe, she simply said, "I have a poem for you."

A poem? I cried inwardly. *See, Lord, I told You she wasn't the one!*

Had she even said, "I have a can of paint for you," at least that would have been practical.

Eleanor began with her compassionate voice to quote a poem that permeated my veneer and exposed the content of my heart.

The woman who can move about a house,
Whether it be a mansion or a camp,
And deftly lay a fire and spread a cloth,
And light a lamp,
And by her loving touch give
The look of home wherever she may be . . .
Such a woman always will seem great,
And beautiful to me.

It was as if the Lord pressed that poem into my heart and did some redecorating. I hung up, knowing I had called the right person.

I pulled a chair to the middle of the room amidst the riotous color and prayed. "Lord, forgive my ungrateful heart, and help me to see what my part is in making this place into a home for my family."

As I scanned my house again, ideas began to flood my mind, and I actually got excited. First, I hired a painter.

I told him, "If you can see it, feel it or touch it, paint it. If it moves, step on it and then paint it."

I had everything painted off-white, even the wood, to give it some continuity. We scraped away our moons. Then we ripped out the stained rug and replaced it with soft gray carpeting.

Now the place looked antiseptic. Adding mauves and blues cured that. Furniture and flowers were our finishing touches.

What started off as a colorful disaster has ended up being a creative delight.

What colors your attitude?

34

Fright Flight

Yoo-hoo, Patsy," I heard someone sing out as I headed for my car in the church parking lot. I turned and saw my friend Claris waving her hand.

"Could you use some sweet corn?" she offered.

"I'd love some," I responded.

"I'll drop off a sack," she assured me as she slid into her pickup and started the engine.

I had a few errands to take care of, but when I arrived home, I was surprised to see Claris had already been there. True to her promise, I saw my bag of corn on the porch propped against the front door.

I repositioned my bag from the drugstore in one arm and embraced the corn sack with the other. I awkwardly unlocked the door and pushed it open with my knee.

Going from the bright sunlight into the dimly lit living room temporarily blinded me. I let the drugstore paraphernalia slide onto the couch, landing gently on the cushion. That freed my hands to open and examine my produce.

I balanced the bag on the back of the couch as I unrolled the top. I was still trying to make my visual adjustment from the outside, so I had to stick my head in the bag to get a corn count.

I'm not sure if my eyes focused first or my nose detected that this was not corn. What I saw were feathers, what I smelled was foul. To be more specific, it was a foul owl.

Reactions can be more rapid than reason. I simultaneously screamed and flung the odoriferous owl ceiling-ward. I went yelling out the door for my husband, who tried to assure me that the worst thing my feathered foe could do at this point was smell—no, make that stink—to high heaven, which was exactly where I had tried to throw that bird.

It turned out that some generous gentleman had found this rotting road-kill on the highway and thought we might like to stuff it for the Boy Scout Museum. At that point, I envisioned mounting the motorist, as a menace to mental health . . . mine!

Caution: Examine carefully before embracing expectations.

35

Stitches

The nine-year age span between our boys didn't keep them from big-time wrestling bouts. I pointed out to eight-year-old Jason that challenging his seventeen-year-old brother was not exactly wise. Jason seemed to have a Hulk Hogan mind-set but the body frame of Pee-wee Herman.

During a body slam attempt, he fell over a footstool and cut his head open on the corner of the wall. Les and I hustled Jason off to the emergency room, because it was obvious he would need more than a Band-Aid.

Jason was shaken and asked, "How bad is it?"

I realized that the location of his injury was to our advantage. He couldn't see it.

"Not real bad," I assured him.

"What are they going to do to me?"

Measuring my words I responded, "Fix it."

"How?"

"They're going to put it back together again," I tried.

"How?" he pushed.

I'd run out of Humpty Dumpty stalls and decided to go for the direct approach.

"They're going to stitch that thing shut, Jason," I declared.

He gasped and then groaned. "Is it going to hurt?"

"Probably," I confessed.

"But what if it hurts more than I'm able to bear?" he pleaded.

"Then you'll reach down inside of you and pull up your courage. Because you accepted Jesus as your Savior, He assures us we can do all things through Christ who strengthens us. So if it hurts more than you can bear, you pray, and He will help you."

Jason became very quiet. We pulled up to the emergency entrance, and I took him in while Les parked the car. The doctor came in, took a look at Jason's injury and began to prepare the wound for sutures. Lest things get active, he had two nurses come in, one to stand on each side of Jason.

Halfway through the process, the doctor realized both nurses were not necessary since Jason offered no resistance. Not once did Jason object to the process or cry or even ask the doctor to stop.

One of the nurses turned to leave when she noticed someone else in the room who was in need of help. I'm not sure if it was my magenta and jade skin tone or my swaying in the breeze that alerted her, but she guided me to a chair and began to fan me. Later the doctor assisted me to the car.

On the way out he said, "I cannot tell you what a privilege it was to work on a boy like that."

My husband shot me a glance as if to say, "Wish I could say the same for his mother!"

As we drove home, I asked Jason, "Did it hurt so bad you had to pray?"

"Oh, Mom, I didn't wait. As soon as you told me, I prayed," he confessed.

"What a good idea. I . . . wish . . . I . . . would . . . have . . . thought of that," I whispered.

Is your life sutured in prayer?

36

Girl Talk

You're not getting older; you're getting better!"

Who said that, and whom were they talking about? I've been looking around, and that's not what I'm seeing.

When I say "around," I mean around me. On my fortyish anatomy are ridges. I thought only potato chips were supposed to have those. These are not even rigid ridges. They're more like Jell-O. They slosh when I walk. They appear to hang in folds round about my waist.

Speaking of waste, I think it's a waste of my energy to carry these waving sacks of cellulite that are drooping off my upper arms.

No wonder women get heavier as they age—everything's turning to liquid. We are like walking washing machines. That's why we are so easily agitated and slosh a lot.

My husband and I were eating dinner the other evening when Les said, "You spilled something on your chin."

I quickly picked up my napkin and dabbed my chin.

He quipped, "No, the other one."

I don't know where those other chins came from. They weren't there when I was thirty.

I've been accused lately of looking snooty in my pictures. Don't they understand I have to hold my first chin that high to smooth out the other three?

Speaking of smooth, what has happened to my thighs? They look permanently puckered, like smocking. I feel speed-impaired at times as one leg of blubber bumps the other. Blubber-bumping can be painful.

Speaking of painful, I now get charley horses. The only place I have muscle left, and just my luck, it knots up!

One thing that has definitely increased as I age is my hair count. I have hair in places I never imagined. Like my neck. I have a three-inch follicle growing from my neck just under my third chin.

I've noticed my mental faculties are slowing down, and now I'm expected to learn a new vocabulary. Words like "menopausal"—sounds like a slow date. "Sputtering ovaries"—sounds like a rare bird or an old car. "Estrogen"—sounds like something you'd drink in outer space.

I don't know. This is all too much for me. I think I'm going to have a case of the vapors.

Gird-le up, gals. There's more to life than meets the eye.

37

Cookie Caper

White creamy clouds of marshmallow atop a thin layer of graham cracker, covered and sealed in a smooth two-inch tower of chocolate—the lick-your-fingers-and-catch-the-crumbs kind of cookies.

I have this "thing" for chocolate marshmallow cookies—alias pinwheels. At first I didn't realize I had a thing. I told myself I was only buying them for my family. But when I began to resent sharing those sweet treats with my husband and our boys, I took a closer look at my cookie consumption.

In a let's-get-healthy moment, I decided to give up my prized pinwheels. The problem was, one cookie was left and, well, I sort of thought it would be wasteful to throw it out.

Besides I'm not too good at this denial stuff—at least not cold cookie. But to eat the last cookie right then seemed so . . . so sudden.

Plus, when you know this is your last cookie, you don't want to just devour it. The moment should be more ceremonial. The cookie needs

91

to be savored. It needs to be appreciated. It needs to be mine! And I knew if I did a couple of household tasks, which I should do, I wouldn't feel as bad when I ate the last cookie, which I shouldn't do.

To protect my piggish plan, I went into the kitchen and hid the cookie from my family. I tucked it in the bottom kitchen drawer behind the rolling pin, next to the measuring cups, with two hot pads carefully placed over the top to form a roof for my little sugar shack. Then I quietly slid closed the drawer and headed off to do my chores.

I cleaned my desk, dusted the living room and changed the sheets on the boys' beds. Then I headed for the kitchen, feeling I had earned this moment.

I checked over both shoulders before sliding open the drawer and removing the roof. There was the rolling pin and the measuring cups. And next to them was . . . the spot where the cookie should have been. My cookie was gone!

The next thing I remember I was running through the house, grabbing my purse and keys, and crying out, "But, Lord, I said just one more cookie!"

I sprinted to my car and hightailed it for the grocery store. I heard myself murmuring, "Just one more cookie, just one more cookie."

Finally I was in the store, moving quickly, far too quickly I realize now as I think back on the little children I had to move aside to clear the way to the cookie aisle.

At last! I had arrived and there, where they should be, were the cookies. Only one bag of pinwheels was left.

As I stood there, faced with my vice, that package packed with chocolate, I reminded myself I was an adult, and I had a choice to make. I could buy them, or I could turn and walk away a wiser woman.

Well, I ate two on the way to the checkout lane and three more on the way home.

By the time I pulled into the driveway I was full, and it wasn't just from the cookies. It was also the guilt. I was mad at myself. To think a grown woman could be controlled by a two-inch glob of chocolate!

I thought I was more mature than that. Funny, the Lord didn't seem surprised at all.

Any sugar-coated secrets in your life?

38

Pulling Strings

I'm married to a mellow fellow. It's a good thing, because I don't think our house could take two of me. I'm so tightly strung I need the balance of someone who has his feet on the ground.

I can identify with my friend Cindy, who said her husband, Craig, is like a balloon-man. He has both feet securely planted.

She's like a hot-air balloon, flying off in different directions. Craig watches her until she gets a little too far out, and then he takes hold of the string and pulls Cindy back down to earth.

Even though I'm grateful Les is a mild-mannered man, at times I wish he would show a little more enthusiasm. Recently I purchased a new dress, and I brought it out on a hanger for Les's viewing.

"What do you think?" I prompted.

"That's nice."

"Nice?" I cried.

"Didn't you ask me what I thought of your dress?" he asked, puzzled. "Your dress is nice."

"Les, 'nice' makes me nauseous."

"What do you want from me?"

"I want dramatic; I want dynamic; I want some enthusiasm!" I demanded loudly.

"Patsy, that dress is nice," he said with quiet firmness.

So I took the "nice" dress and stomped back to the closet.

On my way across the room, Les called out, "Patsy, look! Patsy, look!"

I turned and saw my two-hundred-pound husband leaping in the air, arms stretched heavenward, exclaiming, "Wow, what a dress! Wow, what a dress!"

I burst out laughing. My steady, ground-level man was behaving like a helium balloon.

Ever notice when we try to remake a person that
we are seldom satisfied with the result?

Dynamic Duo

The flight was full. Every seat was filled with an eager traveler leaving the cold Midwest for a warmer destination.

The flight attendant handed out our lunch trays. My next-seat neighbor and I were trying to figure out our questionable cuisine (by its freeze-dried taste), when someone screamed in the back of the plane.

Ever notice when someone screams the quiet that follows seems so loud?

People react differently to a nervous moment. My seatmate began to eat faster and faster. My fork stopped in midair, and I'm sure I appeared frozen in time.

Actually, I was making some fast decisions. My first decision, because I am a great woman of faith, was "I am not going to look."

I knew if I looked I would see that the plane's back section had fallen off, and I would be sucked out. But, if I didn't look, we might land safely before I found out.

That might have worked, except the next time the girl screamed she

97

was standing beside me. Do you know how hard it is to ignore a fellow traveler who's screaming inches from your frozen fork?

By now my seatmate had managed to place all of the food from her tray in her mouth. She had not chewed or swallowed. She looked like she had stored up enough in her cheeks for the winter.

As you might guess, the attendants busily tried to take care of the emergency. It turned out the girl was traveling with her grandmother, who had become ill, and it had frightened the young woman.

As a precaution and to make them more comfortable, they were moved to first class. Soon we noticed grandma and granddaughter were in comfortable conversation with the flight attendant. All was well.

Well, almost all. I had lost my appetite, and my seatmate was looking mumpy.

In an emergency, do you freeze, feed or face it with faith?

40

Weighty Matters

Scales that announce your weight? You've got to be kidding! How humiliating. I bet some ninety-pound, undernourished model came up with that winner.

The only thing worse than a robot voice announcing my tonnage is a robot with recall.

I was staying with my friends, the Hootens in El Paso, when Joyce announced, "Patsy, we have a new scale you must try."

"Oh, really," I replied with skepticism. "Why is that?"

"It's just wonderful. It talks," she joyfully reported. "It will not only tell you your weight, but it also has a memory and will tell you tomorrow if you have lost or gained."

She was thrilled. I was appalled.

I find it depressing to think that, as Righteous Robot trumpets my weight, everyone in the home hears the results. This isn't the final score for the World Series, for goodness' sakes.

"Patsy has gained five and a half pounds!" I imagined it broadcasting.

Yes, it even calls you by name.

I believe in being friendly, but calling me by my first name in the same breath as my weight is a little too intimate for me.

Next they'll put a microchip in our driver's license that heralds our age every time we pull it out of our wallets.

After a number of creative stalls, I finally responded, "No, Joyce, I'm only here for a few days. I don't think it would be productive."

Translated that means, "Ain't no way I'm leaving Texas with that information left behind."

What weighty issue tips your scale?

Buggy

I crawled into bed after midnight. Clicking off the light, I dropped my head onto the pillow. As my ears adjusted to the quietness, I began to drift off.

Then it happened. A small but definite noise. The kind of noise that causes me to become irrational and unreasonable.

I sat up in bed and shook Les.

"What's wrong?" he questioned.

"I hear a mouse."

"I don't hear anything," he stated before he even listened. He knew from experience he would get no rest if we had a mouse.

I slipped out of bed and began to move across the creaking wood floor. I stopped several times and tried to detect from which direction the chomping was coming.

This was behavior befitting a Purple Heart. In the past I would have not only insisted Les get up but also that he immediately list the house with realtors.

As I stood statue-like, I glanced down and saw something moving. No, I saw many somethings moving.

"Les, quick," I summoned.

Les jumped to his feet, motivated by the urgency in my voice. Much to our surprise, a long procession of large carpenter ants was pouring out of our heat register, doing double time across the wood floor and under the bedroom door.

We each grabbed a shoe and began to decrease their population. One of them must have yelled "run," because they scattered in all directions.

After a few moments, we stopped to listen. Once again I could hear chomping. This time the noise was very close. The sound seemed to come out of the door.

I placed my ear against the wood, and the mouse-sound magnified. Then I realized the ants weren't going under the door but inside it. The chomping wasn't a mouse, but a colony of carpenters eating their way through the door's inner layers.

Now I wanted to move!

Les, being far more reasonable, did some carpentry work himself. He retrieved some tools, took the door off the hinges and dragged it out into the night. (I was lucky he didn't drag me out.)

We were now door-less and hopefully ant-less. That night I dreamed that Les borrowed a gun and was trying to shoot the invaders out of the door.

The next morning I got up and went to my desk to work. After only a few minutes I heard a familiar sound—like chomping. I walked to my office door and realized it, too, was harboring a colony. Les then unhinged and removed that door.

Now I was coming unhinged! I was feeling antsie. I began to listen at every door, drawer and floor for the pitter-patter of little feet. I couldn't believe we could have that many unwanted guests and not know it.

Our creeping invaders were using the heat ducts as freeways. The ducts gave the critters, who traveled "antnonymously," access to every room. Since we had only seen a few here and there, we didn't realize that they had moved in their relatives. While we were sleeping, they were devouring . . . our house.

> *Beware of creeping little things*
> *that splinter your house.*

42

Airborne

Edith's combination of qualities drew me to her—her courage, creativity and confidence in God. Besides, she was fun. When I had the opportunity to be her roommate at a women's retreat, I leaped at the chance.

But when I saw the skyscraper we would be calling home, I felt "building dread." I get dizzy when I stand up straight and certainly had not planned on a high-rise experience.

Edith was delighted. For her, everything in life was a grand adventure.

As the clerk mentioned we would be on the twenty-fourth floor, I felt nauseated. Edith was elated. I hate elevators. I tried to figure out how I was going to backpack my luggage up twenty-four flights of steps.

Edith had no idea what I was going through as she headed confidently for the elevators. I had never mentioned to her that I avoided anything that elevates, levitates or regurgitates.

When the elevator arrived, a woman stepped out and proclaimed to me, "That's the fastest elevator I've ever been on!"

I immediately did not care for this woman. She obviously had not been raised properly or had chosen to ignore the commandment "Thou shalt not talk to strangers."

Edith bounded into the elevator and held the door for me. I suggested by my behavior that my suitcase had become so heavy I was unable to get to her. She stared with obvious doubt and confusion. Other people boarded the elevator and glared in my direction with growing agitation.

I knew I would have to get on or be humiliated. I sent emergency prayers heavenward, which by this time I believed to be the twenty-fifth floor.

I tugged at my luggage as I swallowed hard and reluctantly stepped on, closing my eyes so I wouldn't have to see the door seal me in.

Before I could work up a good fear, we had arrived.

Edith opened the door to our room and exclaimed with delight on finding a wall-to-wall, floor-to-ceiling window. I clung to the doorframe to keep our room from sliding off its platform.

She galloped toward the window, thrilled with the view. I began to wonder what I thought was so fun about this woman. She pressed her nose against the glass and beckoned me to join her. Then she turned, surveyed the room and suggested with enthusiasm that we take the bed closest to the window before our other roomies arrived.

"Won't that be fun," I lied.

That night I dreamed I fell off the bed and rolled out the window.

By the time the weekend was over, however, I was grateful I hadn't bolted and run but had stayed and won. I even gradually made my way to the small table next to the window and ate lunch with Edith. This was a mountaintop experience for a former agoraphobic, who couldn't wear high heels without needing oxygen.

Given a choice, I still prefer the first floor; but I've since learned being up doesn't have to be a down experience.

What has you up in the air?

Revenge

I've always been a talker, so it was natural for me, as a teenager, to take a job in telephone sales work. The goal of my position was to interest homeowners in a salesman coming by to explain our service.

Each phone girl had a script to simplify the job, to increase confidence and to keep on target. We sat in a line in front of one long desk that had partitions so we could lean forward and have some privacy when phoning. At the end of the room was a master phone where our boss could listen in on our calls.

The first week of work the boss, without warning, listened in on one of my pitiful attempts. When I hung up, he announced in front of the entire office, "Patsy, that was the worst sales presentation I have ever heard."

I was humiliated. I was infuriated. I was motivated. I attacked that phoning with fervor and determination.

At the end of the week I had more sales than anyone in the office.

By the end of the month I was the top sales girl.
And then in childish revenge . . . I quit!

How do you handle criticism?

Birthday Baby

When my nutritionist said, "No more sugar," I didn't have a sweet response. I did notice I was feeling better, though, when I followed her advice. But there were times . . .

We had been invited to Mary Ann and George's for a couples' Bible study. After the study we surprised our mutual friend Burt with a birthday salute. We gave him cards and sang and . . . then it happened. Mary Ann had baked a huge chocolate supreme pudding cake.

George was helping to serve, not only because he's a good host but also because Mary Ann was on crutches, recovering from an injury. Every time George entered the room with generous mounds of cake, applause and groans of gratitude filled the air.

Something began to happen inside of me as I observed this dessert distribution. It annoyed me that everyone was making such a big fuss over a sugar-infested gooey-gob of chocolate.

And why Mary Ann felt led to add super-sized scoops of vanilla ice cream was beyond me. Excessive, that's what it was.

Just look how silly they were behaving, oohing and ahing like children. It seemed to me that it wouldn't hurt a few of them to skip dessert for a while.

It was at this point that my husband was handed his mountainous masterpiece. His eyes were the size of dessert plates. He lit up with glee. Then he leaned over to me and said, "Would you mind getting me some coffee?"

"Get it yourself!" I shot back so quickly and abruptly that it surprised even me.

Les looked at me with the eyes of a rejected puppy. I felt embarrassed and ticked. I grabbed the cup and headed for the kitchen.

When I returned, Les was face first in his dish, having a lip-licking time.

I thought, *How sad that adults behave out of their addictions.*

Mary Ann called from the other room, "Patsy, could you help me?"

I walked into the kitchen, where she pointed to her dessert and sweetly asked, "Would you carry that to the living room for me?"

The injustice of it all! If you can't carry your own cake, then you shouldn't have any, is my theory.

Now, I know one should not think about tripping a person on crutches, but for one moment that thought scampered through my mind.

Grudgingly, I raced back to the main room, got rid of the calorie-crammed cake and took my seat next to Les, who now reeked of chocolate.

Then George decided to close our loving time of fellowship in prayer.

The little child inside of me throwing the temper tantrum stopped long enough to listen. As I walked out the door, I realized I was the only one with cake on my face.

Better check a mirror. I hear it's contagious!

45

Sandal Scandal

Jonah makes me giggle.

Here was a prophet waiting for orders from headquarters. When they came, he strapped on his Reebok sandals and hightailed it out of town—in the wrong direction.

Jonah was a man who decided to live below "see" level, as he boarded the boat and went down into the hold.

I felt a little down myself when my husband came in recently from the mailbox waving a letter. I recognized the telephone company's insignia on the envelope.

"No thanks," I called sweetly. "You can take care of that."

"No," he replied, "I think you need to see this."

"It's really old news when you stop to think about it," I suggested.

"History is valuable; we can learn from it," he insisted.

I tried a spiritual approach. "Forgetting that which is behind, I press on."

By now he was dangling the expansive sheet of long-distance calls in front of my face. I felt "see" sick.

Have you ever noticed when you don't do what you know you should, you lose your vitality? Look at Jonah. After running away and going below see level, he was plum worn out. He was so tired he snored through a life-threatening storm.

My doctor used to tell me, "Patsy, you're like an ostrich. Every time life gets hard, you want to jump in bed and cover up your head."

I would think, *I must be anemic, I must be hypoglycemic, I must have PMS or TMJ or IRS or FBI.*

All I knew was I was one tired woman. Denial and disobedience are draining.

When Jonah climbed onto his ship of self-pity, he had no idea how low he could go.

I wonder if the Lord said, "Jonah needs some time by himself. Gabriel, reserve him a suite at that new Sea Sub Inn. I understand it has a lot of atmosphere."

Jonah didn't seem thrilled with his accommodations. His room didn't have much of a view, but he had plenty of running water and free transportation. The experience must have been inspiring, because he became a motivated prophet and seemed in a hurry to Reebok down to Nineveh.

All ashore that's going ashore.
Or you can stay below see level.

46

Color-Coded

Does turning forty bother you?" Les asked on my birthday.

"You've got to be kidding. Everyone has thought I was so much older for so long, it's a relief. It makes me feel legitimate," I insisted.

"You know what I hope never happens to you?" he added wistfully.

"What?"

"I hope you never get to the point, when you wave your hand to say good-bye, your underarm waves in the opposite direction."

"That quite honestly has never entered my mind," I assured him.

My husband may be prophetic, because about two weeks later, during my morning shower, every bit of tone rinsed out of my body and down the drain.

It's truly an aggravating attribute to be moving in one direction and feel your body waving in response. Stopping is the challenge, because it takes several seconds for the fleshy momentum to slow to a jiggle and finally stop. One could suffer from "whip flab" if one were not careful or stopped too quickly.

I realized Les noticed his fear had come true when Mother's Day came that year. He bought me a set of dumbbells. Actually, mine were called "smart bells." I didn't think it was a smart move on his part. I was insulted. No, make that ticked!

Finally I decided to do the scriptural thing with my heavy gift and take the writer of Hebrews' advice, "Let us lay aside every weight . . . which doth so easily beset us . . . ." I put them in storage in my bedroom closet.

I had put other things in there never to find them again. I was hoping for that kind of fate for my "bells."

Les never mentioned that I wasn't using them. I think he knew better.

Christmas came, and the memory of my Mom's Day gift had almost faded. For a moment, though, I felt some initial apprehension when he handed me a beautiful package, lest I find a tummy tuck coupon book or a fanny fixer or some other anatomy adjuster.

To my delight, however, I found a multi-colored dress with a shimmering fabric that was feminine and lovely. I was impressed. I was speaking for a luncheon in the area for a holiday celebration, and this would be perfect.

I still remember standing on a small platform speaking on "Jesus Is the Reason for the Season." To add emphasis to one of my points, I made a sweeping gesture only to notice, for the first time, the full draping sleeve.

That's when it hit me; Les had given me colorful camouflage. He had taken a more subtle approach to fleecing my flab. I laughed to myself and thought, *I'll get him later!*

What colorful cover-ups are you using?

Alert

Breakfast can be dangerous to your health. It can look innocent enough, flakes and raisins floating in milk, like the breakfast I had one morning. If I had left those raisins floating, all might have been well.

I'm not sure now if I coughed or just took a breath, but one of those rebellious raisins ran down my airpipe and wouldn't move. I hacked and coughed. I jumped up and down. Then I realized if I got real still I could breathe. My heart, which had been pounding madly, began to find its rhythm again.

I remembered a doctor was staying on the grounds (we were living at a Youth for Christ camp). If I could get to him, he would help me.

I made it to the dining hall without another fruit fit, and gratefully the doctor had just sat down to eat.

"Doctor," I whispered, "I have a raisin stuck in my windpipe. What should I do?"

He looked at me thoughtfully. After a moment of sizing up the situation, he gave his professional evaluation. "We can do a tracheotomy," he offered calmly, as he reached for his juice glass.

My heart began to palpitate wildly.

"Any other options?" I stammered.

"I could try forceps, but there's a chance the raisin would go into your lung, causing it to collapse," he concluded, as he buttered his toast.

Sweat began to appear on my deeply furrowed brow.

"Doctor, is there anything else I might do?" I whimpered weakly.

"Well," he said, hesitating while he salted his eggs, "you could try relaxing and see if it comes up on its own."

Out of all his medical insights, this one was the most appealing to me. I headed back to my apartment, wondering how that doctor could eat his breakfast while I was obviously terminating on mine.

When I got home, I positioned myself in my rocker to contemplate my fruitful dilemma. My mind began to wander to the future...

I was looking into a cemetery where two women were talking.

The one said, "What's that?" pointing to a large tombstone.

"Oh, the one shaped like a raisin?" the other responded. "I can't remember her name, but she was bumped off by her breakfast."

My heart started to jump again, and I realized I was not helping my situation with my daydreaming. I wandered into the bedroom and cautiously lowered myself onto the bed. It felt like I had a baseball in my throat. I decided to go to sleep so if it didn't work out in my favor I'd never know it.

To my amazement, I fell sound asleep. I woke up a couple of hours later—absolutely fine. I could breathe, the baseball feeling was gone, my lung had not collapsed, and I didn't need a tracheotomy. I checked all around me in bed but found no raisin. I don't know where it went; maybe it was resurrected.

All I know is I learned a good lesson—eat oatmeal.

What's difficult for you to swallow?

Scared Silly

When Carol's mom invited me to go on vacation with their family, I was thrilled. Carol was one of my best friends, and I thought a week with her would be an adventure. Carol and I were fifteen. We considered ourselves quite grown up; others seemed to find that debatable.

More than once her mom warned us that we would be staying in a ghost town. There wouldn't be much to do, and there would be no boys. We didn't care, because we enjoyed each other's company, and besides her mother could be wrong about the boys.

We arrived at the little deserted town after dark. Street lights were few and far between. Carol and I took one look at the silhouette of the tall, narrow, rickety house we were to call home that week and announced we weren't going in. It looked spooky to us, and we were scared.

The only thing more intimidating than this haunted-looking house was Carol's mom when she got angry. We had just completed a ten-hour drive, and she didn't want to argue with two sniveling teenagers regarding their accommodations.

Hanging on to each other's shirttails, we inched our way up the rotting steps into . . . a fairly pleasant home. We began to breathe easier until someone mentioned that the bathroom was in the basement.

This was not good news. Carol and I don't do basements. Who in her right mind is going to use a basement rest room in a declining house in a ghost town, especially at night? We decided then and there to exercise great restraint for the next week.

Eventually we realized the futility of that thought and had to make the downward trek. We always entered the cement and stone basement together; and while one went into the water closet, the other sat on the steps nearby.

We talked nonstop and loudly until we came back up, feeling our noise level kept us safe from the basement boogies.

One day Carol and I took a walk through the woods to Lake Superior. On such a beautiful summer day we figured we had no reason to be afraid until . . . we heard noises.

Crackling noises. Crunching sounds. Brush movement.

We glanced at each other as we remembered the stories about area bears. We turned around and began to head back to town with a quickened pace.

The suspicious sounds seemed to quicken, too.

We grabbed hands and began to run and sing loudly. Somehow we both believed that volume was a deterrent to danger. Besides, it had worked so far on the basement boogies, so maybe it would work on the backwoods bears.

We thought a popular song about Yogi Bear was appropriate for the occasion. "I'm a Yogi, I'm a Yogi Bear. Hey Boo-Boo," we sang again and again, hoping to distract and deter our assailants.

By the time we reached town, we could hardly catch our breath, our hearts were pounding wildly, and we were laughing and crying with relief.

We never did see anything . . . well, not with our eyes. But in our minds, every bush had become a bear.

What a week we had! One we would never forget. We created much of our own fun . . . and fear.

Any boogies in your basement?

P.S. She was wrong about "no boys." I'm married to him!

Misdirected

I had just disembarked from a rather bumpy flight. Les was waiting to pick me up, and I shared with him about the growing storm clouds around Chicago. He looked at me puzzled and inquired, "How would you know about the weather patterns in Chicago?"

I responded with sarcasm, "Well, isn't that where I've just been?"

"No," he stated with authority, "you've been in New York."

"I was? I thought I was in Chicago," I confessed in a somewhat lower voice.

Shaking his head in disbelief, he walked ahead of me mumbling something about not knowing how I got from one place to another without him.

Well, come on now. They are on the same side of the country. It's not like I mixed up Pittsburgh and Pasadena.

Besides, I can't help it if I came packaged with directional deficiencies. More than once Les has thought he would have to file a missing-person report on me when we have gone browsing.

The new one-stop shopping system offers, under a single roof, everything a couple could want as long as they both shall live, if they don't get hopelessly lost in the aisles in the process. With the size of today's stores, they should offer us maps, guides and skateboards as we enter.

I can't tell you how embarrassing it is to hear your name announced over the intercom. "If Mrs. Clairmont is in the store, Mr. Clairmont would like her to find her way to the front door, and he will lead her to the car."

The one-stop shop in our area is like an enclosed wilderness. I find myself wandering the aisles wondering, *What am I looking for? Why am I here? Where is my husband? How do I get out of this maze?*

Getting out of the store is just the first phase of testing your survival skills. Next is the biggie—finding your car in the parking lot. I have learned to play Car Bingo.

It works like this: Line up your vehicle with a letter on the building or an object. For instance, you might see a trash can at the end of your lane. You then count how many parking spaces between your car and the receptacle.

Let's say there are fourteen. When you come out of the store, you stand in front of the trash can. Then walk fourteen spaces . . . bingo, your car.

This is not exactly foolproof, though, because I notice that malls have a sensitivity to litter. Our mall has sixteen identical garbage bins, which if you have your calculator handy, means I could (did) look in 256 parking slots before I could shout, "Bingo!"

It's taken years, but I can sort of read a map now. If I get to you, however, don't ask me to get back to where I came from. I don't know why, but I can't reverse directions. I'm a one-way lady.

My husband believes that when I was being "knit together," somebody dropped my directional stitches.

Would you mind if I followed you . . .
that is, uh, if you know where you're going?

Sew Simple

A stitch in time saves nine, unless they're mine!" This quote was said by me, about me, and seconded by my high school home economics teacher.

Our class project was to make a simple straight skirt. Six weeks later, when everyone else was wearing her designer original, I was still trying to sew the darts.

My teacher was not happy. In fact, at times she didn't even look human. Her eyes seemed to glaze over and dilate when she checked my seams.

She made me tear them out so many times it was difficult to find enough solid material on which to try my next stitches.

Finally, a neighbor woman took pity on me and finished my skirt. My teacher knew an adult had sewn it, but she didn't seem to mind. In fact, she looked relieved—until she found out I had enrolled in sewing for another semester.

After announcing to the new class its sewing project, she took me aside and told me I would be doing something different. She decided I should knit a little pair of slippers. The problem was I didn't know how to knit. She assured me it would be simple.

Six weeks later I had a healthy square of knit—too large for a slipper, too small for a rug. I never did figure out how to fit it around my foot.

But my teacher didn't want it on my foot anymore. She mumbled something about putting it in a time capsule, because future generations wouldn't believe anyone could get that many stitches per square inch. I guess I held my needles a little too tight.

When I married Les, I didn't mention my home ec experiences. It didn't seem relevant—until he asked me in our first week of marriage to sew a tear in his pants' seam. I obliged, because I didn't want him to think I couldn't handle my wifely duties.

Several times he came in to see if his pants were ready. I took my time to make sure the stitches were secure.

A little while later Les came hopping out of the bathroom, unable to get his foot through the leg. It seems I stitched through one too many layers. Sometimes it's the thought that counts.

After years of Les doing our mending, the Zander family came into our lives. Margret is a seamstress, and George is a tailor.

Margret assured me that my schoolteacher was wrong, and Margret had never met anyone she couldn't teach to sew. It would be simple.

Margret began to work with me. She was patient. She was kind. She was thorough.

Then one day she looked at me and said, "Patsy, there are exceptions to every rule. From now on you bring your sewing to me."

Feeling unraveled?
There are those He sends to sew and mend.

Subpoena

O rder! Order! Order in the house!

Those words echoed in my head every time I opened a drawer, closet or cupboard. The gavel of conviction was pounding out my disorderly conduct.

I confess my house got away from me. It happened a little at a time, like mold slithering over some elderly eggplant in the back of my refrigerator. Because a person could do dust etchings on my bookshelves and grease engravings on my range, it was clear evidence was piling up against me.

I don't think all of the household disarray was my fault, though. For instance, take the socks . . . actually, you don't have to. Someone already did. Every third pair of socks, correction, that's "sock," in our home lives a solitary life.

If professionals were brought in on this case, they'd discover my dryer has a latent aggression problem. When it surfaces, the heating element disintegrates individual stockings, leaving me holding the spouseless sock. My dryer is selective and careful never to destroy two of the same kind—a true sign of a criminal mind.

I plead guilty to the webbing on my wall hangings, but I had an accomplice. My friend Norm Crane told me, "Never kill a spider. They are wonderful house guests because they are like having your own built-in silent exterminator."

Norm obviously doesn't suffer from arachnophobia.

My husband and two sons struggle with basket-phobia. They can't get close enough to my strategically placed baskets to toss in their dirty clothes. They prefer corners, chairs and doorknobs.

It does give a certain lived-in look (the kind you might find in a high school locker room after a losing game). They drape their used sweat suits and socks so that any movement of air might permeate our home with their own personal fragrance.

My junk drawer in the kitchen has overflowed, spilling shoe horns, screwdrivers, safety glasses, soda straws and squirt guns onto the countertops. This gives the room an antiquated ambience.

I'm drowning in our clutter. I think someone should provide a household suction service in which workmen could pull up in their garbage truck-type vehicle, attach a giant suction tube over the opening of the front door and then throw the switch.

The machine would create a vacuum, sucking up everything that wasn't put away. A second switch would then be activated, and the disorganized debris would be compacted into filler for highway potholes.

We would improve our environment, recycling our clutter while providing a service. Then, instead of tripping over our junk, we could drive on it.

Perhaps I could get probation if I volunteered to work on the Household Suction Service crew. We could start on my house.

Need any debris suctioned from your life?

52

Culprit

I had never kidnapped anyone before, and I was quite excited at the prospect. All the details had to be set in motion if I was to pull it off. This would require accomplices.

I called my victim's workplace, and the secretary (alias, the boss's wife) agreed to schedule a bogus meeting for the employees on Friday at noon.

Next, I lined up my mom to stay at the house with Jason while I was on the lam. I then packed a suitcase, smuggled it to the car and stashed it in the trunk.

I included only a few conspirators to help prevent a leak that would blow this whole operation. I didn't need a traitor; I had too much riding on this to let someone squeal and mess up my action.

A couple of hours away from the scene of the crime was a hotel. I called the innkeeper and told him to get things ready and to make sure I wasn't disturbed after I arrived. I promised him if he followed instructions I'd make it worth his while.

Finally the day arrived. My heart was racing with anticipation. Everything was going as planned.

I arrived at the victim's work at 12:01. Entering the front door, I asked him if I could speak to him for a moment in my car.

I had left the engine running, and when he got in and closed the door, I sped off.

At first there were verbal objections. "You can't do this! You can't do this!"

I handed him a hand-scrawled statement:

Dear Husband,
You have just been officially kidnapped. All necessary people have been notified. All business matters have been covered. Your clothes are in the trunk. Take a deep breath. Relax. I'm in charge now, and you must do as I say.
Love,
Patsy

We arrived at the Victorian bed-and-breakfast, which was decorated for the holidays. We had our picture taken in old-fashioned garb to commemorate my crime. I showered him with gifts—a shirt, pants, robe and slippers. I purchased a tape of old funny radio broadcasts. We reminisced and giggled and had a wonderful time.

I wonder if this would be considered a crime of passion? If so, I plead guilty.

Sometimes crime does pay.

53

SWAT Team

Z-Z-Z-Z-ZZZZ

I had just slipped into bed when I heard the dreaded hum of a mosquito.

Z-Z-Z-Z-ZZZ

I knew it was no use trying to go to sleep until the enemy had been eliminated. I flicked on the light, which woke Les with a start.

"Whas-amatter?" he slurred.

"There's a mosquito in here . . . listen," I whispered.

Z-Z-Z-ZZZ ZZZ-Z ZZ-ZZZ

"Les, either this is the biggest mosquito God ever created, or he has friends," I speculated.

Les grabbed his discarded T-shirt to snap at the little varmints.

I spotted one and alerted Les, "There it is on the ceiling over the washstand."

At the same time, he was zeroing in on two more by the dresser. A few spectacular leaps and swats took care of our troublesome trio.

Since it was already after midnight, we were glad to turn off the light and go to sleep.

z-z-z-zzzz

"You're kidding," Les growled.

I reached over to my nightstand, running my hand down the cord to the switch and once again illuminated the battlefield.

It was us against them, and they had come armed for battle. Their entire platoon had been called in. They attempted several strategies— the old dive-bomb-the-head maneuver and the tricky blend-in-with-the-wood-and-wallpaper routine.

Les outdid himself with breathtaking counterattacks. I think the most impressive ones were as he bounced up and down off our mattress and in one swipe wiped out two of those little scoundrels. Of course, his shocking-pink, striped boxer shorts definitely added flashes of color as he leaped back and forth about our boudoir.

I acted strictly as a spotter, carefully camouflaged under the sheet, lest I become their next juicy victim. Some of their kamikaze pilots had come in and were doing suicidal spirals at our anatomies.

But no fear . . . Les was here! My husband was taking his call to active duty like a real soldier, with true dedication. He was now a two-fisted fighter, T-shirt in one hand, fly swatter in the other.

I became a little nervous, though, when he leapt over me in attempts to get escaping prisoners.

About 2:00 A.M. my dedication faded, and I fell sound asleep. I woke at 8:00 A.M. to find my husband standing over his trophies.

He had killed more than forty mosquitoes before he discovered and closed off their access point. He had twenty-three bodies lined up for all to see. The rest were splattered in various spots in our bedroom. Unlike me, who had gone AWOL, he had stayed faithful until the war was won.

Are you steadfast in life's battles?

Sow's Ear

The flight attendant struggled to position my purse under the seat, insisting it must be stored before takeoff lest it "get loose" and endanger fellow passengers. I noticed a smirk at the corners of her mouth as she said, "I bet you can hold a lot in there."

I'm sure it must look comical to see a five-foot lady carrying a six-foot purse, but I find it a necessity. I remember a fellow passenger once commenting as I struggled to the ticket counter, "Lady, it's hard to tell if you're carrying that purse or it's walking you."

Men don't understand; women have stuff. Important stuff. One never knows what one may need when one leaves home.

In my purse I carry practical provisions, like a pencil sharpener, nail polish remover, vitamins, flashlight, collapsible scissors and drinking cup, five tubes of lipstick, tweezers, floss and other stuff too numerous to mention and too valuable to leave at home.

My purse is an extension of my home. I have every room represented in the folds of my handbag.

I tried a few smaller purses, but I had to carry two, and even then the tops wouldn't close.

My friend Emilie recommends you carry little purses inside your bigger purse to keep the contents organized. I tried that, but I needed so many little ones, it made my paunchy purse look like it had a fertility problem.

Some purses are designed with compartments. I owned one with so many built-in pouches and pockets that I needed a directory to remember where I had stored my stuff.

Today's fad is belly bags that tie around your waist, leaving your hands free. Great concept... for those who have a waist. There's no way I'm going to add inches to the bag already permanently affixed to my bod.

Businessmen understand purses better than they let on. Take note of their briefpurses—excuse me, briefcases. That's where they carry their stuff. Pens, paper, passport, paper clips and paraphernalia.

I was almost cured of my handbag hang-up when I was diagnosed with purse-itus. That's when your purse straps embed themselves in your shoulder, leaving you bound to your belongings.

After a temporary separation, my bag and I have been reunited and are working out a contents settlement. I've agreed to lighten its load; and in return, my purse has promised not to be such a weight around my neck.

What kind of "stuff" are you carrying?

55

Vantage Point

Winter . . . brrrr . . . I never liked the cold.

For years I whined my way through winter, feeling justified as I listened to many others complain about the cold. Then we moved to a Boy Scout reservation on six hundred twenty-five acres, and I realized it could be a long, lonely winter if I didn't find some way to use my time. I decided to take up cross-country skiing.

First, I had to purchase my equipment. That was fun. I chose adorable powder blue ski pants, matching jacket, a sweet little knit hat, fluffy mittens, groovy goggles, floral long johns, cute color-coordinated shoes, darling little poles and oh, yes, some skis.

Les did not think it was wise for a non-athletic novice to go sliding off by herself into half a mile of heavily wooded acreage. I kept assuring him I could handle this.

I can still hear him calling to me as I glided out of sight, "If you get lost out there, I'm not looking for you till spring."

There's something about having the right equipment that can give one unrealistic confidence. I felt as though I looked professional—besides, how hard could it be to walk in the snow?

I was amazed how quickly I picked up a rhythm. The snow must have been just right for gliding, because I was moving well, and my overrated view of my ability was growing with every stride.

At this point I passed the hill . . . a sizable hill . . . a steep hill. It seemed to be beckoning me, tempting me, daring me. What could there be to tucking my poles and bending my knees? Life was meant to be lived. I decided to go for it.

I positioned myself confidently and then leaned forward. Who would think one little lean could start one in such a downward direction? The wind blowing briskly about my face reminded me of the exhilarating challenge of life. I believe it was at this moment that I spotted the lake, which reminded me of the excruciating pain of death.

I seemed to be headed for the thinly ice-covered water at an increased rate of speed. I meant to learn how to swim, I really did. (This thought seemed a little hindsight-y.)

Being perceptive, it didn't take me long to tune into one fact—whoever designed these skis forgot an important feature: the brakes. You would think that a backup parachute would be required at the time of purchase. Where's Ralph Nader when you need him?

No fear though, for there, before my eyes, was an escape route—a grove of fir trees. Actually, I could see now that I couldn't miss those babies if I wanted to.

Leaping sideways to try to slow my momentum, I bounced off almost every tree trunk in the woods. Limbs met my face and body with a whipping force.

Finally I came to a stop. Wrapped securely in bark at the base of a tree, I lay very still. Snow is not as soft as it looks.

Slowly I tried moving body parts that just minutes before were gliding merrily along with little effort. Now some parts had no feeling while others had a great rush of pain.

Les's face flashed through my mind. I could almost see that "I warned you" look, followed by a smirky smile. I determined then to keep this story under my skis.

Discomfort began to attack all parts of my body. Nothing seemed to be broken, just painfully re-arranged.

The hill had acquired mountain proportions. I was scaling it on my knees while dragging my slightly abused ski equipment behind me. I had the suspicion that someone was videotaping this escapade, and the next time Les was watching sports, I would be featured in the "thrill of victory and the agony of defeat" segment.

I buried the bent equipment in the snow beside the house and slipped onto the porch. Swallowing my groans, I made my way through the house to my room, sat down on the bed and started the uncomfortable task of disrobing.

Just then Les walked in.

I'm not sure if it was my lopsided groovy goggles, the pine cones hanging off my sweet little hat, or the evergreen needles protruding from my front teeth, but he sensed things had not gone well.

He was actually quite merciful. He only sang thirty-two rounds of "The Old Gray Mare."

When he left the room I looked down and saw the packaging my goggles had come in. It read, "High-altitude glasses." I thought, *That's what I need.* Not ski equipment but the advantage of a Higher perspective. Perhaps then I would have chosen tatting for my winter sport.

What was that again, the thing that goes before a fall?

Weather Watch

My friend Don Garrett tells me I talk twenty-five miles per hour with gusts up to fifty. My husband says that is ridiculous—my gusts are at least a hundred.

Gusty people are easy to identify. We are the ones broadcasting our biographies to the world. Our friends run from us in the grocery store. We are part of the reason Reeboks are so popular. People spot us by the cereal and quickly jog three aisles over to the dog food just to avoid us. They give up their Wheaties for Woof Woofs and figure it's a small price to pay.

Usually friends feel guilty playing dodge-'em cart, but they know if they ask how we are, we'll start at birth. Most people don't have that kind of time, interest or attention span.

When two Gusties meet up, sprint for cover. Even a windbreaker won't protect you from their gale-force exchange.

They start talking before the grocery baskets stop rolling as each attempts to get his or her news out first. This is an important part of the strategy, so that at the end of the first speaker's whirlwind of words, that person can announce, "Have to run!" The plan is to escape the blast of babble from the opponent.

Gusties have incredible lung capacities. They know if they take a breath, someone else might get control of the conversation. They speed-speak, which requires them to mentally remove all punctuation, enunciation and hesitation.

When two prolific Gusties visit, they often speak in overlap. That's where before one can finish a thought, the other speaks over the top of the victim's words and runs away with the spotlight. The main objective is not what is being said but who gets to say it.

Receiving a telephone call from a Gusty can leave you feeling blown away by the velocity of verbosity. It's amazing that a person can utter so many words and actually say so little.

The good news about Gusty callers is that you can lay down the receiver, complete several tasks and pick up the phone without having them miss you. They are what you might call self-contained conversationalists.

If you meet a Gusty with PMS or one in mid-life, watch out! It adds a whole new meaning to "the winds of adversity." Meeting one is like trying to hug a hurricane. Storm warnings should be posted during these seasons for the safety of the public.

Do you leave people with a wind-blown look?

Visitors

Les and I have been married . . . forever. Our marriage didn't start in paradise but in a basement. It didn't start out like Eden but more like eek!

Our first apartment was in a monstrous, ancient, decrepit, mansion-type house. Ours were the only basement quarters. That should have made us cautious, but we were young, inexperienced and poor. We had to live in the inner city to be close to the bus station so Les could get back and forth to the military base.

After we paid the rent, we had five dollars for groceries and bus fare. We bought milk, bread and bologna. That simplified meal planning.

Les spent every other night at the barracks, which meant I was alone. This was a new experience for me.

Our apartment was furnished in early ark artifacts. We had three rooms and a bath. Because the rooms were lined up on one wall of the basement, the floor plan was like a conveyor belt. We had to go through the living room to get to the bedroom, and through the bedroom to get to the kitchen, and through the kitchen to enter the bathroom.

Our bathroom was unique in that you had to stand in the doorway to take your shower. It seemed the shower head was permanently jammed in a northeast direction.

One night when I was alone and bored, I decided to eat something. I thought my big menu decision was whether to have my bologna sandwich with or without a glass of milk. I was wrong.

When I opened the cabinet that housed my bread, I found other tenants. Roaches. Hundreds of roaches. The bread bag hadn't been retied securely, and it was alive with these pilfering pests. They were feasting on my valuable staple.

I was repulsed and angry. Slamming the cupboard shut, I flicked off the light and fumed back to the living room.

As my hunger increased, I reasoned that those nasty varmints couldn't get into the refrigerator where the milk and meat were safely stored. So I went back to the kitchen.

As I turned toward the refrigerator, I saw something move. I froze in my tracks and so did it. I was about three feet from the biggest rat I had ever seen. Well, actually it was the only rat I had ever seen.

In slow motion I climbed onto the tabletop as a scream moved through my body and out my lips. My new roommate decided to vacate by scrunching under the kitchen door. This door led to the rest of the basement, which was a dark maze filled with furnaces for the upstairs apartments.

While perched on my platform I cried . . . profusely! I didn't know anyone, we had no phone and no money, it was late, and Les wouldn't be home until the following day. We didn't even have a TV or radio that I could turn on to scare the rat and give me a diversion.

When I ran out of alternatives, I remembered the Lord. It had been a while since I had talked with Him, but I wanted to now.

After an emergency prayer time, I cautiously made my way off the table. Then I quickly turned on every light in the apartment. I stuffed towels in the scrunch space under the door. Then I sat in the living room and plea-bargained with the Lord.

Eventually, I braved my way to bed, praying all the way. As I lay back against my pillow, an incredible peace came over me. I felt so safe and cared for. I could feel the stress of my trauma ease out, and I felt myself falling asleep.

Have you noticed when you run out of places to turn,
He's always there?

58

What a Pain

Before I even opened my eyes, I knew I was in trouble. My stomach felt as though it was an automatic butter churn. The paddles were doing double time, and everything in there was clabbered. My head felt light, and when I opened my eyes, my body seemed to jounce.

I sat up abruptly, hoping to recall my head from the ceiling. It didn't work.

I carefully inched my way to the edge of the bed and tried to figure out what was going on. My twirling head made it difficult to reason.

I thought maybe I'd feel better if I got up and moved around. I slid off the side of the bed onto legs like Jell-O and hugged the wall. I decided I was dying.

"Les, Les," I groaned pitifully down the stairs.

"What?" he called back cheerfully from his office.

"I'm sick. I think I'm dying," I whimpered, resenting his good mood.

I'm into group suffering. If I'm not doing well, it's not that I want you to be sick exactly . . . miserable will do.

Les bounded up the steps and then walked too heavily down the hall, hurting my now throbbing head. He took one look at me embracing the wallboard and announced, "You look like you're dying."

I didn't have time to thank him for his words of encouragement, because I had a physically compelling desire to visit, if not move into, our bathroom.

I have always found kneeling in front of a ceramic centerpiece humbling.

Finally I moaned my way back to my bed where I found Les trying to stifle a case of the giggles under his pillow.

"I'm sorry," he confessed, "but if you could only hear yourself."

I personally find it helpful to moan if I am in pain. The more pain, the louder I moan. Besides helping me deal with my discomfort, it alerts everyone within a one-mile vicinity that I am not doing well. I am certainly not opposed to get-well gifts.

I reminded Les of that and told him he had better hurry because I wasn't sure how long I could hang on.

Turns out that my terminal illness was a short-term flu. Just about the time I thought I was taking my last breath . . . I was well.

Can you handle pain, or. . . are . . . you one?

59

Wild Bunch

I'm staying on beautiful grounds that belong to my friend Verna. While I'm resting and writing, I'm in a home tucked in the woods. God's fingerprints are all around . . . as well as His sense of humor.

I was reading one morning when I heard what at first sounded like a squeaky wheel. As the sound moved closer, I went to the window.

Much to my surprise and delight I saw a flock of wild turkeys. Counting heads was hard because they were moving so quickly, but I figured there were at least forty of them.

They appeared to be having an intense meeting. Having divided into opposing sides, they were in a heated debate. One group would aggressively storm their opponents, gobbling forcefully. The others would then respond confrontationally, their gobbles sounding at times more like screeching. It seemed as though those yelling loudest were the most intimidating.

One small group separated from the others in pursuit of a lone turkey, apparently trying to whip him into shape or get him to submit. They surrounded him, backed him into several trees and didn't let up until he hightailed it to the back of the pack.

Then one of them spread his masterful tail feathers and began to strut. Immediately the flock settled down and followed the flamboyant one single file into the woods.

As I observed these turkeys, I couldn't decide if I had just witnessed a political rally or a church board meeting.

Gobble Gobble

Bus Stop

Jason, our youngest, has two goals in life. One is to have fun, and the other is to rest. He does both quite well. So I shouldn't have been surprised by what happened when I sent him to school one fall day.

As Jason headed off for the bus, I immediately busied myself, preparing for a full day. The knock on the door was a surprise and disruptive to my morning rhythm, which is not something I have a lot of. I flew to the door, jerked it open, only to find myself looking at Jason.

"What are you doing here?" I demanded.

"I've quit school," he boldly announced.

"Quit school?" I repeated in disbelief and at a decibel too high for human ears.

Swallowing once, I tried to remember some motherly psychology. But all that came to my mind was "A stitch in time saves nine" and "Starve a fever, feed a cold," or something like that. Somehow they didn't seem to apply to a six-year-old drop-out dilemma.

149

So I questioned, "Why have you quit school?"

Without hesitation he proclaimed, "It's too long, it's too hard, and it's too boring!"

"Jason," I instantly retorted, "you have just described life. Get on the bus!"

Well, I cannot tell you how many times the Lord has had to echo that counsel back to me—times when I've questioned, "Lord, You say You'll never give us more than we can bear. You must not be looking. This is hard, very hard!

"By the way, Lord, it's been lasting a l-o-n-g time. And truthfully, it's getting bo-ring!"

About that time, in the recesses of my mind, I hear the refrain, "It's life; get on the bus!"

Bus token, anyone?

Prophet Profile

God purchased His people to plant them in the place of His prosperity. Let's peer into the power-packed pages of our Protector's priceless promises to see this very thing.

In His publication, on the first page of Exodus, we see God's people pleading in prayer, as prisoners of pharaoh because of population problems. When God's people pray, He delights in providing.

But point two becomes perplexing when the provision for His people is put in a pond, pulled from the basket and placed in pharaoh's daughter's arms. She beats a pathway back to the palace to prepare him to become a prince.

Problems arise for Moses when he becomes a perpetrator. The palace becomes a perilous place, so he heads for the pasture.

Now how could pasturing stupid sheep ever prepare you to lead God's people? Perfectly!

We begin to see the process to become one of God's VIP's . . . plagues, Passover, pillars and piled-up water that became a pathway for some and a precarious place for others.

Perhaps you've been pondering your future plans and feel perplexed. Well p'shaw y'all! Just remember Moses, who went from the pond, to the palace, to the pasture, to the pinnacle, to view the promised land before entering paradise. Praise the Lord.

Normal
Is Just
a Setting
on Your Dryer

Patsy Clairmont

CARMEL • NEW YORK 10512

NORMAL IS JUST A SETTING ON YOUR DRYER

Editor: Janet Kobobel
Designer: Jeff Stoddard

Printed in the United States of America

To my mom,
Rebecca McEuen,

housekeeper, homemaker,
& humorist
extraordinaire

Contents

Acknowledgments

Writing a book is never a normal experience, nor does its completion express the efforts of just one person. It took a lot of above-normal people for this project to become reality.

My husband, Les: thank you for your love and all the creative ways you find to express it.

My firstborn son, Marty: thanks for all the hugs when I felt discouraged.

My younger son, Jason: thanks for believing the best in me and for me.

My sister, Elizabeth Vegh: thanks for laughing at my stories.

My editor, Janet Kobobel: thanks for your above-and-beyond-the-call-of-duty involvement. You are not normal; you're exceptional.

My computer specialist, Mary Lou Schneemann: thanks for responding to a last-minute, frantic call with sacrificial generosity.

My adviser, Ruth Ann Davis: thanks for your insights that you wrap in life-giving humor. You have been a healing gift to me.

Thanks also to friends who nudged, nurtured, and prayed:

Carol Porter	Nancy Berrens
David Berrens	Ginny Lukei
Jan Frank	Lauren Hess
Danya Voigt	Joanie Karpanty
Lana Bateman	Debbie Wirwille

Thank you also to Verna Paul for giving me an anything-but-normal hideaway. It was truly a little bit of heaven.

Finally, a big thank-you to Focus for including me in the family. A special thanks to Al Janssen, Gwen Weising, and Larry Weeden.

1

Normal Nonsense

L ord, if only I could be normal like other people!" That was my constant prayer during the years I hid away in my home with agoraphobia (a constricting circle of fears that leaves one housebound). Then I got out of my home, into the flow of people, and found out "ain't nobody normal." Unique, yes. Special, definitely. Normal, no way!

Normal is just a setting on your clothes dryer and has nothing to do with people. Try as we might, we remain peculiar people with distinct differences.

I was peeling tomatoes in my kitchen one day when a friend began to laugh. Surprised, I asked what was so funny.

"I've never seen anyone take the skin off tomatoes before adding them to the salad," she said. She thought that was abnormal.

But when I was growing up, my mom always removed the peel for our guests. She considered it good manners to make things special and convenient for our company. Peeling tomatoes was the norm for us.

I had a neighbor we nicknamed Mrs. Ickity-Pickity because of her seemingly abnormal need to have things clean. We used to laugh because she even washed the soap in her soap dish.

Today I don't think that's strange at all. I find it unappealing to spot a grimy gob of gooey soap stuck in the sink. It is now my normal procedure to follow Mrs. Ickity-Pickity's example and douse my Dial.

My husband, Les, not only felt it was normal to rise up early, but he also was certain other people's character was flawed if they didn't leap out of bed at the first glimmer of light. Normal for my family, on the other hand, meant that on days when schedules permitted, a late morning snooze was a treat to be enjoyed. You can imagine the conflict these two "normals" caused as they—and we—collided.

As an agoraphobic, I felt anything but normal. I didn't know of anyone else who was afraid to go to the grocery store because the aisles seemed to swallow them up. I didn't know of anyone who listened to 30 weather reports every day and then hid under the table from approaching storms. Nor had I talked with anyone who couldn't ride elevators or stay alone at night. Then when I had to give up driving because of panic attacks, I knew I was hopelessly abnormal.

Yet if you could coax agoraphobics into a room together, there would be a "normalcy" among us in that our behavior would match in many ways. Just goes to show—normal is only a setting on a dryer.

I believe abnormal is normal. Think about it. Consider your friends—great people, but don't they have some pretty curious ways? Abnormal is not an isolated occurrence but a constant reoccurrence. It's something we share in common . . . our differences.

I kept trying to attain normalcy by being what I thought others thought I should be. How exhausting! Everyone seemed to have his or her own definition of my normal, leaving me feeling like an isolated emotional abnormality.

That's what this book is about—emotions and how they affect and infect our lives and our need for a healthy balance. We'll look at a variety of emotions and how, if we deny them, we end up out of balance, and yet if we indulge them, our pendulum swings too far the other way.

This *isn't* a book on how to be normal. (I haven't figured that out yet.) Rather, it's an encouragement to be the best "us" we can. We think we know ourselves so well, yet we find our emotions often mysterious. And sometimes our emotions surprise and overwhelm us.

You may experience different feelings in response to these stories of others who struggle, fail, start over, and celebrate. You'll see that life is seldom as simple as setting your dryer to normal. And my prayer is that you might laugh, cry, think, remember, and come to understand yourself better as you move through the pages of this book.

2

Sure I Can!

Most of us over 40 find it difficult to believe we're losing our youth. Our minds are still spunky, at least in a sputtering kind of way, and tend to send inaccurate information to our bodies like "You can still leap buildings in a single bound." *Right.* I can hardly step into an elevator without having my arches fall.

At 47 (at the time of this writing), my mind is marching to "The Battle Hymn of the Republic," while my body is humming in the background, "That'll Be the Day." Even with my increasing physical disruptions, I keep holding my thumb over the birth date on my driver's license when I'm cashing a check.

My friend Claris, a heroic woman who drove school buses for 19 years and has lived to tell of it, forgot her age. It had to be amnesia that caused her to be coaxed into going roller-skating in her forties. An hour later she was in an ambulance, and she wasn't driving. A cast, crutches, and several months later, Claris was back wheeling around in her bus, which has the only size wheels she now trusts to hold her up. Speaking of holding up, . . .

Jim was certain he could reach a little higher than his arm span while tottering on the top rung of the ladder. Need I tell you any more? Our fiftyish friend came down like the Jericho walls, but instead of broken pitchers, he had broken ribs. After being taped back together, he felt every breath he took. Speaking of breathtaking, . . .

Meagan decided to take up downhill skiing . . . at 40. Her first time out she fell backward on her skis, but they didn't release. That was not good. Meagan had to be removed from the slopes on a stretcher by the ski patrol. She wore a mega foam collar for months.

You would think we would learn from our friends' examples. Well, actually I did. I don't roller-skate, climb ladders, or ski downhill. No, not me: I'm too smart to try those tricky feats. Instead, I decided to ride a five-speed bicycle. My infamous ride would have been a cinch had I ever before ridden a bike with the brakes on the handlebars, which I had not. That became quite clear to who knows how many.

My son Jason and I rode our bikes to a nearby store, where, instead of braking when the bike slowed down, I side-saddled it and jumped off like Annie Oakley. I ran into the store and bought a couple of small items. We didn't have a basket, but I was confident I could manage the bike and the bag. It had been many years since I had ridden a bicycle. (Actually, I was eight when I got my last bike.) But you know what they say: "Once you learn, you never forget."

We were almost home when my bike began to pick up speed. Evidently there was more of an incline on our street than I had realized. For a moment I felt like a kid again, with the wind whipping through my tresses and the houses passing by in a whirl of colors. Suddenly I recognized the whirling greens as my house. I instinctively pedaled backward to brake. Nothing happened. I mean, nothing happened! My acceleration was such that I could see I was headed rapidly for the side street. If my calculations were correct, I would cross it at the speed of light.

Feeling I was losing control of this ride, I kind of panicked. Then I recalled Les's reminding me, as I rode away, that the brakes were located on my handlebars, and that I should squeeze them to stop. I could only grip on one side because of the bag, and when I squeezed, nothing happened. Seeing my life skateboard past me, I grabbed for the other grip, bag and all, and pulled as hard as I could. Sure enough, something happened!

I became airborne. Over the handlebars and into the wild, blue yonder. I'm sure I looked like a 747 wide-body. That is, until my landing. I did a belly-flop glide down my sidewalk/runway, stopping just before I became a permanent design on our front steps.

Jason looked down at me in utter amazement. I'm not sure if he couldn't believe I could ride a bicycle that fast or fly that high.

If this had happened to you or you had observed it happening to someone else, what would you expect the first words out of the person's mouth to be? Perhaps "Call 911!" or "Get your dad!"

Well, that's what a normal person might say. But not me. The first words out of my swelling lips, while my face was still ingrained in the cement, were, "Is anyone looking?"

Is anyone looking! Give me a break! The sidewalk/slide had torn my pant leg off, my knee was ripped and gushing, I had skid marks on my stomach, my elbow felt like Rice Krispies, my ribs had a Vise-Grip on my lungs, and I wanted to know, "Is anyone looking?"

With Jason's help, I limped into the house, carefully lowered myself into a chair, and cried. My tears were as much out of embarrassment as from pain.

From my emotional response, I had obviously damaged something more than my body. Mine was a giveaway statement of someone suffering from fractured pride.

But then I wondered: Isn't that true for any of us who can't accept our limitations?

3

Ouch!

P ain is God's megaphone," C. S. Lewis said.

If that's true, then, folks, I've heard from heaven!

Last year I went through months that were a literal pain in the neck. I've been accused of being one, and now I know what it feels like to have one.

I hauled too many suitcases, briefcases, purses, word processors, and carryon's through too many airports and hotel lobbies. I exceeded my recommended load limit, and in doing so, I stretched my back and tendons. I then spent painful months learning the importance of listening to my body.

My physical therapist asked why it took me so long to seek medical help. To tell you the truth, I thought I was just being wimpy, and that if I kept bench pressing my luggage, eventually I would look as fit and fabulous as Stormie Omartian. Instead I complicated my recovery, as the tendon damage spread from my shoulder to my elbow, and then to my wrist.

Our bodies protest when we do things that are beyond their ability to perform. Body signals alert us in many ways. Our muscles, tendons, ligaments, and back scream when we try to lift or carry things that are too heavy.

Les is a strapping fellow who, during his younger years, was so strong (how strong was he?) he could lift buffalo. What he shouldn't have tried to carry was the two bundles of shingles for our roof. Actually, he might have achieved that hefty task if, after he slung both bags of shingles over his shoulder, he hadn't had to climb up two stories on a ladder. Even then he might have made it if, when he put his foot on the roof, the ladder had stayed still. Which it didn't. And neither did he.

The first part of Les's fall was broken by a porch landing. He then proceeded to tumble down a flight of steps and collide with the less-than-cushy earth.

Stunned, Les lay very still to assess the damage. After a few breathless moments, he rose slowly, slung the bags over his shoulder again, and climbed back up on the roof.

Les's friend Tom Wirsing had witnessed this acrobatic feat. But because Tom was on the roof when it happened, and Les took the ladder with him when he fell, Tom couldn't come to Les's aid. He spent several harrowing moments as a helpless bystander. When Les stepped back on the roof, Tom had just two words for him: "Go home!"

The next morning, Les's body was buzzing with messages. Les needed a headset to keep up with all the incoming data. His back went on strike, and his legs, sympathetic to the back's protest, filed their own grievance. Muscles he didn't know were a part of the human structure reported their existence. Bruises the size of roof tiles added color to his battered frame. The bruises served for quite a while, like Post-It notes, as a reminder never to do that again.

Along with Post-It notes, our bodies have built-in alarm clocks. Instead of waking us up, they're designed to insist on rest. These alarms go off every time our heads nod dangerously behind a steering wheel, we fall asleep in class, or we drag through a day with the enthusiasm of a yawn.

When Les and I were a young married couple (versus the relics we are today), Les worked a long way from home. One morning, as he neared work, he began to nod. We had stayed up late that week, and his need to sleep sat on his eyes like sandbags. The sound of the early-morning traffic became a lullaby, and Les took a nap. It didn't last long. He woke abruptly when he hit a parked car, which hit a parked car, which hit another parked car.

Les called me on a pay phone from the scene of the crash. "Patsy, I've been in an accident."

"Are you okay?"

"I'm not sure. My head is bleeding. Here come the police. I have to go." And he hung up.

I was seven months pregnant and beside myself with concern. I had no idea where the accident happened or if he truly was all right. My body soon announced that if I didn't settle down, our family would be having more than an accident.

Five hours later, my smiling husband walked in the door. I hugged him and cried with relief. Then I wanted to lambast him for not calling me back. It all worked out well. Les decided it was easier to hit the hay than a lineup of cars.

Mood swings can be the body's beeper, reporting possible hormonal havoc. I remember three sisters I met at a retreat who were concerned their fourth sister was in spiritual trouble because she wasn't her usual bouncy self. They kept her up late at night and prayed with her over every possible hidden sin in her life. Later they found out she was just pregnant. After a couple of months and some uninterrupted sleep, her hormones settled down, and she was back to her perky self.

I'm not saying the all-night vigil was a bad idea, but there are times when mood swings beep attention to a legitimate health issue.

There's no doubt we are fearfully and wonderfully made. All we have to do is listen to our bodies and respond with good choices. Some of you already are disciplined and wise in caring for yourselves. But, like me, many of you don't listen until you're in trouble. We could all benefit by answering the following:

How much water do you drink in a day? (No fair counting the water in coffee or cola.)

How many hours of sleep do you require a night to feel "normal"? (Les requires seven hours but prefers six. I need eight hours but enjoy nine. Les catapults from the bed each morning, while I have to be jump started just to ignite a pulse. Remember, normal is just . . .)

Do you have an exercise regimen? (Getting out of bed each morning does not qualify as weight lifting.)

When was your last eye exam? (I took my mangled glasses in last week for repair. I had sat on them . . . for the third time. The woman looked at them and said, "Lady, do you know which end these were made for?"

"Evidently not," I replied sweetly, "or I wouldn't be here again.")

Write down the date of your last dental appointment. (If B.C. follows the date, it has been too long.)

Are you listening to your body when it says, "Enough is enough" (food, work, rest)?

When was your last physical? (Talking to a friend who once took a first-aid course does not count.)

Did it include a pap smear? (This is an uplifting experience.)

Have you had a mammogram? (That's where the technician thinks she's a magician and tries to turn a cup into a saucer.)

Have you ever had a change in your weight without a change in your eating? (My mother-in-law thought she was fat. Her "fat" turned out to be a tumor the size of a watermelon. My husband was losing weight while eating like a buffalo. [Maybe that's why he could lift them.] It turned out he was diabetic.)

Are you having frequent headaches, stomachaches, backaches, rashes, sleeplessness, spotting, mood swings, urination, unquenchable thirst, and so on? It's time to find out why.

How many pills do you take in a week? in a month? Are you masking a growing health issue? (Our plop-plop, fizz-fizz mentality covers our pain but doesn't resolve it.)

Trust the way God has designed your body to let you know when you need to make a life adjustment or a visit to your family doctor. This body is just a temporary time suit. (Can't you hear it ticking?) It's the only one we get before heaven's new, improved version, which will be complete with eternal vision.

Speaking of vision, remember that in this life, your glasses belong on your nose. Take it from someone who knows.

4

Jumpin' Jehosaphat

S ome friends were getting ready to move and needed a home for their dog, Fredda. We already had a dog (Fredda's mama) but felt obligated to take Fredda back since we had given her to them fraudulently. See, I thought she was a he when I gave Fredda to them, and they therefore named her Fred. After arriving home with their little guy, they noticed Fred had problems that would require surgery or a change of names. They kindly opted for a name change.

Fredda was a kind-of-cockapoo. Actually, she thought she was a kangaroo (no doubt the result of her early identity crisis) and developed a unique straight-up-and-down leap. She was a very sanguine dog and hated to be left outside. So she used her incredibly high leap to peek in our windows at what was going on. It wasn't unusual to be sitting at the table eating and, out of my peripheral view, glimpse a set of eager eyes and fluffy, flying ears. By the time I could turn to look, Fredda would have dropped out of sight. She repeated this Olympic feat frequently.

This caused many visitors concern about their sanity. We tended not to mention our "kangaroo" to guests until their eyes looked dazed. You could see them trying to process whether their minds were leaving them or we had been invaded by seeing-eye fur balls. With quick jerks, our friends would whip their heads to the side in an attempt to catch our mystifying mutt. Eventually we would confirm their UFO sightings to ease their troubled minds.

Fredda became our son Jason's dog (he was eight at the time) and would escort him to the bus stop. Jason would have to leave early because it takes longer when you're with an animal that insists on leaping up instead of forward. One morning, Jason came bursting back into the house crying, "Mom, Mom, come quick! Fredda's been hit by a car!"

I grabbed my housecoat, and as I secured it, Jason added, "I think she's going to be all right, because I saw her tail wag!"

Halfway up our driveway, a lady I had never met came running toward me and right into my arms. She was crying, "I hit your dog! I'm sorry, I'm sorry." I held her for a moment and assured her we knew it was an accident.

She sobbed, "Yesterday my cat died, and today I've hit your dog!"

"I'm sorry this has been such a painful week for you, and I know you didn't mean to hit her," I responded. I hugged her one last time and encouraged her to go on to work.

I thought how disconcerting as well as disastrous it must have been for that lady to have a flying dog, all eyes and ears, leap out of nowhere.

By the time I reached the road, Les had arrived and was gently placing Fredda in his pickup. He looked at me and shook his head to let me know she was dead. I turned to look for Jason and saw that he was back in line for his school bus. He had his eyes squished tightly shut, and his little arms were pressed firmly against his body in his attempt to not see or know the fate of his beloved, bouncing buddy.

"Jason," I said softly.

He didn't move.

"Jason, honey, your doggie is dead."

He fell into my arms, allowing the swell of tears out of his flooded eyes. Then his tense little body let down and began to shake. I took him by the hand, and we walked down the hill to our house to grieve.

Many times I, like Jason, have wanted to just close my eyes and not look at reality. Reality is often harsh, filled with unfairness, pain, and loss. But when I refuse to face truth, I find myself rigid with anxiety and unable to deal with life. Acknowledging and letting go of what I can't change is the beginning of the grieving process.

5

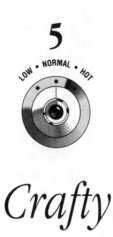

LOW · NORMAL · HOT

Crafty

I do crafts. No, wait, that's not quite right. I own crafts. Yes, that helps to bring into focus the blur of materials stuffed into assorted baskets, drawers, and boxes in my attic and basement.

My craft addiction has left partially done projects pleading for completion. I have snarls of thread once meant to be used in needlepoint and gnarly-looking yarn intended for an afghan. I have how-to books worn from my reading and rereading of the instructions. (I love reading; it's the doing that bogs me down.) Swatches of material, florist wire, paint brushes, grapevines, and (every crafter's best friend) a glue gun—along with a myriad of additional stuff—greet me whenever I open my closet.

Every time I'm enticed into purchasing a new project, I think, *This one I'll do for sure.* I've attempted everything from oil painting, floral arranging, quilting, and scherenschnitte (the German art of paper cutting) to quilling.

"Quilling?" you ask. For those of you unfamiliar with it, this craft requires you to wind itsy-bitsy, teeny-weeny strips of paper around the tip of a needle. Once they're wound, you glue the end, using a toothpick as an applicator so your paper coil doesn't spring loose. Then, with a pair of tweezers, you set your coil onto a pattern attached to a foam board, securing it with a straight pin. You are then ready to start the paper-twirling process over again. To be a good quiller, it helps if you, the crafter, are wound loosely. I believe quillers (at least this one) have to be a few twirls short of a full coil to attempt this tedious art.

You may be wondering how many of those paper tidbits one needs to finish a piece. That depends on the size of your pattern. I chose a delicate, little snowflake. Taking into consideration that I'm a beginner (which is still true of every craft I've ever tried), I decided to select a small pattern and not overwhelm myself. (This would be like saying, "I think I'll go over Niagara in a barrel rather than a tub in hopes I won't get so wet.")

When I started my snowflake, I thought, *I'm going to make one of these for each of my friends and put them on the outside of their Christmas packages.* After five hours and a minuscule amount of noticeable progress, I reconsidered. *I will give these only to my best friends and include them in their gift boxes.*

A week later, I realized I didn't have a friend worth this kind of effort; only select family members would get these gems. And they would be all they'd get. I thought I would also include a contract for them to sign, agreeing to display their snowflakes well lit, under glass, in a heavy traffic area of their homes, all year.

Fifteen hours into my little winter-wonder project, I decided this would be the first and last paper wad I'd ever make . . . and I'd keep it for myself. It could be handed down in my family, generation after generation, in a time capsule, after my passing. I often wondered who the flake really was in this venture.

I suppose you're asking yourself, *Did she finish it?* Not yet, but I plan to (great inscription for tombstones).

I once attended a retreat where I was persuaded to join a wooden angel craft class. The angel done by the instructor (art major) as an example was adorable. Mine (craft minor) looked like an angel that might join a motorcycle gang.

Even that angel didn't get completed, because they ran out of heavenly parts. She had only one wing and was minus her halo. Actually, it was kind of sad. Today my fallen angel lies at the bottom of a box in my basement, covered with rotting quilt pieces and plastic ivy, still waiting for her ordination. May she rest in peace.

I took a painting class for credit and received an A. Finally, something I could succeed in! Of course, if that was true, why didn't I have a picture to hang?

It hit me that I didn't have a painting anyone could identify, much less display. For one of our projects, we painted apples in a bowl. When I took it home, my friend thought it was a peacock.

I approached the instructor and asked how I had earned an A in her class. "For showing up every week," she responded. She must have the gift of mercy.

Les and I started hooking a two-foot-by-three-foot rug 25 years ago. We're almost to the halfway point. We figure, in a joint effort, that we have hooked less than an inch a year and should complete it in the year 2012. You may want to get on our gift list.

I seem to be more into ownership than completion . . . and then I feel guilty. I've noticed I'm not alone in that. Some kindred spirits could stuff a landfill with their forsaken artistry. I wonder if that's why we have so many garage sales and so much garbage in this country. We sell off and throw away our unfinished business, and then we go buy more.

Words like *responsibility, follow through,* and *moderation* get lost in the shuffle as I push back one box of crafts to move in my newest project. Every time I haul out or hide away another abandoned endeavor, it reinforces a negative quality within me.

Besides, what happened to the notion "Waste not, want not" ?

That's a great line. I wonder how it would look in cross-stitch? Oops, there I go again.

6

Snappy Answers

Sometimes I feel as though my emotions are a tangled wad. I guess that's why one night, while I was in bed praying for a creative way to visualize emotions, I thought of knotting rubber bands together. I jumped up and found a bag of 100 red, blue, green, and yellow rubber bands. Then I climbed back in bed and began to tie them in a long, snarled chain (probably the closest I've ever come to knitting or crocheting).

My husband came into the room and saw me busy at my stretchy task. He shook his head and muttered, "I knew one day it would come to this."

I often ask my audiences if they brought their emotions with them to the retreat. Usually they giggle, and a number of women raise their hands, signifying they did. Then I ask how many of the gals brought their hormones, and the rest of the hands go up.

When I next pull my emotions out of a bag in the form of my rubber chain, the women titter and nod their recognition. I demonstrate, by tugging at the bands until they appear they will snap, how people sometimes get on my nerves. As I pile the long, variegated snarl into a five-inch-tall heap on my hand, I show them what happens when I don't stay current with my emotions—they become so entangled that I can't tell what I'm feeling. And when I can't identify what I'm feeling, I can't resolve it, which means the knotted mess is growing inside me.

I remember coming home one evening after being with a group of friends and telling Les how angry I was with one of them.

"Really, what did she do?" he inquired.

Well, I told him in no uncertain terms what she did.

When I finished, he said, "I don't think you're angry."

"You don't?" I asked.

"No," he reinforced.

"I feel angry," I assured him.

"I think you're jealous," he stated boldly.

"Jealous?" I screeched.

"Jealous?" I hissed.

Then I slunk into another room to file my nails in private. Alone, I finally asked the Lord if what Les suggested could possibly be true. Immediately I realized he had caught the cat by her claws.

I've been able to work through my jealous feelings in regard to this friend thanks to Les's confrontation. Otherwise, I'd still be rationalizing my anger and not facing the real issue.

When issues aren't faced, they build inside us, which means somebody's going to experience emotional whiplash when we get crossed. The way buildups become blowups is that one day a family member, co-worker, friend, or total stranger makes one teeny-tiny comment, and we let that person have it with our entire rubber-band arsenal. He or she doesn't know what happened.

When the person asks, "What's wrong with you?" we shout, "Everything!" shaking all our tangled emotions in his or her face.

Have you ever noticed how quiet a room gets when you over-react? All eyes are on you. Even though no one says it, you know they're wondering what your problem is. But then, so are you, because more often than not, the time and place where you explode are side issues.

I once had a disagreement with a co-worker, and when I came home, I started nit-picking on my teenager Jason. I hit him with a lengthy list of criticisms. Baffled, he asked, "What's wrong with you?"

Those words caught my attention, and I realized I was the one with a problem. Jason was the victim of my misdirected frustration.

Sound familiar? Does to me.

I find that when I have a gob of feelings overlapping, I begin to highlight one or two emotions. I then work those feelings over-time and ignore the rest. That's why I thought I was angry with my friend instead of jealous. Besides, jealousy is so—so—well, petty, whereas anger is more respectable (righteous indignation) and gives me a feeling of being in control.

I find it fairly easy to say to someone, "My friend Jane makes me angry." (I'm in control.) But it's hard to confess, "I am jealous of Jane." (Now I feel vulnerable, and that's scary.)

For years, I majored in fear. I seldom felt another emotion during my agoraphobic days. I was afraid of everything, or so it seemed. Later, I began to get in touch with anger, joy, sadness, and other equally important feelings. As I identified them, my wad of rubber bands became smaller. That gave me more inner space for the things of God.

What is your most-frequently-expressed emotion? Do you find yourself erupting in anger? enveloped in fear? engulfed in guilt?

If we don't deal with our raggedy strands, we react like turtles — our answers have a bite to them, and then we pull our heads back into hard shells of denial until our next snappy performances.

7

Step Right Up

I can identify with Zacchaeus in that I have a difficult time finding a place high enough to let me see a parade. Visibility is limited when you're five feet tall. I've spent a lifetime on my tiptoes, calling up to others, "What's going on?"

I know I'm supposed to take comfort in the saying "Dynamite comes in small packages." But I don't want to blow up; I want to grow up.

Sitting tall is also a challenge because invariably, a seven-foot-two fellow will plant himself in front of me at church. I then have the joy of staring for the next hour at the seams in his shirt and his nappy neck. It's like trying to watch a ball game through a billboard.

Hugging is often a strain as we shorties have to reach past our stretching points to squeeze a neck. It's such a rumpling experience and requires readjusting everything from hat to hose.

As a speaker, I frequently find myself peeking over lecterns in my attempts to spot the audience. It's difficult to retain the interest of people when their view consists of your forehead and eyebrows. I have stood on many creative booster stools so I could see and be seen.

At one retreat, the kitchen workers brought me a box of canned juice to stand on. It worked fine until my high heel poked between two cans and I jerked sharply backward. I grabbed the lectern, catching myself just before doing a topsy-turvy somersault. My disheveled appearance from my stage aerobics made me look juiced.

I have perched on many piano benches to speak. Because they're pieces of furniture, I always remove my shoes before stepping up. Smooth nylons on shiny-finished wood equal slick chick in action. It's like trying to speak on ice skates—possible but risky.

To elevate me enough to be seen at one church meeting, the staff quickly piled up two stacks of hymnals, five deep. As I turned to look at my audience from one side of the auditorium to the other, the books would swivel. At one point, the right-foot stack headed east while the left-foot stack headed west. Those shifting stilts kept me divided in my concentration, as I was concerned I would leave with a split personality.

I've stood on milk crates, suitcases, tables, and kiddie stools. Once I was precariously placed on a wooden box whose weight limit I obviously exceeded. It creaked threateningly throughout my presentation. As I closed in prayer, a soloist began to sing, and I cautiously stepped down. Relieved that I hadn't burst the boards, I walked down the platform steps to take a seat. At the last step, my heel caught in the microphone cords, and I crash-landed in the front row as the singer was belting out "Amazing Grace." I obviously was not Grace, although in a discussion later, we thought it was amazing I could survive my teeter-totter platform and then splat when I arrived on solid ground.

It's difficult to be taken seriously when you're 60 inches short. People have a habit of referring to shorties as "cute." "Cute" is what you call a toddler, a house without a future, or the runt of a litter.

I tried to increase the presentation of my stature by wearing tall clothes. But more than once while walking up the front steps in sanctuaries, my heel slid into the hem of my long skirt, toppling me across the altar, where I looked like some sort of short sacrifice.

I shortened my skirts and added shoulder pads to my jackets in an effort to give an illusion of tallness without tripping myself.

Then one time I was in Washington, and when I was introduced, I grabbed my suit jacket and slid into it as I headed for the stage. I had been speaking for about 15 minutes when I turned my head to one side and noticed that my left shoulder was four inches higher than my right. Evidently the pad, rather than conforming to the shape of my shoulder, perched on it. Up to that point, I was the only one in the auditorium who hadn't noticed. I was speaking on being dysfunctional and suggested this perched pad was proof of my expertise in the subject.

When I finished speaking, the mistress of ceremonies approached the steps with the back of her dress tucked into her pantyhose. That took a lot of pressure off me.

Another time, I was sharing the stage with a statuesque and elegant friend who, as I was speaking, noticed my mega shoulder pad had slid off my shoulder and into my blouse. She reached in through my neckline and fished down my back in her attempt to retrieve it. I was stunned but continued to speak as if I didn't notice she was shoulder deep in my clothing. Well, I lost the audience as everyone became hysterical watching her catch my illusive inches and pat them securely back into place.

I wish my height were my only struggle with smallness. Unfortunately, I'm also shortsighted in my faith. I'm one of those "If I can see it, then I can believe it" people.

Zacchaeus was a small man who shimmied up a sycamore tree to give himself a boost. To that extent, I can identify. But his next move made the difference for him in a way lengthened robes or mountainous shoulder pads under his togas never could. He inched out on a limb to glimpse the Savior. He risked the shaky-limb experience of faith and responded to the Lord's invitation not only to come down, but also to grow up.

That day he stepped down from his own efforts to see and be seen and stepped up to the call of the Lord. Zacchaeus still lacked inches, but he gained insight and walked away a giant of a man.

Faith is a believe-it-first proposition, with no promise I'll get to "see it" regardless of how many boxes I climb. That's scary . . . like going out on a limb, huh, Zac?

8

Short(s) Circuited

Knowing my friend Nancy is like embracing a waterfall. She splashes over with energy, excitement, and enthusiasm for life and people. She's filled with joy, and also mischievousness. Her mind and wit are quick and memorable. David, her husband, is a courageous man who has survived and been blessed by Nancy's outrageous humor. We all remember when . . .

David is mellow and usually cooperates and enjoys his wife's wishes and whims. But one day the two of them had a tiff, and neither Nancy nor David would budge from the feeling of being in the right. Several days had passed since the difference between them arose, and static hung in the air, droning out communication.

David would normally give in under such circumstances, but not this time. Nancy was amazed he wasn't talking, but she was equally determined not to speak first.

Then it happened. David came home and started to pack his suitcase. Nancy was confident he wasn't leaving her; he was often sent on business trips. But she couldn't believe he would go without resolving their conflict first. David, however, jaw set, silently prepared to leave. Nancy fumed.

Most of us, when we fume, have to verbally spew so we don't become combustible and explode. Not Nancy. She uses her hostility to create . . . well, let's just say *memories*.

That night, they went to bed without a word. David was feeling a slight advantage in their "cold war," because he knew what his travel plan was, and she didn't. He also knew this would bug her, because she's a detail person and likes to be fully informed. David fell asleep that night with a smirk on his face. I don't think he would have rested as well as he did, however, had he seen the grin spreading across his stalemate's lips.

David rose the next morning and went in to take his shower. While he was washing up, Nancy was quietly yukking it up. First she counted his undershorts in the suitcase to see how many days he would be gone. Finding that out, she then could determine where he was going. He always went to one of two places, each requiring him to stay a different length of time.

Once she figured out his destination, she quickly lifted the neatly folded underwear out of his luggage and replaced it with a note. Stifling giggles, she stashed his confiscated shorts in a drawer, zipped his case closed, dashed back between the bedsheets, and used a pillow to muffle her pleasure.

David emerged showered and shaved, picked up his suitcase, and left for his trip. This was the first time they had parted company without hugs, kisses, and promises to call. They were both finding a bit of comfort, though, in thinking they had a secret the other didn't know.

The outbound flight put David in a confined place with time

to think. He began to feel bad about their stormy week and his stony departure. He dearly loved Nancy and promised himself and the Lord that he would call and apologize as soon as he arrived at his hotel.

Nancy meantime busied herself around the house, stopping occasionally to imagine David's reaction when he unpacked. Chuckling, she waited for the phone to ring, both dreading and delighting in the prospect.

She didn't have long to wait. "Mom, it's Dad; he wants to talk to you," her son yelled.

Nancy wasn't sure if she should run to the phone or run for cover. But she made her way to the table and picked up the receiver. What she heard was not what she had anticipated. On the other end, David confessed his regrets at their spat and expressed even greater sorrow at leaving without making things right.

Nancy's heart sank as she was warmed by his tenderness and sincerity. She decided she had better 'fess up, too.

"David, have you unpacked yet?" she inquired.

"No, not yet."

"Maybe you should," she suggested.

"Why, what did you do?"

"Just go open your suitcase; I'll wait on the line."

David came back chuckling. "Very funny, Nancy. Where did you put my shorts?"

"Oh, they're here in the drawer," she admitted.

"No, really, are they in a side pocket?"

"Honest, I took them out before you left. Isn't that funny, David?" she said with failing confidence.

The line was silent, and then, much to her delight, David

broke into gales of healing laughter.

The note? Oh, yeah, it read:

"David, your attitude stinks, and now so does your only pair of underwear!"

9

Middle Man

Because of a delay in taking off, my homebound flight was late, leaving me at risk of missing my second plane. When we landed at the connecting airport, I did an O. J. Simpson through the terminal, arriving at my gate just as they were closing the doors. Relieved I'd made it, I headed down the aisle in search of my seat. I stopped at my assigned row and, to my dismay, found I had the middle seat.

There are some things I don't do. Middle seats head my "no way, I ain't gonna!" list. Middle seats make me feel like an Oscar Mayer wiener advertisement. My mood swing went from "I'm so grateful I caught my plane" to "I don't care what this ticket says, I'm not sitting in that center seat!"

I glanced around and realized, however, that this was the last available seat on the flight, and I would sit there or on the wing. Previously I always had an aisle seat; this just wasn't normal. All things considered, though, I prayed for an attitude adjustment. I remembered that God will operate on our attitudes but that He requires us to cooperate.

To do my part, I tried to think of a way to make this irritating situation fun. I took a quick survey of my seating again and thought, *What could I do with a person on each side of me?*

Then it came to me that I could pretend I was Oprah Winfrey and my seat partners were my guests. I would interview them. Now, this had possibilities!

Right off, there was a problem. Evidently the lady by the window didn't recognize my Oprah impersonation, because she wasn't a very cooperative interviewee. She was reading a book, and she let me know with sighs and downcast eyes that she didn't want to be disturbed. I thought Oprah wouldn't allow that to stop her, so I continued.

"Are you married?" I inquired.

"Yes," she mumbled.

"Do you have children?" I persisted.

"Yes," she grumbled.

"How many?" I pushed.

She stared at me with a strange look on her face, and I thought maybe she didn't know. Then she leaned in to me, lowered her voice, and said, "Nine."

"Nine!" I bellowed, surprising even myself. "Nine," I repeated, this time to myself. I don't think I had ever met anyone with nine children before . . . and she was pregnant. I was impressed!

Now, I also have this problem in that whenever I'm given noteworthy news, I feel led to pass it on. As I sat there trying to mentally contain those nine children, it seemed as if a balloon was being blown up inside me. I would explode soon if I didn't tell someone about these kids.

I leaned back toward the woman and said, "Would you mind if I tell this man on my left that you have nine children?"

Startled, somewhat confused, and slightly irritated, she whispered, "If you feel you need to tell that man!"

"Trust me," I responded, "I need to do this."

I then leaned to my left and said, "Excuse me, I thought you might like to know that this woman has nine kids."

"*Nine!*" he exclaimed, leaning forward to view this productive female, much to her consternation.

That was the kind of enthusiastic response I was looking for. I decided right then that he was a kindred spirit, and I turned my interview efforts toward him. Besides, I now realized that Multiple Mom was too pooped to participate in my game show (she had nine good reasons to be).

I had already observed something about this young man when I was being seated. He called me "Ma'am." At the time I thought, *Either he thinks I'm ancient, he's from the South, where they still teach manners, or he's in the service.* I decided the latter was the most likely, so I asked, "You in the service?"

"Yes, Ma'am, I am."

"What branch?"

"Marines."

"Hey, Marine, where are you coming from?"

"The Desert Storm, Ma'am."

"No kidding? The Desert Storm!" Then I thought, *This interview stuff is great!*

"How long were you there?" I continued.

"A year and a half. I'm on my way home. My family will be at the airport. I'm so scared." As he said this last, he took in a short, nervous breath.

"Scared? Of what?" I asked.

"Oh, all this hero stuff. I'm not a hero, I'm just me, and I don't want my family to be disappointed."

"Take it from me, Marine, your parents just want you to come home safe."

Nodding his head in hopes I was right, he looked at me and asked, "What do you do?"

I had been waiting for someone to ask this very question. I had just completed my first book, and I wanted to announce that I was an author. Here was my big chance. Sitting as tall as a five-foot person can, I said clearly and possibly a little too loudly, "I'm an author."

"An author! An author!" the Marine proclaimed. "An author," he repeated, obviously impressed.

I loved this kid!

Changing the topic back to him (as Oprah would do), I commented that he must have thought about returning to his family and home many times while he was in the Middle East.

"Oh, no, Ma'am," he replied. "We were taught never to think of what might never be, but to be fully available right where we were."

What great instruction, I thought, *whether you're in the armed forces or the army of the Lord.*

Then Michael (that was his name) told me that when he lived at home, he and his mother were friends. When he joined the service and was stationed in Hawaii, they had written to each other and had become good friends. But when he went to Desert Storm, they became best friends.

"She will never know how she affected my life while I was away," he continued. "I've never thought of myself as a religious person, but while I was in the Storm, I learned to pray. The example I followed was the one my mom set for me when I was growing up."

"What was the most difficult time for you?" I inquired in Oprah fashion.

"There was a four-month space when we had not seen a woman or a child. The day we drove into Kuwait was very emotional for us. The women stood in the doorways, waving, but even more moving was when the children ran to greet us," he said, his voice still filled with the feeling.

I wondered if the children affected the soldiers so deeply because children give us such a sense of a hope and a future.

"Since I've been stateside waiting to go home," he continued, "I've been thinking about my nephews, and I can hardly wait to hear them call me Uncle Michael. The title *uncle* means even more to me than being called *sergeant.*"

About that time, the flight attendant was passing by, and I tugged at her skirt. She looked down, and I said, "Know what? He"—I pointed toward Michael—"is returning from Desert Storm, and she has nine kids." I gestured in the direction of Super Mom.

The attendant evidently knew people with nine children, because that didn't hold her attention. But Michael sure did. She asked him several questions and then requested that he write his name on a piece of paper. Taking his signature, she headed toward the front of the plane. She reminded me of a woman with a balloon inside her that was ready to pop.

Moments later, the pilot came on the intercom and, with enthusiasm and sincerity, said, "It has been brought to my attention that we have a VIP aboard. He is a returning GI from Desert Storm."

Michael groaned and began to inch down in his seat.

I sat up taller.

"Sergeant Michael is in seat 12F," the pilot continued.

All heads swung in our direction. Michael had slunk so deeply into the upholstery that he was about two inches tall. In contrast, I was six-foot-two. (Visibility is always good for ratings.)

Then the pilot said, "As a representative of this airline and a citizen of the United States of America, I salute you, Michael, and thank you for a job well done."

At that point, the entire plane burst into applause.

Wow! I love this Oprah stuff.

The pilot came back on and said, "We are making our final approach into the Detroit Metro Airport."

Michael's breath caught.

I looked up and saw his eyes had filled with tears. He peeked through a tear to see if I had noticed, and of course there I was, goggling at him.

He said softly, "I just don't want to cry."

"It's okay," I told him. "I checked a Marine manual on this one, and it's all right to cry. Some of the most admirable men I've ever known have shed tears at appropriate times, and Michael, this is a right time."

"Then you don't think I need to blame this on my contacts?" he responded, grinning.

"I don't think so," I said with a giggle.

As our plane taxied in, I told him the best gift my son brought me when he returned from 18 months in Guam was that after he made his way through the waiting crowd, he scooped me up in his arms and held me for a very long time.

It was time to deplane, and when Michael stood, men all around us slapped him on the back and pumped his arm, thanking him for his contribution.

We made our way to the front, where the pilots came out to meet the sergeant and shake his hand. The flight attendants encircled him and told him he was great. I noticed that he didn't seem to mind this last gesture. In fact, he seemed to be getting taller.

Because of security precautions, no one was allowed to meet us at the gate, which meant we had to walk down a long corridor before we reached Michael's family and my husband.

Michael's homecoming included a lineup of relatives armed with video equipment, flags, cameras, and banners. When we were close enough for eyes to focus in and distinguish which one was Michael, his family began to chant, "Michael, Michael, Michael."

Michael stopped dead in his tracks. I got behind him and pushed. "C'mon, soldier," I said, "this isn't the enemy. This is your family."

He started walking again, but his shoes seemed to be full of cement, and he was moaning quietly with every step.

Even from a distance, I could identify his mom. She was the one leaping the highest in the air. A guard leaned against the wall, watching to make sure no one stepped over the security line. But every time Michael's mom jumped into the air, she came down with her toe just over the line to let that guard know who was really in charge.

As we got closer, she stopped jumping, and her hands went over her mouth to muffle the building sobs. Tears poured down her arms and dropped off her elbows . . . just over the line.

I realized that this was not my party (or Oprah's) and I needed to step back. When I did, in his nervousness, so did Michael.

I gave him a final nudge toward his family, and they engulfed him, everyone in tears.

I made my way through the other waiting people, wiping my eyes. When I saw my husband, he spotted me dripping emotions. "I'm part of this," I sniffed, nodding toward the reunion.

"You think you're a part of everything," he proclaimed.

That was true, but this time I really was . . . sort of. I wanted to stand and watch as I saw Michael find his mom in the crowd and pull her into his arms and hold her.

"That's tacky, Patsy," Les reminded me. "It's rude to stare."

Mr. Manners guided me over to the escalator and prompted me on. I turned backward so I could watch for as long as possible. As the moving steps drew me away from the celebration, I saw Michael still holding his mother, and he had held her for a very long time.

When we got to the baggage claim area, I prayed for the first time ever that my luggage would be delayed. Before long, the whole Desert Storm entourage came down to claim Michael's duffle bags.

Yes! I thought. *My big chance to be part of the finale.*

Michael was still surrounded by family when I saw a youngster toddle over and pull on his pant leg. I realized this must be one of the nephews he was so eager to see again. When I noticed how young the boy was and remembered that Michael had been gone for a year and a half, I held my breath to watch how the boy would react to his uncle. (I thought about my sons when they were that young and how, if I left them with a sitter for more than an hour, they acted as though they didn't know me when I returned.)

Michael's face lit up as he reached down and picked up the young boy. His nephew wrapped his chubby legs around the sergeant's waist, and his arms encircled Michael's neck. Then the boy's mom came over, and I heard her ask, "Honey, who's got you?"

He looked up, his young eyes reflecting his hero, and said, "Uncle Michael."

I could breathe again.

A few minutes later, as Les escorted me to the car, the thought hit me that I almost missed being a part of this tender event because I hadn't wanted to sit in the middle.

I wonder how many divine appointments I've missed because I found my circumstances not to be what I expected (just not normal), and my defiance robbed me of His greater plan?

10

Yuk It Up!

We all have moments we'd rather not remember—the kind that when we do recall them, we get embarrassed all over again. Like finding you're dragging a long sweep of toilet tissue. Spike heels are great for that. You shish kebab the tissue on your way out of the restroom, and you can literally parade it for miles before anyone will tell you.

Having dragged my pantyhose behind me through my hometown has left me with empathy for other dragees. I remember a gentleman and his wife who approached me at a convention and related their adventure.

The man said, "If you think it's embarrassing for a woman to drag her pantyhose, how do you think a man feels when it happens to him? I went to work and walked through the office when one of the women sang out, 'What's that, Bill?' I turned to look, and dangling out of my suit-pants leg were my wife's pantyhose. I casually ambled over to a wall, shook them out, and walked away. I left the hose huddled in the corner to figure out their own transportation home."

Evidently his wife didn't pick up her pantyhose, but the static in his slacks did. Half the hose clung to his pant leg, while the remaining leg danced behind him. The man, his wife, and I laughed long and loud as he relived his tail.

There's something so healing about laughter. When I can laugh at an event that has the potential to turn my pale face flashing red, somehow the situation doesn't record itself in my memory with as much pain.

My friend Ann is a good example. She flipped her melon and lived to laugh about it. While she was shopping for groceries one time, she spotted a large, elongated watermelon. She wanted the melon, but it looked heavy, and she wasn't sure she could lift it. No stock boys were around, so she decided to give it the old heave-ho. Either the melon didn't weigh as much as she had thought, or she was stronger than she realized. Anyway, she grabbed hold of the watermelon and slung it up and toward herself. With torpedo speed, the slippery melon slid out of her hands and up her shoulder to become airborne.

Once again, Sir Newton's theory of gravitation proved true. The melon headed for earth with great rapidity. When a melon is dropped from more than five feet onto a tile floor, "splat" doesn't begin to describe what occurs. Not only did it explode, but everything in a 15-foot radius was affected as well.

As Ann turned to look at her Herculean effort gone awry, she spotted . . . a victim. Or should I say the victim was "spotted"? A nicely dressed businesswoman looked stunned as ragged chunks of watermelon dripped down her pantyhose.

Ann didn't mean to laugh, but the whole scene struck her as so absurd that she couldn't help herself. The lady was not laughing, which seemed to tickle Ann all the more. The woman marched off in a huff, leaving a trail of seeds behind her.

Ann was now leaning against the rutabagas, trying to catch her breath, when the manager walked up and said, "This is not funny."

Well, that was the wrong thing to say. Poor Ann howled. Her sides were splitting, her face was red, and she was hysterical. She said she was trying to gain her composure so she could find the lady and apologize to her. But finally she had to just leave the store.

Laughter can make moments more memorable. Whether laughing alone or with others, it helps us feel good about our memories.

I remember walking through the mall once when I noticed a quarter on the floor. Had it been a penny, I might have passed it by. But a quarter? No way. I stooped down and swooped my hand across the floor to scoop up the coin, but it didn't budge. I tried again. I could hear laughter coming from a nearby ice cream shop, but I didn't look because I was focused on the shiny coin. I tried to pick it up again, but it held fast. I tried prying it with my nails. I even took out my emery board and used it like a crowbar, trying to dislodge this gleaming coin.

As I stared at George Washington's immobile silhouette, I thought I saw him smirk. Then I realized George was not alone. The laughter nearby had grown to unbridled guffawing. I looked up and realized five teenagers were watching me and laughing at my financial struggle. It was the kind of laugh that told me they knew something I didn't.

I could have flown off in a fury or resented their intrusion. Then again, I could find out what was so hilarious and join the fun.

I asked, "Okay, what's the deal?"

One girl confessed they had glued the quarter to the floor and had been watching people try to pick it up. The kids dubbed me the "most dedicated to the task." I giggled with them as I thought about my 25-cent antics.

Laughter is an incredible gift. It helps us to not take ourselves too seriously and makes it possible for us to survive life's awkward moments.

11

There's a Reason

When my high school teacher's eyes suddenly met mine, my heart began to palpitate. I slowly slid down in my seat, trying to disappear inside my open textbook.

"Patsy," she sang out, "let's hear your report."

This was not music to my ears. During my school years, I had developed creative avoidance skills in an ongoing endeavor to escape up-front presentations. Not making eye contact was a crucial part of my strategy. In a careless moment, however, I had glanced toward the chalkboard, only to find myself in eye-lock with this dear but determined teacher.

Realizing I would have to respond, I slowly rose and, on knees of silicone, made my way to the front of the room. My topic was "Quinine."

Fear had collected in my throat, which I forgot to clear before announcing the title of my speech. The "Qui" came out like the deep rumblings of Mount Saint Helens, and the "nine" screeched at a pitch that attracted dogs from three counties.

The class howled. My face flashed lipstick-red. I speed-sputtered through the report, never looking up.

By the time I finished, the jelly in my knees had congealed into blocks of cement. With 50-pound knees, I stiffly hobbled back to my desk. I plopped into my seat, dropping my eyes in humiliation. For the remainder of the semester, I studied the designs in the tile floor, not daring to glance up lest I be called on again.

When people don't make eye contact, there's a reason.

I had been cleaning my bedroom and headed for the kitchen to find the glass cleaner. As I passed through the living room, I glanced in the direction of my two-and-a-half-year-old (at the time), Marty. He had been watching cartoons and playing with his cars. Something about his looks made me stop in my tracks. I realized it wasn't what I saw but what I didn't see—his eyes. Marty stared down at his toys. I called out, "Marty."

He lifted his head but avoided my eyes. I walked toward him, and he sheepishly peeked up at me. Then I saw it. Lying on the floor behind Marty was an open bottle of baby aspirin. Little, pink pills were strewn among his playthings. I pulled Marty to me and looked into his mouth. Crushed aspirin particles were stuck in his tiny, white teeth. My heart began to pound wildly.

This was a new bottle of medicine, and only a few tablets had been used before now. I scooped up the remaining pills and quickly counted them. It appeared Marty had ingested 69 aspirins.

I drew him into my arms and ran to my neighbor's apartment. We didn't have a telephone, and Les had taken the car to work. I ran into Sharon's home and frantically called my physician. The woman who answered the phone instructed me not to bring Marty in but instead to induce vomiting by running my finger down his throat. She informed me that the doctors were too busy to talk to me. I thought, since she worked for the doctors, that she must know what was best, and I followed her directions.

I hung up feeling sick to my stomach but with a sense of urgency rushing through my mind. I dialed my mom's number and yelled, "Marty has an overdose of aspirin in him! Help me!" I slung the phone down without waiting for an answer and ran with Marty in my arms the two doors back to our apartment.

When my mom arrived, I was in the bathroom working with my little guy. It was necessary to do what I was doing to him, but very unpleasant for both of us. Mom and I took turns helping him bring up the potential poison until, in one effort, Mom's fingernail jabbed his tonsil, and Marty started to spit up blood.

Mom and I were unsure if we should continue, so we picked him up and ran back to the phone. This time I was able to speak directly with the doctor. He was appalled to hear we had been told not to come in. Now too much time had passed, and the aspirin remaining in Marty had gone into his bloodstream. The doctor said to let him play but to watch his eyes and not let him go to sleep. He said that if Marty's breathing became difficult, we should rush him to the hospital's emergency room.

I hung up the phone, and as I was telling Mom what the doctor had said, Marty's eyes closed and his breathing became erratic. I firmly shook him awake, and we headed for the emergency room.

That had to be one of the longest nights of my life. The hospital wouldn't allow me to be with Marty, so I camped out all night in the waiting room. By daybreak he was out of danger. Mom and I had been able to get enough of the medicine from his system that he had no long-term damage. But it would take him a while (us, too) to recover from the trauma of this event.

When we returned home, I investigated how Marty had managed to get to the aspirin. We didn't have childproof bottle caps at that time, so as a precaution, I had placed the bottle in the highest cupboard of our home. Marty, however, had ingeniously pulled a high stool over to the cupboards and climbed up on it, taking along his play golf club. From what we could determine, he had then stepped up on a shelf and, while holding on with one hand, swung his club, knocking the bottle off the upper shelf. The drop must have loosened the top, and the rest, as they say, is history.

What alerted me to our emergency was not the stool or golf club but Marty's eyes—especially when he wouldn't look at me.

When people won't look at you, there's a reason.

I can tell when my friend is angry at her husband, because she won't look at him. She avoids visual acknowledgment of his existence until he somehow works his way back into her favor.

Others aren't sure of what to do with how they feel, and they find themselves dodging eye contact to avoid giving away their hidden emotions or getting into conflict. Lack of visual involvement is a screeching smoke detector, alerting us to smoldering relational issues. How many times have you heard or said, "If you're not upset, why won't you look at me?"

Some folks are so full of shame that they don't feel worthy of personal eye contact. Then there are those who have been traumatized and feel frightened and abnormal. They only allow themselves quick peeks at those around them.

Guilt can be another visual barrier that keeps people from our view. Whether false or genuine, guilt affects our connection with others.

The way I see it, when people won't look at us or we won't look at them, there's a reason!

12

Heigh-ho Silver

I love playing word games, though Les would rather go to the dentist and have all his teeth extracted than join me. So once a year, whether he feels like it or not, we play a game of Scrabble. That is, until . . .

It was twilight, and we had been playing a short time (hours if you asked Les) when our eight-year-old, Jason, questioned, "What's that noise?"

I was in eye-lock with my letter tiles and didn't even look up. Les, who had been staring at the ceiling counting cobwebs to entertain himself, took an immediate interest in Jason's noise just in case it offered him a way out. Sure enough, it did.

Jason went to the window, and then, with eyes the size of saddles, he hollered, "The horses are out! The horses are out!"

That broke any concentration I had, as we all rushed to the window to see for ourselves. Our hearts began to pound, and we stood frozen for a moment. We watched as a dozen horses stampeded across our yard and toward the road.

The potential for disaster sent everyone scrambling. Les yelled for our oldest son, Marty, and his friend Steve to try to head them off. The boys hightailed it out the back door, and Les sped out the front.

I, being of great value during a crisis, ran back and forth in the house, shouting, "Oh, my! Oh, my!"

Then I went out on the porch to peek, but I couldn't see what had happened because the horses had galloped out of our tree-lined yard and onto the well-traveled road. But I could hear. Screeching tires first, and then a sickening thud, followed by breaking glass. A shudder went through my body, and my mind kicked into high gear.

I flew back into the house and phoned our friend Tom across the lake. "Come quick! The horses, ran, road, thud, glass . . . ambulance, vet, tow truck . . . Come quick!" I sputtered like a stenographer.

Panting, I made my way out to the line of trees, but I was too scared to look. Jason leaned out to see what had happened, and I snatched him back. "No, Jason, this is too gruesome for a child. Go back to the house," I instructed firmly. Then, considering the wisdom of those words, I went with him.

By the time I reached the front door, Marty and Steve were coming up the hill after corralling the remaining herd. Then Les walked in, shaking his head and mopping his brow. He proceeded to explain the runaway results.

It seems a neighbor was on his way home from work when he came over the top of the hill by our house. As he crested the hill in his Volkswagen, all of a sudden he was part of a stampede. He hit his brakes, and as he skidded, his little car scooped up one horse, slung it over the roof, and gently deposited it back on the road, heading in the opposite direction. As the horse skimmed the top of the rounded vehicle, it tapped its hoof through the passenger's window, leaving splintered glass piled neatly in the empty seat.

The car came to a stop long enough for the uninjured but dazed driver to regroup and then drive home (with quite a "guess what happened to me on the way" tale to tell). The rattled runaway, wide-eyed and wiser, was ushered back to the barnyard to rejoin the rest of the herd.

Les and the boys had just caught their breath when up drove Tom and his troops. His wife, Joyce, their kids, and some friends had all piled in the car to see the horse-rendous accident and do what they could to help.

But now the car, driver, horses, and even the glass were all gone. The road was humming with traffic, the horses were grazing innocently in the pasture, and Les was lounging next to the Scrabble board . . . grinning. It appeared to be a normal evening at the Clairmonts'.

Our friends looked at me as if I had imagined the whole thing. I began to wonder myself. Les finally confessed, but only after I released him from any future spelling games.

When emotions stampede like wild horses in the night, one may end up with hoof prints in one's mouth.

I had made assumptions based on what I had heard but hadn't actually seen, and then I had passed on that information. I had the sinking feeling this wasn't the first time I had done that.

13

LOW · NORMAL · HOT

Clean Sweep

Feeling zonked, I decided to zone out when I boarded the plane bound for home. I found my row and secretly checked out my seat companion. She was a normal, fifty-ish-looking woman. (I immediately liked her for being older than me.) I peeked at her so I wouldn't be obligated conversationally. I didn't want anything to disrupt my siesta in the sky.

Doesn't it just drive you bonkers when you have a hidden agenda and someone toddles into your space and trips up your plan?

This time my "toddler" was a flight attendant who came scooting down the aisle offering treats. My stomach won out over sleep, and I ended up chatting with my neighbor, Susan. Am I glad I did! This was no normal woman.

Susan told me an incredibly sad story with a surprise ending. She said her beloved husband of 30 years decided he loved someone else and wanted a divorce. The feelings of crushing betrayal deepened when Susan found out his affair had been going on for years. He was also a clever businessman and had prepared himself for this decision so that he would come out the financial winner.

Susan was first numb and then paralyzed by her grief. Her husband used her shock to his advantage, swooping down fast and furious to get all he could. Much to Susan's dismay, she was notified by the court that she would have to turn over to her husband and his girlfriend her cherished home of 23 years, where they had raised their five children.

Reeling from grief upon grief, Susan moved into a tiny, furnished apartment. There she tried to figure out what had gone wrong. In the divorce settlement, she was awarded a small, failing business, and that was to be her source of income. To add not only to her dilemma but also to her pain, her ex-husband and his female friend opened a new, competing business just down the street.

Now, folks, I don't know about you, but that's where I would throw up my hands and spit.

Not Susan. She reached inside and pulled up her faith. She decided she couldn't allow others' choices to extinguish her joy or decree her future. She was determined not to be a victim but to be victorious and begin with a grateful heart. No, she wasn't grateful for her tremendous loss, but that God is a healer of fractured hearts.

One day while doing dishes, Susan turned on the small TV near her sink. As she changed channels, she came to a musical presentation and was caught up in the contagious melody. But now she had no dance partner.

Then she spotted her companion leaning against the cupboard. He was the tall, silent type. She waltzed over and embraced the kitchen broom, then twirled about the room, laughing and singing. Around and around she spun, dizzy with delight. Suddenly she realized she was not alone.

Susan saw she had been joined by three of her married daughters, who were standing in the doorway, giggling at their mother's antics. (They checked on her regularly those days for fear her losses would be more than she could bear, driving her to an act of despair.)

As she stood holding her silent partner, Susan looked at her girls and said, "In the years to come, may this be the way you remember me . . . dancing."

Susan didn't want to leave a legacy of brokenness or despair. Instead, she chose to give a living heritage of courage, conviction, and, yes, celebration. Her circumstances were anything but normal, but then, so was her response.

By the way, she was able to turn the little business around, buy a lovely home, and enjoy a full and active life. She chose not to stay in her sorrow or linger in her loss, but in the midst of devastation, to dance.

14

You-Turn

I am always going. Going places, going to town, going up, going down, and even going bonkers. But one going I don't do well is going back. I'm a forward person, and I'm married to a fast-forward kind of guy. If Les and I are pulling out of our driveway and realize we've forgotten something after we've passed our mailbox (affixed to our front porch), we don't go back; we go without.

Since I'm an "Onward Christian Soldier," you can imagine how difficult it is for me when I have no choice but to go back.

Janet, a friend, and I had just completed four glorious days of study and fun. We stayed in a beautiful, wooded setting that we thought was paradise. The grounds were complete with English gardens, wild turkeys, deer, and swans.

The most attentive creatures were the swans—especially the male fowl, who truly was foul. He changed our thoughts forever about swans' being gentle beauties. Good-looking he was; good-natured, guess again.

We nicknamed him "Dick the Bruiser." Dick's walk was an

overstated strut. He would flex his chest feathers and then swagger. To further intimidate us, this bully would stretch out his S-shaped neck until it became an exclamation point. The feat made you wonder if there were a giraffe in his family closet. He seemed to be of the mind that the grounds were his and we were intruders. After he backed us into the kitchen and didn't allow us to leave until he finally became bored with us, we decided it *was* his place. We did our best to stay out of his way the rest of the time we were there.

When it came time for Janet and me to leave, we were reluctant because it had been a perfect writing place for us. With the Bruiser's permission, however, we eventually packed the van and said our good-byes. We hugged Zona (the best cook in Michigan), waved to Dick and his willowy wife from the safety of the van, and hit the dusty trail.

We had a three-hour ride in front of us, and we decided to use the time brainstorming. Janet and I had been chatting for an hour when I noticed my gas gauge was registering a little skimpy. I chose to fill up then to prevent any delays later.

I swung into a country service station and ordered ten dollars worth of gas. Then I reached for my purse. It wasn't there. I panicked. Janet prayed. Then Janet paid. No purse, no moolah.

I pulled away from the pumps, parked the van on the side of the road, and began a frantic search. I rummaged through the boxes, bags, and baggage in an attempt to force my purse into existence. While I ripped apart the van, Janet was nervously tossing animal cookies into her mouth.

I finally had to admit I had forgotten my handbag back with the Bruiser. Ol' Beak Face was probably picking through it while I was ransacking my vehicle. (I wonder how swan feathers would work for pillows?) To make matters more frustrating, buckets of bone-chilling rain were coming down.

Looking for an easier answer than going back, I decided to call Les. The only available phone was an unprotected one that I couldn't reach from the van. So I jumped out into the downpour and grabbed the receiver, only to realize I had forgotten my home number. I jerked open the van door, my hair hanging down my face like wet feathers, and asked my California guest if she knew my number.

Janet was still munching morsels. (I don't think she was hungry but thought it best to chew on the cookies rather than chew me out.) She dipped into her purse and pulled out my number. She tried reading it but instead showered me in hippo crumbs. I took the sticky scrap with the scrawled numbers and hurried back to the phone. I reached Les as the rain washed away the writing, leaving the paper as blank as I was feeling.

After a quick but soggy talk, Les and I agreed I would have to return to claim my belongings. I sloshed my way back to Janet, who appeared to have stored the cookies much like a chipmunk storing acorns in his chubby cheeks. I announced my backtracking plan to her. She swallowed hard and smiled weakly.

Once I made the U-turn and aimed the vehicle in the "wrong" direction, we tried to cheer up. We remembered we had passed a bakery advertising homemade pies. We had valiantly declined the chance to have a piece on our first drive by. Now we agreed we should not only stop, but we should also each have our own pie as a source of comfort. In preparation for this highlight, we talked about what kinds we hoped they had, and we tried to imagine the light, flaky crust.

Our mouths were watering when we spotted the bakery ahead.

I sped up and turned into the driveway, only to spot something else. The bakery had closed. I began to wonder how swan pie might taste.

I know an hour's distance is not that far, but when I have my mind set on forward, I find it exasperating to switch directions. My mistake added two unnecessary hours to our travel. With each mile back, we felt the emotional impact of going the "wrong way."

Janet was kind and didn't say I was a nitwit. But I found it difficult to forgive myself for this stupid stunt.

"If only I hadn't left my belongings," I whined repeatedly. Yet my purse was too valuable not to retrieve. It was full of my identification, as well as my finances. I had to drive the long road back before we could continue our journey.

I find this is also true when we're working on issues from the past. We have to be willing, at times, to look back so we can go forward. If we don't, we leave valuable pieces of our identification behind.

It's not unusual to feel angry about going back to retrieve our emotional "bags," because most of us have our indicators set on forward. Returning seems like such a waste of effort. But it's the same as when I recovered my purse; once I had what was mine in hand, my anger began to subside, and I was more fully equipped to move ahead.

The temporary inconvenience of returning put me in a much better place than if I had gone home and arrived there both angry and without my personal belongings.

Unresolved childhood conflicts can leave us in cycles of anger, guilt, shame, or fear. Those feelings use up more of our time than if we made the ride back and took care of our personal stuff. They also add stress to our relationships, leaving us stuck in negative emotional cycles without an exit.

Angie felt like a mouse in a maze. She was caught in her unmanageable emotions, and she couldn't find a way out. Her husband, Rich, was exhausted from trying to understand her and was threatening to leave.

When Angie first called me and confessed her bizarre behavior, I suggested she talk to a counselor about some childhood pain. She instantly became irate, declaring, "My childhood was like being brought up in Ozzie and Harriet Nelson's home. It was perfect."

Angie's strong response indicated that the past was a painful and scary place for her. Her proclamation showed an extreme need to avoid not only going back, but also checking her rearview mirror. Her reluctance to consider yesterday as an answer for today was as normal as my hesitancy to backtrack for my bag.

Later, out of desperation for her own emotional well-being and for the sake of her marriage, Angie made the journey "home." She claimed "her belongings," which turned out to be far more valuable than she had imagined. She also felt a sense of inner relief, making it possible for her to move ahead.

The strange thought patterns and behavior that had plagued her lessened and then stopped. When Angie was able to change channels (from "The Nelsons"), life came into clearer focus for her. She began to tune in to reality and see how her life actually had been. Living in truth, although initially painful, helped her emotions to heal. Today Angie enjoys healthier thoughts and improved relationships.

Back is, at times, the most forward step we can take.

15

LOW · NORMAL · HOT

Accidental Perspective

I bounded out the door, energized because I had completed a writing project and motivated by a purchase I was going to make. I had been working on a story for two days, and it had finally come together. While I was writing, in the back of my mind, I kept thinking about a used piece of furniture I had seen in town that would be just right for my office. I needed a book and display case, and this piece offered both, plus more. The price was right, too.

I was excited as I headed into our little town full of delightful shops offering wonderful "deals." I was almost to my destination when, in my rearview mirror, I noticed a car come up behind me at a fast clip. I remember thinking, *That guy is going to hit me if I don't scoot out of his way.* I added a little pressure to the gas pedal and turned my wheel to hurry into a parking space. That's when it happened. A loud thud was followed by crunching, scrunching, grinding sounds as my minivan rearranged the front fender of a parked car.

I am of the belief that if you're going to hit a vehicle, you should select one with someone inside. When you smack an empty, parked car, you pretty much rule out the chance the other person may have been at fault. All eyes are focused on you. Also, if you must have an obvious accident, it's better not to do it on Main Street in your hometown.

I jumped out of the van and ran over to look at the smooshed car. The victim's vehicle had two silver beauty marks streaking down the side, and the chrome fender curled out instead of in, giving it a flared appearance.

Then I ran inside an office and asked if the car belonged to anyone there. It didn't, so I headed for the next building, when I heard someone call my name.

A lady I had just met at Bible study two weeks prior waved and ran across the road in my direction. She gave me a hug and told me everyone in the ladies' dress shop heard me hit the car and came to the window to see what had happened and who had done it. When I had stepped out of my van, she had squealed and announced, "I know that woman!" In a small town, anonymity is difficult.

Then she added as she checked out the crumpled car, "You could tell this story at conferences."

Trust me—at this point, I was not eager to tell my husband, much less the world, what I had done.

I dashed into the shop where the bookcase was and called to the clerk, "I have to go turn myself in at the police station, but would you please measure the bookcase for me? I'll be right back to purchase it."

As I headed for the front door, I heard a sweet voice say, "I just sold it."

"No!" I exclaimed. "You don't understand! I hit a car in my attempt to get here and buy this piece" (as if that would make a difference). Then I whined, "The buyer wasn't driving a dark blue Buick, was she?"

The saleswoman assured me she wasn't. I could tell she felt bad about my situation, but I felt worse. On the way to the police station, I thought, *Maybe I'll have them throw me in the slammer and sleep off this trip to town.*

When I arrived, I confessed to a woman behind a barred glass window that I had committed a crime. She called for an officer to come and write a report. While I was waiting, I noticed the zipper on my pants was down and my red shirttail was sticking out like a road flag. I quickly turned away from the men sitting in the waiting area to "fix" myself and tried not to think about how long my red tail had been waving. A fleeting recollection of me looking like Wee Willie Winkie as I ran from one store to the next, trying to find the car's owner, darted through my head.

The officer appeared and began to ask questions. Near the end of the inquest, he asked, "How much damage did you do to your vehicle?"

"I don't know," I answered.

"You don't know?" he echoed.

"I don't know," I validated.

"Why don't you know?" he pushed.

"Because I didn't look."

"Why didn't you look?" he asked in disbelief.

"I'm in denial," I confessed.

"You have to look," he told me. Then he sent me out to get my registration.

I returned, paper in hand.

"Well," he said, "how much damage?"

"Sir, I didn't look," I said with polite resignation.

He shook his head and gave me back my registration. As I was leaving, I heard him say, "You'll have to look."

When I got home, I asked Les to go out and look.

It turned out I had swiped her car with my running board. The board wasn't off, yet it wasn't on. It was neither here nor there but suspended in air. Threads at each end dangled the board precariously.

Afterward, I realized that when we spend too much time looking in our rearview mirrors, we may hit something right in front of us. Looking back is an important part of conscientious driving, but it's not the only safety precaution.

Likewise, it's important for us to benefit from our past, but we don't want to get so stuck staring at yesterday that we collide with today in a destructive way.

Unlike the situation with my van, I can't send Les to check my past and assess how much damage was done. That's my responsibility. As the officer said, "You'll have to look." But once I take care of what I can do to repair the past, I then need to drive on, benefiting from occasional rearview references and perspective.

16

High Flyer

When my brother-in-law, Bryan, was sent to Saudi Arabia during Desert Storm, my sister, Elizabeth, and their three children came for a visit. Elizabeth and the youngsters—Steven, eight; Nicholas, two; and Lindsey, four months—stayed for five weeks.

It didn't take me long to decide that combat gear would be helpful not only in Saudi, but also at our place. It had been a long time since Les and I had experienced young ones for days on end, and we had forgotten how much energy they're capable of expending. The visit also highlighted Les's and my need to consider a retirement village . . . soon!

Elizabeth, being a conscientious mom, strapped on her Reeboks every morning in her attempt to keep up with the fast-paced, creative escapades of her little munchkins.

In my effort to be supportive of this never-ending challenge, I invested in some baby furniture. First, I bought a small crib, then a highchair, and lastly a walker.

I had noticed Nicholas, the two-year-old, thought his four-month-old sister, Lindsey, made a cushy trampoline. So I thought I would spare her little body squash marks by tucking her in the walker.

When I arrived with the walker, I was eager to try it out. Fortunately it didn't require assembly, and all I had to do was open it up and slide her in. Seemed simple enough. Little did I realize I was under surveillance for the purpose of sabotage.

I innocently turned my back on the open walker while I stooped down to pick up Lindsey. In that unguarded moment, the saboteur, Nicholas, catapulted his two-year-old frame into the walker. He then pulled it up like a pair of pants and tore off running at a high speed that set the walker legs flapping in the breeze.

Much to my amazement and horror, Nicholas headed for the stairway. He evidently thought the word *landing* meant "runway" and the term *walker* was a code name for Lear Jet, because he ran right off the landing into midair.

At that point, Nicholas learned a scientific concept . . . gravity. Nick and his floppy-fitting flying machine dropped into the stairwell, crashing on the cement floor below.

My heart stopped for the split second of silence that followed. Then my feet began to gallop as screams came trumpeting up the steps. As I neared the landing, I envisioned Nicholas in a pile of little broken bones. But what I met was an enraged consumer stomping up the stairs, registering the loudest complaint I had ever heard. Evidently Nicholas wanted money back on this faulty piece of equipment.

Nicholas didn't have a mark on him and didn't even seem to be in pain . . . but he was livid this contraption didn't fly. I tried to console him, but he was intent on revenge. He kicked the plastic tires a couple of times and called it names in toddler jargon. I believe he referred to it as a "swachendinger." Finally, we were able to divert his attention while Les stowed the abused apparatus.

I find it interesting how young we learn to blame something or someone else for our behavior, and then how long we hold onto the habit. The other day I saw a grown man behaving much like my little nephew. The man's car had a flat tire, and when he stepped out of the vehicle, he proceeded to kick the tire and bang the hood with his fist. I'm glad my windows were up and I couldn't hear the names he was calling his car from his adult arsenal.

That scene was both funny and sad. Here was a grown-up conversing with an inanimate object as he tried to beat it senseless. Smart, huh? And yet he's certainly not alone . . .

A friend came over one day, steaming because the bank had dared to bounce her check. "Did you have money in the account?" I asked.

"That's not the point," she insisted. "I've done business there a long time, and they should have overlooked it."

Instead of seeing her poor bookkeeping and spontaneous shopping sprees as the problem, she pointed an accusing finger at the bank's "unfriendly tactics."

My check-bouncing friend, the flat-tire man, and my flying nephew found it easier to shift blame than to see how their actions played a part in the outcome. Blame is a common defense. I know, I've used it. In fact . . .

Recently I was running a little late for an appointment. Just before I ran out the door, I stopped to put away my mail. I noticed an unopened letter and took additional moments to open, read, and write a quick response to it.

On the way to the meeting place, I ran into heavy traffic and then had to wait at a train crossing for 100 cars to chug by. When I arrived at my destination, I was stressed out and frustrated. I heard myself accusing the stand-still traffic and the stretched-out train for my delay.

As I thought about it later, however, I realized that if I had left when I should have, I would have missed the train and had enough leeway to inch through the traffic and still arrive on time . . . minus my jangled nerves. I find that I'm often guilty of creating the chaotic atmosphere that sets me up for emotional frenzy.

In the blame game, everybody loses, and nobody changes.

17

My Way

Joanie had a magnetic beauty. People often stared at her out of admiration. She also had a spunky personality and was known for being a little headstrong. Her dynamic beauty and bouncy determination made her quite popular.

Jeff was a successful businessman and real-estate investor. He was brought up in a dysfunctional home, but he had chosen a different life-style from his family's. He was well respected and loved by his friends and co-workers. When Joanie and Jeff married, everyone felt they were a perfect pair.

Joanie and Jeff had it all, with one exception. They were unable to have children. This grieved them both, but especially Joanie, who felt she had let Jeff down. Jeff remained devoted to her, but she became preoccupied with her infertility. She wept often. Her housekeeper, Karen, would hear her cry and try to console her. Karen's gentle care touched Joanie's heart, and they became friends. Joanie found herself confiding in the other woman.

Joanie and Karen's lives were very different. Karen was much younger, she lived a meager life-style, and she had only been in the U. S. a short time when she began to work for her wealthy employer.

As the months passed, Joanie's desire for a child only increased. One day, as she watched Karen arrange flowers in a vase, an idea swept through her mind. At first she was startled at her own thought, but as she entertained the idea, it began to comfort her.

Joanie wanted Karen to have Jeff's baby. That way Jeff would have a child, and Joanie would not have to live with the nagging feeling of failure.

Artificial insemination had not yet been perfected, and Joanie felt she had waited long enough. Besides, she knew Karen and Jeff loved her, not each other. So how could it hurt?

Both Karen and Jeff agreed to Joanie's plan. In fact, neither seemed to hesitate or object. And so it was that Karen became pregnant with Jeff's firstborn.

Joanie initially was pleased with her decision. But then she noticed a change in Karen's attitude toward her. At first Joanie thought she was imagining the change. Or maybe it was just the mood swings of a pregnant woman.

But time told a different tale. Not only did Karen's tummy puff, but so also did her pride. Karen felt superior to her childless friend.

Joanie was first crushed and then livid. In a fit of fury, she fired Karen.

Jeff, Joanie, and Karen's lives had turned into a tragedy. What started out as the perfect pair seemed to end as brokenness and despair.

Actually, there's more to this story, much more. If you'd like to see the end of the saga, look in an age-old book, the Bible

(Genesis). Joanie (a.k.a. Sarah), Jeff (a.k.a. Abraham), and Karen (a.k.a. Hagar) are presented in all their sadness and eventual celebration.

It's a story that tinges the reader's heart with sorrow over their choices but gladdens the heart over God's grace.

When you think about it, this trio doesn't sound old. In fact, Sarah, Hagar, and Abe's choices remind us of the tabloid headlines we see as we move through the grocery store checkout. This proves once again that Scripture offers counsel generation after generation.

"There's no new thing under the sun."

18

Flight 326

I had just finished a demanding three days of teaching in Indiana and was headed for my home in Michigan. As I stood in the airport looking out at the runway, I became aware of how exhausted I was. But I comforted myself with the thought that I would soon be home.

While standing at the window, watching for my plane, I noticed a tiny Tinker Toy-type plane putt up and park at a gate. I told myself, *See, Patsy, things could be worse. Instead of being just tired, you could be booked on that pretend airplane.*

As that thought crossed my mind, I heard an airline hostess announce my plane's arrival. I picked up my belongings and headed for my gate. Even my purse seemed heavy as I dragged along. When I arrived where I thought I belonged, I noticed I was all alone. I backtracked to the check-in desk to ask about my gate. The lady behind the desk told me that someone would be escorting me and some others outside.

Confused, I asked, "Why would I need to go outside?"

"To board your flight," she said dryly.

"I don't understand," I replied, feeling mentally deficient. I thought, *Surely I can't be so wiped out that I'm unable to process what this gal is saying to me.*

She spoke slowly, hoping, I'm sure, that a light might go on signifying someone possibly was home. "Your plane has arrived," she reannounced, directing my attention to the window. "We'll have someone take you out to board."

My eyes followed her outstretched arm, but I couldn't see my plane. I thought my mind had left me, and now my sight was impaired. I decided to be blunt. "I don't see my plane," I said, bewildered.

"Aren't you on flight 326?" she inquired.

I looked at my ticket and verified by bobbing my weary head up and down. Evidently she felt sorry for me, because she took me by the arm, walked me to the window, and pointed to the plane.

Suddenly I came to life. It was as if someone had stuck my finger in an outlet. She was aiming her sinister finger at the play plane I had seen earlier.

"No, I don't fly in anything but a jet," I shot at her.

"You are today," she smilingly bubbled back.

"No, no, there's been a mistake. I only fly in normal airplanes." I stammered the words, starting to panic.

She seemed to take my "normal" statement personally. She told me I could call my travel agent on the pay phone, and then she turned and walked back to her desk and the waiting line.

I was nauseated. How could this have happened? Then I heard the announcement that the guide was ready to take us outside to board.

Not knowing what else to do, I followed several businessmen

out to the waiting plane. The Bible verse "All we like sheep have gone astray" came to my trembling mind as I followed on the gentlemen's heels. When we arrived at the portable steps, I knew by seeing it up close that this was what is referred to as an "aircraft." That means, "something a couple of space cadets glued together in their garage while watching Big Time Wrestling."

I had to bend down to enter the aircraft. (Excuse me, but I'm only five feet tall.) Then I made my way (a distance of 12 inches) to my seat. Because of restricted space, I had to embrace my purse and briefcase in my lap. I could feel the vibration of the engine shaking my armload of belongings. Then I realized the engine wasn't running yet, and what I felt was my own pounding heart ricocheting off my clutched parcels.

I peeked around and noticed the men aboard didn't seem comfortable, either. They looked like sumo wrestlers bent forward and stuffed into seats not designed to hold them. Their knees seemed to be growing out of their chins.

The cockpit was open to us, and it appeared that if the pilot got into any problems, we, the flyees, could lean forward and take over.

I peeked out my lens-sized window as an airline employee approached the propeller and gave it a mighty whirl. I was not encouraged to know this apparatus had to be hand wound. The engine kicked into an ear-deafening rhythm.

Instead of just vibrating, I now felt as though I were being shook silly on one of those weight-reduction belts. The plane wobbled out to the runway and began to taxi. (I wished at that point that I was *in* a taxi.) I had the distinct feeling, as we sputtered ahead, that the businessmen and I would each have to sling out a leg and paddle to get this baby airborne.

That wasn't necessary. Suddenly a hose broke loose outside the plane and spewed liquid across our windows. The tiny craft reduced speed and hightailed it back to the terminal.

The next thing we knew, the pilot and copilot had evacuated the plane. Their desertion removed any question about whether they planned on going down with the ship.

Somehow, when the pilots left us, we passengers were in no mood to stay. One of the pilots ran around to the side of the plane, wiped his finger through the liquid, and smelled it. Then he disappeared.

A businessman looked at me and said, "It's a good thing none of us is smoking."

That pretty much did it for me. I was getting off if I had to stuff myself through the porthole window next to me. That wasn't necessary, though, because an airline worker opened the door at that moment and asked us to quickly evacuate the plane. I gave new meaning to the word *quickly*.

As we gathered inside the terminal, we were told there would be a short delay while they fixed the plane. I could just picture them pushing this craft back into the garage so the space cadets could safety pin the hose back in place.

In about 15 minutes, they lined us up and marched us back to the Tinker Terminator. Only now there were fewer of us, because several men refused to get back on.

That was the most purging ride of my life, as I asked the Lord to forgive me for every offensive thing I had said or done. All this confession was in preparation for meeting Him, which I knew I was going to do at any moment. The flight felt as if we were sky surfing. And then we made a roller-coaster drop from the sky, thumping onto the runway.

Les told me he was looking out the window, watching for my plane, when Tinker bounced in. He said that out of boredom, he was watching the handful of people squeeze out of the hatch when I emerged. "Boy," he said, "was I surprised to see you in a plane like that!"

"You!" I squealed with weak knees. As we walked to the baggage area, I Velcroed myself to Les's arm. I was grateful to be back on earth with my husband and my squeaky-clean heart.

Interesting how disruptive events can give us a more grateful perspective and a renewed commitment to our families and faith. Could that be what they were designed for?

19

Hold Your Tongue

When Janet and I arrived at the house in the woods to work on a manuscript, the bear rug in the living room caught our immediate attention. It was large, furry, and cuddly looking. But when we viewed our new friend from the front, our assessment changed. The black bear didn't look so friendly with its huge head and ferocious, open, growling mouth. We dropped "cuddly" from our list of descriptives.

Janet and I tried to guess what might have caused this bear to look so testy. Maybe someone had swiped its Smoky the Bear poster, or perhaps it had sat on a hive and the bees had made their point. Finally we decided this was a she-bear, and someone had criticized her cubs and ticked her off. Her gleaming teeth were bared as though she were seething with anger and eager to rip off someone's limbs. But we both agreed the most despicable feature of this animal was her long, glistening tongue. Yuck!

After hours of concentration on our project, my head felt clogged with words, and my mind was skipping beats. Janet and I were losing our enthusiasm and focus. That wasn't good, because we had a lot of writing to accomplish before proclaiming our work complete.

As the gaps in my thinking process widened, I began to hit wrong keys and misspell simple words. It was obvious I needed a break.

I pulled away from my computer and walked across the room, being careful to inch around the intimidating animal skin sprawled on the floor. I shuddered as I passed. Pulling a couple of tissues from the Kleenex box, I turned to say something to Janet while walking back to the table. My eyes were on her, and for a split second I forgot our fiendish floor friend. In that unguarded moment, my foot slipped into the bear's open jaws, sending me catapulting over its head. The tongue flew out of its fierce mouth and slurped down my leg as I screamed in disgust. Trying to catch my balance, I staggered against the fireplace and cringed as the tongue slid to my feet.

Janet howled!

I broke my grisly gaze to look in Janet's direction, and we both came unglued. We laughed and laughed, the kind of laughter in which it's hard to catch your breath, and your insides jostle around like an unbalanced washing machine on spin cycle. Tears cascaded down our now-blotchy faces. Gasping, I jumped around in an attempt to jump-start my breathing. As we both caught our breath, we noticed the bear staring at its own taunting tongue lying three feet from its head, and we burst into laughter again.

After our 15-minute seizure of guffawing had passed, we felt great! The laughter had amazingly flushed our heads, refreshed our attitudes, and relieved our emotional humdrums. Janet and I went back to work with renewed interest and creative results.

Laughter lightens the load.

20

???'s

od asked a lot of questions in Scripture. That intrigues me. He who has all the answers, asked. Did you ever wonder why?

For instance, the Lord called out to Adam and Eve after they had sinned and hidden from His presence, "Where are you?"

Whenever I've read that portion of Scripture, I've wanted to tattle and call out, "They're hiding behind the blaming bush!"

The bush must really have been a dandy hiding place if our all-knowing, all-seeing God didn't have a clue to their whereabouts. I'm sure it was a big garden, but c'mon, we know God knew. So why did He ask?

The Lord questioned Eve in regard to her disobedience, "What is this you have done?"

Do you actually think God was stumped? I wonder why He didn't just dangle in front of her guilt-ridden face a Polaroid snapshot of her and the enemy dining on fruit flambé. Or run an instant replay of Adam's eating out of his wife's hand.

I notice God didn't stop asking questions in the garden but

continued throughout Scripture. Curious response from a sovereign God who can not only tell us what we've done, but also expose the content of our thoughts and hearts. Consider Hagar . . .

Hagar was in trouble. Death was knocking at her door, as well as at her young son's, when the angel of God called to her, "What is the matter with you, Hagar?"

Isn't it rather obvious, especially for an overseer like an angel? Hagar and Ishmael were a couple of crispy critters after crawling in the scorching sun. The only moisture was the boy's tears, and they evaporated before they could drip off his face.

Maybe the angel was wearing shades or was momentarily blinded by the sizzling sun. But wait, something even stranger happened next. Before Hagar could give the angel an update on her ordeal, the angel mapped out her future, answering his own question.

I'm getting more confused. If the inquiring angel knew the answer, why did he ask?

Let's see, we have Eve in arrears while the enemy leers, and Ishmael in tears while Hagar sears. Boy, do I have questions.

The story of Elijah doesn't help. Elijah had a fiery faith until Jezebel doused his flames. Jez Fed-Exed Elijah her plan to snuff him out. Elijah's faith flickered, allowing fear to flame up, and he fled.

We find Elijah headed for high ground in an attempt to control his own destiny. He was pursued not by the enemy but by the questions of God.

"What are you doing here, Elijah?" the Lord probed. Not once but twice, He asked Elijah what He already knew.

Even in the midst of death, God asked questions. We find Ezekiel in a valley of death, meandering among the corpses. The voice of the Lord solicited what sounds like advice from Ezekiel when He asked, "Can these bones live?"

Excuse me, but He who formed our skeletons from the dust of the earth and breathed into mankind the breath of life wasn't sure if the bones could live? Perhaps He misplaced His recipe. Can you hear Him pondering, *Was it one part dust to every three breaths, or three parts dust to every one breath?*

I think not. I'm the one left pondering.

God sent us His Son, Jesus. The family connection is obvious, because Jesus, our Answer, came asking questions. Like Father, like Son.

The Lord asked impetuous Peter, "Who do you say that I am?"

Still later He penetrated Peter's heart with the words, "Do you love Me?" Evidently the Lord thought Peter was hard of hearing, because He repeated Himself, "Do you love Me?" Twice I can see, but the Lord pushed Peter a third time. "Do you love Me?"

This loving interrogation left Peter stumped. He responded as we might have, "Lord, You know all things; You know that I love You."

What I hear Peter saying is, "Why are You asking when You know me better than I do?"

If we truly believe the Lord knows us, we must realize these questions have a purpose. And it certainly isn't that the Lord is forgetful and needs us to remind Him. Nor is He stuck and in need of our feeble insight. I think He questions us so we might think—think through our choices, our responsibilities, and our beliefs.

Maybe, if we try to answer some of these questions in regard to our own lives, we will better understand their wisdom:

"Where are you?"

"What is the matter with you?"
"What are you doing here?"
"Who do you say that I am?"
"Do you love Me?"
"Do you love Me?"
"Do you love Me?"

Well, what do you think?

21

Risky Business

My husband is a risk taker. Usually that has enhanced his life. Occasionally, though, his on-the-edge attitude gets him into a jam. And I'm not talking strawberry preserves.

One day Les was working on a project that required him to do some welding. In his desire to expedite things, he took a risk and didn't wear his safety glasses. He thought it might not matter since it wasn't an involved welding job. *Nyet*. It mattered.

The tingling in Les's eyes began about ten o'clock that evening, but he decided to brave it out. The sandpaper feeling began about eleven. He thought he could endure it. The feeling of hot coals sizzling his eyeballs hit about midnight. He finally requested to be taken to the hospital or shot, whichever was fastest. I debated and then settled on the hospital.

We lived at a Boy Scout reservation in the country at the time. Our two young sons were asleep, and they both had school the following day. I decided to call in a friend to take Les to the clinic. I chose our dear friend and pastor, Marv. (Don't you know how thrilled he was to receive this honor.)

Les and Marv had been friends for years. They share a common interest in getting the other's goat. They are both playful, fun-loving fellows who genuinely care for each other, although the casual observer might think there are moments when their jokes outweigh their caring.

Marv came immediately, extending concern and support. After arriving at the hospital and going through an eye check, Les learned there was no permanent damage. The doctor filled his eyes with cooling salve that immediately eliminated the pain. Then he taped Les's eyes closed, covering them in bandages that wound around his head. Les looked like an escapee from King Tut's tomb. The doctor instructed him to leave the dressings on for eight hours.

Picture the opportunity this gave Marv—Les blindfolded and needing Marv to lead him around. Marv guided Les to the parking lot and then let him go, suggesting Les find the car. It was now 1 A.M. There were only three cars in the lot. Les couldn't find any of them. (Remember Pin the Tail on the Donkey? Les's childhood training in this important game must have been inadequate. Car trunks and donkey rumps alike eluded him.) Marv finally ushered Les to the vehicle and brought him home.

At 2 A.M., I heard laughter rolling in through my bedroom window. I was dozing, waiting to hear the outcome. I had expected the best, but I was not prepared for laughter.

I pulled back the shade and saw Marv holding onto Les's arm. Marv was telling Les how to avoid obstacles in his path.

I head Marv say, "There's a step, Les; lift your foot."

Les lifted his foot in blind obedience. But there really wasn't a step, which left Les high-stepping it around the yard like a drum major.

Marv and Les were both guffawing, although Marv seemed to be laughing harder.

After I received the good news on Les's eyes, Marv headed home. We listened as he chuckled his way out to his car. Les and I laughed our way to bed.

The memory of that night could have been an eyesore for us all. But thanks to Marv, as we think back on it, we smile rather than wince. A little levity applied at the right moment can be a balm that lasts longer than the hurt, soothing a heavy heart. And yes, Les found a way to pay Marv back.

22

Blue Light Special

Moving? Not again!" That was my first reaction when Les suggested we go house hunting. After 23 moves in 30 years, I could hardly grasp the thought that it was time to pack another U-Haul. For years we had worked in camps where we lived on the grounds in camp housing. But Les felt we should buy our own home.

Purchasing a place sounded exciting, exhausting, and scary. This was to be our "grow old together" home. That meant I had better be sure I loved it, because I probably would spend a good long spell there.

I decided to make a list of everything I'd like in a home. I started my lineup with a maid, a cook, and a masseuse, but then the words "Get real" came to mind, so I chucked that list and began again.

Location was important to both of us. We had been living in the country the past five years, which was glorious in many ways but had a few disadvantages. For instance, like the pioneers, going to town was a big deal for us. That may have been due to the wagon-train-sized ruts in our road. The ride jostled you so hard, your cheeks bounced up and down and hung like jowls by the time you disembarked.

Also, we had a large hill just before our home. During the winter it could be treacherous, often causing guests to leave before they ever arrived, as their vehicles glided backward down the icy incline. During the summer, the hill made us a target for every storm that blew through our county. The winds rattled windows and snapped power lines, plunging us into darkness in the middle of the woods. Dark darkens in the woods—trust me.

I decided to wait till glory for my next mansion on a hilltop. For now, I wanted to stand by my man on level ground.

I knew I wanted a first-floor master bedroom and bath, as well as a first-floor laundry room. (I wanted Les to have easy access to the laundry in case he ever felt led to clean up his act or mine.)

Next, I thought a pantry and a dishwasher (which I had never owned before) would be great. I knew a fireplace would be fun. We'd had them before, but it had been eight years since the last one. I missed all the ashes, soot, log chips, scorching sparks, and the smoke when the flue wouldn't stay open. There's something romantic about a fireplace.

I also wanted a shower separate from the tub. Don't ask me why; I just did. A yard with trees seemed important, and I love porches. We hadn't had a garage in years, so I added that to my wish list as well. Then I jotted down a basement, because they're valuable for storage and shelter from storms. I wanted all this with a blue-light-special price tag.

As I clutched my "all I want in a house" paper, we began our search. We looked at all kinds of homes, always feeling hesitant for one reason or another.

Then, as we were driving down a street in town weeks later, I noticed a vacant home. Les took down a phone number off a building permit and called. We found out the house was for sale and had not been listed. The builder offered to show us the place in an hour. The home was not new but one a tree had squashed, and the builder had made it like new.

When we stepped into the home, my husband's face lit up. For him, it was love at first sight. I was "in like" with the house but certainly hadn't decided I wanted to live there. After the tour, Les was ready to sign on the dotted line, while I was still trying to remember what color the carpeting was. In the evening, we placed a deposit on the home, and I felt numb.

The next day, we took another walk through Les's house to see where we would be spending the next century of our lives. As Les paced off the property line, I sat on the floor of the living room, staring. Then I remembered my list, which had been buried in my purse when this whirlwind house purchase occurred. I shook out the wrinkled and crummy paper and started to check my requirements.

First-floor bedroom, check. Well, at least I did have that. In fact, it was the largest bedroom we had ever had. It had a door that opened into the first-floor bath, which isn't exactly what I had in mind, but it worked, so I checked that one also. The separate shower was incorporated into the home . . . on the second floor.

Pantry. Hmmm, I was thinking walk-in. This one had a bifold door with a single line of shelves. It was a pantry. Check.

Hurray, a dishwasher! It pleased me to check it off.

First-floor laundry, check. Of course, it was only large enough for the washer and dryer. I was thinking it would be nice to have space for things like the dirty clothes and a basket. I couldn't deny, though, that there was a laundry area.

The home had a basement, check . . . a Michigan basement. That means that once your furnace and water heater are in, it's full.

The garage sits in the backyard and will hold Les's tools and our boxes of storage. No room for a vehicle, but still a garage. Check.

Porch, check. Seats two people.

Trees, double-check. Yard is three inches deep in fallen leaves.

Fireplace, check. It's modern; I'm country. Sigh and check.

As I gazed at all the marks on the page, I realized the Lord had given me everything I had asked for. It was just packaged differently from what I had expected. Rather than seeing this house as a problem, I began to see it as a provision. And do you know what happened? I fell in love with this darling home.

I wonder how many times I've received from the Lord what I had asked for but just didn't recognize it?

P.S. Our home is on low ground, in town, and was a blue light opportunity!

23

Bucket Brigade

When I was growing up, my big brother Don had a favorite record he would play repeatedly. It was sung by Johnnie Ray and was entitled "The Little White Cloud That Cried." Over and over, that poor cloud would weep its little heart out. Just about the time you thought you couldn't bear to hear the cloud squeeze out one more teardrop, Don would turn the record over, and Johnnie would sing his hit song "Cry." We needed a bucket brigade just to handle the tears of this one crooner.

Some of you reading this will remember Johnnie Ray performing "Cry" on television. He would truly get into his song. Dramatically he would pull at his tie, open his shirt collar, drop to his knees, and finally fall to his face while pounding the floor with his fists. Don't you just love a man who can show emotion!

Okay, okay, maybe that's a little more emotion than I'd be comfortable with, but I wonder how many of us wouldn't benefit from a good gully wash.

While some of us have cried a river already, others of us have lost touch with this vital resource. I remember doing a retreat in central Georgia during which a number of tender and endearing things transpired that moved almost all of us gals to tears. But I spotted one young, attractive woman whose posture was like a robot's. She appeared to resist emotions positive or negative. I chatted with her and mentioned her "composure." She announced stoically, "I don't ever cry."

It was obvious she needed to, however, although I'm sure it would have been like releasing Niagara Falls. The torrent of tears would have eventually subsided, emptying out space for her to feel again.

I realize this crying thing can also be taken too far the other way. There's nothing sadder than a sniffing saint who's stuck inside herself and sees her sniveling as spiritual. Some soggy saints could be rented out as professional mourners. Grief was not meant to be an address but a process.

I used to think that because I cried so easily, I was deeply sensitive. Instead, I've learned that when someone told me a sad story, I was so full of my own unshed tears that the first tear I shed was for them, but the rest were for myself. Other people's pain kept tapping into my own unresolved issues.

I remember one night watching a movie on TV. Toward the end, the star was treated terribly by someone she loved. I felt her pain, and I began to cry. The story continued, and so did my tears. Building sobs were difficult to hold in. The movie ended, but I kept crying. My husband came into the room, and I blubbered, "I just feel so bad about that girl."

Tenderly Les said, "Honey, I don't think this is about that girl."

That did it. My dam burst! Les's words seemed to make it safe for me to feel my own pain. I began to realize that my first response was more than "sad movies make me cry." This girl's injury triggered my own buried memories. I wept and wailed for almost an hour. It was great! It wasn't great while I was crying— in fact, that was kind of scary. But the release I felt afterward was liberating.

Of course, most painful issues can't be resolved in an hour of crying, but many times it can be a good place to start.

Try this: List the last three times you cried. What did you cry about? Whom were you crying for?

Maybe you're a soggy saint. If so, it's time to call in a bucket brigade and get on with life.

Or maybe it's time for your tears, and you need someone to give you permission to let loose. Well, here it is. Go ahead . . . have a good, soul-washing cry!

24

LOW • NORMAL • HOT

Soup's On!

I hate feeling rejected. I'm so overwired in this area that when I approach a traffic signal and it turns red, I take it personally.

Okay, I'm not quite that sensitive, but I do like to be liked. I'm always grateful for the cheerleaders in my life—the people who root for me and believe the best about me. But into each person's life must come a few pom-pom pilferers.

I love speaking and have had the privilege of sharing the stage with many outstanding people. Usually we speakers are so busy that we don't have time to get to know each other. We fly into a city for an engagement, eat, speak, eat, talk with some of the audience personally, eat, and then go. (We leave with more "tonnage" than we came with!) I'm always overjoyed when I have a chance to "talk shop" with someone who shares the same type of ministry. So when a platform personality came to me after I spoke at a large event and wanted to chat, I was pleased.

She was warm and affirming and asked if she could recommend me to groups as she traveled. I was complimented and grateful. We chatted nonstop, then hugged and agreed to meet the following day for another visit before our departure.

When I met with her the next day, there seemed to be a problem. By her actions, I could tell I was it.

She went from cool to cold to curt. I went from confused to hurt to ticked. The ticked part came afterward, as I tried to figure out how I had fallen from favor. Later, I learned an acquaintance had spent some time with this speaker discussing me. I guess "Poached Patsy" didn't taste too good, because she certainly seemed to have indigestion.

The more I thought about the injustice of this encounter, the angrier I became. The incident stirred up memories of every unfair situation I'd ever experienced. I brooded, I boiled, and occasionally I blew up as I retold the story to Les. He got tired of receiving the residue of my rejection. So I set the incident on the back burner of my emotions and let it simmer. Once in a while, I'd lift the lid and stir the soup.

One day, while having lunch with cheerleading friends, the topic of unfair situations came up. I ran for the stove to check my pot, and sure enough, it was still hot. As I spewed my injustice all over them, they were taken aback by my intensity.

Finally one friend asked, "When did this happen?"

I had to stop and think for a moment, and then I realized it had been three years! My friends were surprised I still carried such animosity, because I had not seen this woman since that encounter.

After lunch, I thought through what my friends had said. I began to see that keeping this issue hot within me had left me with a pressure-cooker personality (minus the gauge). Instead of letting my rage diminish, I seemed to have used time to refine and define it.

Something about injustice convinces us of our right to hold onto our anger and even embrace it. I'm learning anger is not necessarily a wrong response . . . until I choose to harbor and nurture it. When I enfold anger, it drains my energy and takes up valuable inner space. Brewing anger taxes my physical, mental, and emotional well-being. It also hampers my close relationships with others and God.

Some of us don't have a handle on living skills that equips us to deal with our emotions appropriately. We tend to deny we're angry or defend our right to be so, leaving us frustrated, misunderstood, and stuck in the muck of our own emotions.

I understand now that the woman's momentary rejection of me was not as damaging as my long-term choice to raise rage. When I think of the people I have formed opinions of or changed my opinions about because of what someone else has said, I'm aware of what a human response it is—often not fair or loving, but human.

When Les and I were first married, we lived in a mobile home park. Just after we moved in, I was warned about the unfriendly neighbor next door. I was told she kept to herself and was snobbish. Remembering what I had been told, it took me a while before I tried to establish communication with her. It turned out she was shy and very dear. She and I enjoyed a warm friendship that I almost missed out on because someone had told me her stunted understanding of my neighbor.

When the platform speaker and I had our puzzling encounter that second day years ago, I felt hurt by her change of heart, which is an appropriate feeling when you're rejected. But I quickly put the lid over my hurt and turned up the burner of my anger. Rejection felt too cold; at least anger had some self-generating warmth. But I must have stood too close to my own heat, because my emotions felt scorched. I'm slowly learning to take my hurts to the Healer before I hide them under my unrighteous rightness.

Relationships, like alphabet soup, spell out "opportunities." It's just that some are easier to swallow than others.

25

Fired Up!

Plucky: "Having or showing courage or spirited re-
sourcefulness in trying circumstances" *(American
Heritage Dictionary)*.

Elijah was plucky. After all, he's the guy who challenged
Ahab and Jezebel's wise guys to show up or shut up. Elijah laid
out a game plan with the end result of winner takes all.

Allow me to set a little of the scene. (For inerrant accuracy, read
1 Kings 18 and 19.) Wicked Ahab, king of Israel, was miffed at
Elijah for declaring a drought on the land and then disappearing.
Ahab had searched the kingdom for three parched years, trying to
find this troublemaker. Finally, Elijah sent a messenger to Ahab so
they could have it out.

When they met, Ahab and Elijah began their finger-pointing
meeting by blaming each other for Israel's problems. This was
not your average my-daddy's-bigger-than-your-daddy argument.
No, this was much bigger.

At that point in the debate, Elijah issued the divine dare. He
invited Ahab's wise guys to a community barbecue and chal-

lenged them to a cook off. But listen to the plan: 850 wise guys against one fire-preaching prophet. If Elijah pulled it off, imagine the payoff on those kinds of odds!

Speaking of odd, the people thought this barbecue was a great idea. (I personally would not have wanted to go against a guy who spoke a drought into existence, but then I'm funny that way.)

The rules stated that the wise guys were to prepare an ox, lay it on the altar, and ask their gods to consume it in fire. Elijah would do the same and ask his God to send fire from heaven. The first one to smell fried ox (yuck!) wafting from his grill won.

The Baal and Asherah prophets pranced around the altar (similar to ring-around-the-rosy), trying to ignite a spark of enthusiasm from their gods. When they began to grow weary, Plucky Prophet Elijah taunted them: "I think your gods are out to lunch, nah, nah, nah, nah" (loose translation—very loose).

This brought a fresh surge of rage (you just can't kid with some people) and a renewed effort to kindle their gods' attention. But try as they might, the answer still appeared to be a big fat "Ho-hum."

Elijah was fired up. He positioned stones, prayed, and then watched the power of God consume the ox and everything surrounding it, including the dust. (Do you know how difficult it is to burn dirt?) The fire-licking flames even lapped up water and sizzled the surroundings bone dry.

Remember the odds? They changed. The barbecue turned into an evangelistic meeting, and no one had even sung 13 choruses of a favorite hymn. The people fell on their faces and acknowledged the one true God. Elijah took it from there and wiped out the wise guys.

Elijah's barbecue was a blazing success. That is, until . . .

Word arrived, via Ahab, to Queenie. To say Jezebel was not happy to hear she'd missed the big event of the year would be to understate this sinister woman's fury. She faxed her seething sentiments to Elijah, outlining her outrage, and he hot-footed it into the hills.

Excuse me? What happened to our plucky powerhouse who took on a passel of prophets? Surely one wicked woman couldn't douse our fiery prophet's ministry. Could she? Was this another case of "never underestimate the power of a woman"? I think not. Looked more like a slump in emotions following a big event.

Our fading hero ended up knee knocking under a juniper, singing a familiar refrain in the key of "me." He whined so long that he wore himself out and fell fast asleep.

I love the next part of the story. Here was a wayward man, battling self-pity and anguish, headed in the wrong direction, and the Lord sent him company and provision. An angel woke him and offered him a cake. (Wow! Angel food cake, one of my favorites.)

Elijah, a man after my own weakness, ate and fell back asleep. But the Lord of the second chance awakened our friend again, fed him, and allowed him to continue his journey. The heavenly host's cooking was so vitamin-enriched that Elijah went on in the strength of it for 40 days. (I'd sure like that recipe, although I've cooked some meals my family hoped I wouldn't fix again for 40 days. Does that count?)

Even with two chances, Elijah's fears didn't diminish. Instead of turning back, he scampered away. He eventually hid in the side of a mountain. He caved in emotionally. (I wonder if he was agoraphobic.) He trusted in a rocky fortress instead of the Fortress who is our Rock.

Once again, our God pursued the lost, the lonely, the confused, the fearful, the deceived. In a gentle breeze, He whispered His loving direction to our fleeing friend. Elijah heard, returned, and for his grand finale joined the Lord in a blaze of victory.

I don't identify with many of Elijah's strengths, although I once set my dish towel on fire while cooking lamb chops. What I connect with are his weaknesses. I'm reminded how susceptible we are emotionally to the threats of the enemy, especially following spiritual conquest.

I have made some of my worst personal bungles following some of my sweetest spiritual advancements. For me, I think pride edged in, and I tripped over it. But I'm convinced we need more than luck in this life. We also need pluck. And I know of only one reliable Source for that kind of character.

26

Bouquet

I am a woman who loves getting presents. Fortunately, I'm married to a man who gets a kick out of buying me surprises. He also is famous, in a spontaneous moment, for whisking me off to a mall to shop for a new outfit. It's not unusual for us to go into a dress shop and have Les want to buy more for me than I would for myself. That causes quite a reaction from the sales clerks, since his attitude is not the norm. They all want to know how I trained Les to be that way. Unfortunately, I can't take credit. (I love credit, too.) He just has that kind of giving heart.

I remember our nineteenth wedding anniversary, when Les wrote me a funny, little poem that I still cherish.

<blockquote>

Roses are red, violets are blue,

If I had it to do over again,

I'd still marry you!

</blockquote>

The poem was especially dear to me because Les and I married when we were 17 and 18, and we had been through some challenging years (financially, physically, and emotionally), including my period of agoraphobia. From time to time, I wondered if he regretted his choice. So even though the poem didn't exactly start off originally, it ended for me like a masterpiece.

Over the years (30), Les has given me gifts that have made me laugh, cry, gasp, and even learn some lessons.

One sunny, spring day, Les came bounding into our home embracing two apricot sweetheart rosebuds for me. I, of course, was delighted.

The flowers had come with a powdered mix to lengthen their blooming time; I stirred it into the water. I gave each rose a fresh cut and then slipped them into one of the many vases collected from Les's continued courting of me. I sat my mini-bouquet in the living room, being careful to protect it from direct sun and yet giving it visibility for my enjoyment.

As the days went by, I was fascinated by what happened. My seemingly identical roses responded very differently to their environment. One began slowly to open, and at each stage of development, she was exquisite. Her unfolding presentation pleased me and added beauty and wonder to the room. Finally, my apricot beauty dropped her petals in a breathtaking farewell performance.

In contrast, the other rose seemed stuck in her beginning. She held tenaciously to her baby form. In the end, the brooding bud turned brown and hung over the edge of the vase like a tragic teardrop.

For days I thought about the contrasting visual. I've always applauded rosebuds as being so romantic. Yet there was something sad and unnatural about seeing a flower begin and end at the same place. The bud that didn't open never reached her potential. She never released the sweet fragrance placed within her to share with others. Her death portrayed regret and sadness.

I could celebrate even the loss of the open rose, knowing she accomplished all she was designed to do. Her fragrance lingered in our home even after the vase was removed.

My friend Vella was a flower in the fullest sense. When she was told she had only a short time to live and that her cancer was the most painful of cancers, instead of closing up, she spread her petals all the way open and bathed us in the fragrance of faith. We would not have blamed her if she had drawn into a bud and died privately in her pain.

But Vella saw this illness as her farewell performance, an opportunity for as long as she had left to fulfill the design God had for her. Vella lived out her remaining days with exquisite grace. Dropping her last petal, her parting words were, "Praise the Lord." Then she fell asleep and was gone.

Family and friends could celebrate her life and her homegoing. At the time of this writing, it has been 11 years since she left us . . . and her fragrance still lingers.

Because there's a great deal of cancer in my family, I sometimes wonder how I would handle it if I were to be diagnosed with the dreaded disease. I'm not a brave person . . . except in my imagination. There I am valiant, noble, and steadfast. In reality, I whine when I get a cold.

Three years ago, I watched my dear, 73-year-old mother endure breast surgery for cancer. She went through her diagnoses, surgery, and radiation not only with courage, but also with sweetness and humor. That gave me hope.

I want, whatever my environment, to be growing and fragrant. I don't want to be closed and unable emotionally to open up to others. I don't want to die holding to myself what I should have given away.

Les's gift of roses, pressed between the pages of my memory, has been a poignant reminder: Openness is a risk, growth is its reward, and His grace makes it all possible.

27

Seasonal Seesaw

I love the holidays!

I hate the holidays!

I am a Christmas contradiction. I'm up with excitement and then down with disappointment. I'm up with anticipation and then down with depression. I'm up with . . . well, you get the idea. I'm on my seasonal seesaw. My teeter-totter partner is my own Currier-and-Ives expectations.

Ever notice in those Currier and Ives pictures how even in frigid weather the cows are contented? They willingly pose next to the wood for the fireplace, which is neatly stacked next to the house. While Bossy grins, Junior is shown joyfully skipping out to bring Mother dear kindling for the stove.

I don't have a cow, but I do have a dog. Pumpkin refuses to go outside if it's damp. She has an aversion to moist feet. She will sit for days with her paws crossed, waiting for the sun or wind to dry up the ground. No way is she going to pose willingly by a wet wood pile.

Of course, that would be difficult anyway since we don't have any wood—that is, unless I hike five miles to the woods and gnaw off a few branches. Oh, well, our fireplace stays cleaner that way.

I tried to imagine our Junior skipping joyfully toward a task outside in inclement weather. Ha! I think Junior caught Pumpkin's malady.

No matter how I try, I can't seem to cram my family onto the front of one of those cards.

I don't know why I can't remember, from one Christmas season to the next, that Currier and Ives is an unattainable height. Every Christmas, I want my house to be picture perfect. Ha! I can't achieve that in a nonholiday time, much less in a season with so many added demands.

I imagine white birch logs (cut by me in our back 40—feet, that is) snuggled in a handwoven basket (I designed) placed next to the hearth. The blazing fire invites guests to warm in our candle-lit (all hand-dipped by me) dining room. I would serve a gourmet dinner for 30, followed by strolling musicians playing Handel's "Messiah." All this would take place in my 10-by-12 dining area.

When I have such unreasonable goals, I end up with a high frustration level and a frazzled nervous system. Then I find myself in last-minute panic spurts, trying to excuse, hide, and disguise all my unfinished projects.

One year we decided to write Noel in lights on our house. We started late and finished only half the project because of bad weather. That left a multi-colored NO flashing on our rooftop. We had fewer guests that year.

Usually, I wait too long to complete my shopping, leaving me victim to jangled nerves from holiday traffic, crowds, and check-out lines. People's personalities are seldom enhanced under pressure. Also, I tend to be more impulsive in my buying when I'm running late. I suffer from bargain whiplash trying to take advantage of all the Christmas markdowns. Too many last-minute purchases leave me holding the bag . . . and it's full of bills. The bills then pile up in my emotions, leaving me feeling spent.

Also, during the holiday hoopla I seem to get bit by the bug. No, not the flu bug; the love bug. I fall into the trap of thinking everyone is going to get along. Give me a break! How unrealistic to believe relatives and friends, some of whom have never hit it off, would suddenly become seasonal sidekicks! I'm learning there are those who believe "Ho, Ho, Ho" is something you do strictly in your garden and has nothing to do with exhibiting a merry heart.

Another habit I have is wanting everyone to love the gifts I give them as much as I did when I selected them. I'm into applause and appreciation. Here's the problem: I live with three guys (one husband and two sons), and they only applaud silly things like grand slam home runs in the World Series, touchdowns in the final seconds of the Super Bowl, or when I fix dinner and they can tell what it is.

They don't show the same enthusiasm for my gifts—like the nifty button extenders, the monogrammed electric socks, or the fuchsia-colored long johns I wrapped for them. I realize my gifts are . . . uh . . . distinctive, but I want them to be memorable. My guys agree they have been.

Well, there it is, my Christmas confession. Maybe some of you can identify with part, if not all, of my seasonal seesaw. Come join me in entering into the holidays without the teeter and totter in our emotions. Here's how:

1. Set more-sane house goals. Better to plan less and accomplish more than to fall short of your ideal and start your holidays

feeling disappointed.

2. Shop early, and buy a couple of generic emergency gifts. (Unlike fuchsia underwear, a box of fine chocolates holds general appeal.)

3. Settle on a reasonable budget before going into the stores to prevent falling victim to strong sales tactics (which include Christmas mood music that plays on our nostalgia, sale-sign seduction, and plastic explosives in the form of credit cards).

4. Sow the seeds of goodwill, but don't expect every "Scrooge" in your Christmas circle to embrace your efforts . . . or you, for that matter. Don't snowball your own emotions by expecting love from people who can't give it. (History in a relationship is usually a good benchmark of his or her ability.)

5. Seek some silence. Balance your busyness with moments of meditation. Don't allow all the flashing lights on the outside to distract you from the inner light of His presence. Even a short silence each day will give a greater semblance of order to your emotions and schedule.

Set goals, shop early, settle budget, sow goodwill,

seek silence,

and don't forget to

SIMPLY CELEBRATE!

Ways to celebrate simply:

Make a snow angel, drink eggnog, write a forgotten friend, decorate a snowman, go caroling in your neighborhood, feed the birds, bake apples, watch the movies *Heidi* and *Little Women,* write a poem, cut out cookies, share tea with a friend, frame an old snapshot, hug a child, hug an oldster, read the Christmas story out loud, and sing Happy Birthday to Jesus.

28

Eek!

Y'all come, hear," is music to my ears. I love knee-slappin', banjo-pickin', harmonica-playin', good ol' country livin'.

Every summer when I was a youngster, my family would travel south to the Bluegrass State to "sit a spell." We had more relatives in Madisonville and Nebo, Kentucky, than a corn-cob has kernels.

One of my favorite places to go was my Aunt Pearl's. She was feisty and funny, and she made visiting her memorable.

I remember one visit when I stayed alone with Aunt Pearl. Usually one of her four children was around, but not this time. Even though I was a teenager, when it came time for bed, I didn't want to sleep by myself. She lived out of town, and I was a city slicker not used to the wide-open, dark countryside.

Aunt Pearl was a down-home girl who knew how to make people feel welcome and comfortable. She had me crawl right in bed with her.

We had said good night, and I was listening to the outside night sounds, about to doze off, when an inside noise caught my attention.

It sounded as if someone or something was scratching frantically.

"Aunt Pearl," I whispered.

"Huh?" she groaned from her half-conscious rest.

"What's that noise?" I whimpered.

"I dunno," she slurred.

I realized I was losing her to sleep, and I needed to know what that frightening sound was. So I gently shook her arm and called, "Aunt Pearl, Aunt Pearl, listen."

Coming to, she lifted her head, eyes still closed, and listened. Then, from years of experience, she stated, "It's okay. It's only a mouse that has fallen off the kitchen counter into the garbage can."

Only! Only! She might as well have said, "It's okay, it's only Big Foot." I don't do mice. I was petrified.

Much to my amazement and horror, my aunt laid her head back on her pillow instead of getting up and calling 911.

"Aunt Pearl, aren't you going to do something?" I questioned.

"What do you want me to do?"

"I'm not sure. Call someone maybe."

She laughed, rose up, and headed for the kitchen. I heard some shuffling around, and the scratching stopped. Within minutes, she was climbing back into bed.

"What did you do?" I puzzled.

"Oh, I opened the door and dumped him out into the night. Now go to sleep."

"Okay," I responded, trying to imagine anyone so brave as to have deliberately gone close to a monster in a mouse suit.

Within moments, my aunt began to snore. But in between the

short and long snoring sounds, I heard something. It sounded like frantic scratching.

"Aunt Pearl, Aunt Pearl, please wake up," I pleaded.

"Now what?" she said groggily.

"Did you close the door before you came to bed? I think that mouse is back."

"Just go to sleep. That mouse ain't botherin' you."

I listened to its attempt to escape its paper prison. Then I told her, "You're wrong. That mouse is bothering me a lot."

She swung her legs out of bed, grabbed her slipper, and left the room. Another minute passed. Then I heard a couple of thuds followed by silence. My aunt hurried back to our room, dropped her slipper next to the bed, and climbed in.

Wide-eyed I said, "What did you do?"

"I killed it," she replied calmly.

"Killed it!" I cringed. "With what?"

"My slipper," she reported as she rolled away from me.

Now I was nauseated. I had wanted the mouse excommunicated, not executed. I could hardly stand the thought that I was sleeping in the same room with the weapon that was probably covered in mouse particles. I wanted to go home.

As I was trying to figure out how to tell my aunt I needed to leave immediately, I heard a now-familiar sound. I wondered if this mouse had swallowed a cat and therefore had nine lives. It scrambled around in the garbage bag and evidently was trying to leap out, as we heard it falling repeatedly.

This time I didn't have to say anything. My aunt marched through the house, determined to put my fears to bed, as well as herself. I heard the back door slam, and then her footsteps as she made a beeline for her bed.

When her head dropped onto the pillow, she announced, "The can, the bag, the slipper, and the mouse are outside, and the door is closed and locked. Good night."

I scooched closer to her and fell sound asleep.

Today I still have fears dressed in Big Foot suits. Often these fears grow larger in the night as I lie awake and hear them vigorously stomping around my house. I sometimes find myself whimpering, but now I cry to the Lord. Again and again, I've found Him faithful to respond, and the closer I move to Him, the safer I feel and the better I rest.

29

TNT

After dinner one night, my friend turned, looked intently at me, and stated gently, "Do you know what I see when I look in your eyes?"

"Blue?" I quipped.

"Anger," she responded.

"Anger!" I exploded with venom. "Anger! You don't see any anger in me! You might see fear, but not anger."

I went home that night ticked! As I stomped through the house, I bellowed out to the heavens, "Who does she think she is?"

At that point, I noticed my clenched fist flailing around in midair. I stood for a moment, staring at this volatile visual. As I opened my fist, I saw imprints deeply etched in my palms by my fingernails. I asked aloud, "Am I angry, Lord?"

Immediately my mind was catapulted back to years before when I had a panic attack after a spat with Les. The attack was terrifying. I decided it wasn't safe to get angry (an old message that was now reinforced). I had pushed down deeper inside of me some unresolved anger issues, and what came up to take their place was unrelenting guilt and unreasonable fear—I had become one of the "un" generation. That gruesome twosome, guilt and fear, dominated my life for a number of years.

When I began to deal with my guilt and fear through the wise counsel of Scripture and friends, I thought emotionally I was going to be home free. I believed I would finally be normal. Instead, without the cover of the gruesome twosome, my now-volcanic anger had begun to erupt toward those around me.

I discovered different kinds of anger. There's the temporarily-ticked kind in which we want to yank a hank of hair off some-one's head, but only for a moment. There's the slow sizzle style in which we work overtime on the details of the offense and then revel in our wrath. A favorite of many is the dump-truck approach. This is when we back up to a person and unload all our "stuff" on them. Following close is the rage routine, sung to the tune of "I'm going to hate you forever . . . or at least until Jesus returns."

My sister, Elizabeth, saw the dump-truck approach at work in her own home. She had just finished a phone call and found that her three-year-old son, Nicholas, had been making use of his "free" time. He had sprinkled two pounds of flour laced with Kool-Aid powder throughout the living room. After a firm scold-ing from his mom, Nicholas, indignant that his culinary endeav-ors had not been appreciated, trucked into the playroom and hit his two-year-old sister, Lindsey.

I can identify. There have been times when I've released a flurry of fury at some unsuspecting soul, surprising, at times, both of us. I've learned that when I haven't dealt with my emo-tions and they stockpile, I will inappropriately dump them on an unsuspecting bystander—like a checkout clerk, a bank teller, or a waitress.

I remember trucking over to a receptionist for a mistake on a billing. She was calm and kind. I, on the other hand, was spitting words through tight teeth and displaying pulsating purple veins. The good news was that I had more color than I usually do. The bad news was that my faith faded fast in the eyes of this young woman. Even though I returned and apologized, it changed our relationship. She is far more reserved than she once was with me . . . and rightfully so.

The results of dump-trucking on an innocent party are that it leaves them on-guard, and they skirt around any meaningful involvement with us. It takes a lot of time and effort to reestablish a relationship. Even if we don't care to reinstate a connection, that type of dump-'em-and-leave-'em behavior runs over our chances of having any personal integrity.

I wasn't that put out with the receptionist's mistake when I "let her have it." My reaction came following a disagreement with a relative in which I had shoveled my feelings into the back of my dumpster instead of saying how I felt. Then, when the botched-up bill came, I jumped into my rig, backed my truck up to the receptionist's desk, and unloaded my cargo right in her lap.

I'm learning that as long as I misdirect my emotions, I will find myself rationalizing my TNT behavior and limiting my ability to have honest relationships.

30

Overnight Fright

I was booked on an early-morning flight out of Detroit on my way to Iowa. Because I was leaving before daybreak, Les and I decided to stay at a hotel near the airport the night before. We had done this on several occasions and found it less stressful. I didn't have to get up early and therefore would be more rested, and Les didn't have to battle the morning rush-hour traffic.

We arrived at the hotel and checked in. Somehow our request to be on the first floor had been mixed up, and instead we had a third-floor room. Les and I decided we could adjust. We wouldn't allow a room change to ruin our evening.

We had an early dinner that was not good enough to recommend and yet not poor enough to send back. After our mediocre meal, we retired to our room to relax.

I kicked off my shoes and began to leaf through a newspaper. Les remembered seeing a pop machine and thought he would buy a few sodas for us. He was gone quite a while, and when he returned he was shaking his head. He had visited three different soda machines, and the change makers were broken on all of them. He then checked at the front desk, and they were unable to provide him with change. So we settled for ice water.

Then we noticed the red message light was flashing on the phone. I buzzed the desk and asked for the message. It was for a Mr. Hudson from a business associate. I assured the gal I was not Mr. Hudson and asked if she would please turn off the red blinker. She said she would.

I organized what I would be wearing on the flight the following day and decided to go to bed. I whipped back the bedspread and top sheet so I could crawl in. Much to my disgust, the sheets were dirty. They looked grungy, and every square inch was wrinkled. I wondered if these were Mr. Hudson's sheets. If so, he had left wisps of his brunette tresses and makeup behind.

I called the desk and reported the need for clean linens. The girl at the desk apologized and said someone would come with fresh bedding. Well, someone came all right . . . the Sheet Inspector.

The (six-foot-five) Sheet Inspector announced he had come to inspect our sheets. (Of course, we should have known.) He approached the bed, looked closely at the sheets, then made his way slowly around to the other side of the bed, still examining. (To have an in-house inspector made me think ours may not have been their first sheet complaint.)

After contemplating for a moment, he announced, "These sheets are dirty."

I wondered how much he got paid for linen appraisal. I'd been thinking about a part-time position. It was obvious I qualified, since we both had come to the same conclusion.

As the inspector left, he took our sheets and promised to return soon. He kept his word. He returned promptly. We opened the door and found out that Sheet Inspectors must be specialists, because he handed us our linens and marched away.

Les and I stood looking at each other in disbelief, then shrugged our shoulders and resigned ourselves to the bed-making task. To expedite this project, we each got on one side of the bed, and Les flung one corner of the sheet over to me. I caught it, and then I gasped. Les looked, and his eyes dropped in disgust. These were the same sheets we had before.

We called the desk, and the girl told us she would lodge a written complaint to housekeeping. Now, not only did I have grungy sheets, but I also had developed an attitude the size of the inspector.

When it registered that they were not planning to bring us clean sheets in the near future, I became creative. I gathered all the clean towels and spread them lengthwise on the bed, giving us a somewhat nappy but clean sleeping surface. Then we climbed in bed, and I fell asleep despite the message light flashing in my face, still beckoning Mr. Hudson.

I woke up off and on throughout the night. I couldn't seem to get the looped threads in the towels to go all in the same direction. I dreamt that the Sheet Inspector came back to our room dressed in red blinking pillowcases and fined us for sleeping on the towels.

Finally morning arrived (Mr. Hudson's light was still flickering), and we could hardly wait to leave. We certainly were not rested. *Tested* would be more like it. I can't tell you how difficult it was to leave, knowing we had paid for this stress-filled night.

I'm sure you're wondering why we didn't demand retribution. We did . . . eventually. When the time was right.

You see, the day before the hotel havoc, Les had gone through a heart catheterization. He had just found out he had had a second heart attack and that one of his bypasses had closed. We checked into the hotel (part of a reputable chain) to protect him from stress while he was recovering. When we ended up in "The Hotel from Hell," we had to weigh which was more important: fighting for what we paid for, or adapting and filing a complaint at a more appropriate time.

Believe me, demanding my rights would have been far easier for my temperament. But when I weighed the battle with the hotel against my husband's well-being, what was one uncomfortable night?

Too many times in my life, I have reacted from my emotions rather than from wisdom. Wisdom says, "There is . . . a time to be silent and a time to speak" (Eccles. 3:1, 7b).

I don't think it's a mistake that silence is listed before speaking. Usually if we wait, we're more likely to handle ourselves and our words with greater dignity.

After returning from my speaking trip, I did call the hotel's headquarters. They were surprised to find they had a Sheet Inspector working for them. They refunded our money and sent us a coupon for a free night at the same hotel. Harrumph! Not in this lifetime.

I sure hope Mr. Hudson received his message.

31

Bedded Bliss

When we moved into our new home, I could hardly wait to decorate. I started with our bedroom. It was a generous-size room and showed potential. All I had to do was coordinate the decor.

Our aging bedspread had served us well but needed to be relieved of duty. Selecting colors and a pattern for our new spread was great fun. I chose a multicolored comforter. The saleswoman pointed out the matching shams and sheets. Les and I hadn't thought about an ensemble . . . but it would be nice.

As we were getting ready to pay for our mound of goods, the sales gal pulled out a wallpaper book to show us the paper designed just for our bedding. It was beautiful. I *had* planned to wallpaper . . . eventually. Besides, if I didn't get this now, I might never find another paper that would fit so perfectly.

As Les and I left the store with our arms full of parcels, we were elated, in a heavy sort of way. We comforted and buoyed each other with the thoughts "It's not like we've ever done this before" and "We just won't spend as much for the living room."

When we arrived home, I immediately put the bedding on, and we oohed and ahhed it. Then, after the wallpaper was hung, we were even more pleased with the coordinated look we had achieved. But I had failed to think through the pictures on the walls. They didn't fit in well. I could always bring some in from another room or buy some cheapies.

As I was hanging my newly purchased pictures beside my bed, I noticed how tacky the table cover was on my nightstand. It just didn't fit with everything else. How much could a little cover cost, anyway? Actually, more than I had anticipated.

We had invested a lot, but at least my room was in harmony with itself . . . except for the bath that opened into the bedroom. It seemed visually disruptive. After hanging an antique mirror and lace shower curtains and adding a looped rug, my pocketbook was empty, but my eyes were full of continuity.

As I studied my endeavors, it hit me that I could enhance my efforts with multiple pillows and some flowers. Those two additions are the way a woman places her finishing touches on a room. I added eight pillows and a bouquet of silk roses. Yes, yes, these were like a feminine signature . . . and with a few candles would be complete.

I must have overdone the candles, because Les installed a smoke detector. But the candles seemed necessary to add ambience. Our bedroom would have been a masterpiece, but it seemed to need an injection of character. I dragged in Les's grandfather's trunk and set it at the foot of our bed. That worked. I displayed an antique wicker tray on the top of the trunk. The tray required just a few small, framed photographs, a teapot, a pair of women's gloves, and a man's pocket watch to create a still-life effect.

Funny I could be that far into our bedroom project and only

then notice how out of place my lamps looked. Totally the wrong feeling, and even the shape seemed passé. It would be a shame to allow them to rob us of the rewards of all our time and toil. Lamps are small in stature but big in impact. Once you flick on one of those babies, you can't help but notice it.

Speaking of noticing . . . I have worked so intently with this room that I've developed a new problem. I'm tired of the whole thing and wish I could start over.

When is enough . . . enough?

32

Awakening

Hello, Patsy. This is your sister, and I thought you should know that I am very sick."

When I hung up from Elizabeth's call, I immediately prayed on her behalf. Thoughts of her would come to me again and again over the next 24 hours, and I would quietly pray and then go on with my day. Even though I could tell from Elizabeth's weak, quivering voice that she was ill, I was not prepared for the next call.

This time it was my brother-in-law, Bryan. He reported in disbelief that in the night, Elizabeth's fever had gone up and she was shaking uncontrollably, so he had taken her to the hospital. By the time they arrived at the emergency room, she had become disoriented. The nurses helped her into bed, and Elizabeth went into a coma.

The doctors weren't sure what was wrong with her, but her brain was swelling. I was devastated. How could this be?

Seventeen years prior, our 39-year-old brother had died of a brain injury following a car accident. The thought of losing my

135

33-year-old sister through some sort of brain problem seemed more than I could bear. It just didn't seem normal that our family would have to go through a second tragic loss of this type.

Another call came informing us that Elizabeth had been placed on life support and was now listed in critical condition.

Her voice kept replaying in my ear: "Patsy, I just thought you should know that I am very sick."

Waves of realization would flood in on me, and I would reel from the impact. Then I would busy myself, only to have another wave crash down on me.

Tears came like raindrops that soon built to what felt like tidal waves racking my body. I was overwhelmed.

Bryan called again to report there was no response from Elizabeth, even to pain. "Patsy, I just feel that if you would come, she would be able to hear your voice," he choked out through his tears.

When I hung up, I told Les that Bryan's belief she could hear me was that of a desperate man longing to have his wife and the mother of their three young children back. I knew the days of Elizabeth's life were in God's hands and that I could not add to or subtract from them.

"Yes," Les agreed, "but God often uses people to speak."

I knew that was true because of all the times the Lord has given me insight, counsel, and encouragement through the voices of people. Some of my reluctance to go to her bedside was self-protective. I didn't feel I could handle flying out to Utah to see her die. But Les's tender reminder caused me to make plans to leave as soon as we could.

The closer our plane got to the Salt Lake City airport, the calmer and stronger I felt. Upon arriving, we rented a car and drove immediately to the hospital, half an hour away.

When we got there, we tried to prepare ourselves for what Elizabeth might look like. Much to our surprise, she looked quite well, even with all the life-support equipment. But our hearts and hopes dropped when we touched her. Her skin felt like wax, and her limbs were ice-water cold.

I was heartsick when the intensive care nurse came in with a rounded pair of scissors and pressed them as hard as she could into Elizabeth's cuticles on her fingers and toes. Elizabeth gave no response.

Sleep was skimpy for Les and me that night. We grabbed some breakfast and headed for the hospital at the first light of dawn. Then we took turns talking to Elizabeth and asking her to give us some sign that she could hear us.

At one point, Les was sure she put some pressure on his hand with hers, but it didn't happen again. Several times that day, her eyes seemed to be trying to open, but the nurses said it was an involuntary movement of a comatose patient. We watched the countless machines and computer printouts, trying to analyze what it all meant.

That evening, we went back to our room for another long, fitful night.

The following afternoon, I was alone, sitting next to Elizabeth's bed, and started to talk to her about when she was a little girl. (I was 13 when she was born, and I felt very motherly toward her. Translated, that means I was bossy and protective.) I was telling her about the time she gave her stuffed monkey, JoJo, a bath in the toilet and then threw her moist monkey and our mom's poodle in the dryer. Fortunately, both JoJo and Sassy survived.

All of a sudden, I realized Elizabeth's eyes were darting around under her closed eyelids. There wasn't a nurse around to ask about it, so I leaned in to my sister's ear and said, "Elizabeth, it would really help me to know if you can hear me. If you can hear me, would you please open your eyes?"

I cannot begin to tell you how I felt as I saw her eyes open fully to my request. In that moment, hope surged through me like electricity. Even though I could tell she couldn't see, I now knew she could hear, understand, process, and respond.

I flew out to the nurses' station and excitedly reported what had happened. The nurse looked at me as though I had said, "There is dust on the windowsill."

Realizing my own nervousness, I figured I hadn't spoken clearly. I deliberately slowed down my speech and retold my story. The nurse looked at me and simply stated, "That did not happen. I have been taking care of her for the past ten hours, and she is incapable of responding."

Then her voice softened. "Families tend to overreact to patients' involuntary movements."

"Trust me," I insisted. "She responded on command."

"As far as I'm concerned, that never happened," she stated flatly, then walked away.

I sulked back to my sister's room and stood silently at her bedside, mulling over what had happened and what was said.

About then, the nurse came in to check the equipment. I looked at her and then at Elizabeth.

I moved close to Elizabeth's ear and pleaded, "I know I've been bugging you a lot today, but I need you to leave that quiet place where you're resting, and I need you to open your eyes. I want you to open them wide, and I want you to do it right now!"

As I said "now," the nurse looked nonchalantly over her shoulder toward my sister. Elizabeth's eyes popped open like an owl's. My hope surged! And the nurse? She almost fainted. After catching her breath, she scurried to the phone to alert the doctor.

By the next morning, when I spoke Elizabeth's name, she not only heard me, but she also knew me and almost jumped into my arms.

It took days for all the equipment to be removed and for her vocal cords to heal enough from the trauma of her breathing tubes that she could talk. Then she told us that the first thing she could remember was my voice calling her name and talking to her as though she were a young child.

Weeks later, as I looked back, I began to see how my responses to my sister's illness were like the flowers I harvest from my garden. When a bloom is cut from the plant, the stem seals the severed area to preserve the moisture it contains. This self-protective action prevents the flower from taking in any additional water. So while the sealing is an attempt to preserve life, it also keeps the plant from receiving sustenance from sources such as water in a vase. For this reason, florists instruct buyers to make a fresh cut in the stem and immediately place it in water to extend its life.

When I first received word about Elizabeth, I, like the flower, felt as though I had to seal my resources within myself to survive. I had just come through an emotionally and physically draining season of my life that had left me feeling incapable of dealing with this crisis.

But when Les suggested God could somehow speak through me even though I felt so fragile, it was as if someone had made a fresh cut and placed me in water. Deciding I could go to Utah and survive—whatever the outcome—gave me a quiet strength. That strength grew every day.

I wasn't strong because of any special wisdom or stamina within myself, but because I had been plunged into the water of the Great Sustainer.

It was an important lesson on human nature and divine intervention. All in all, I feel fortunate to have been a part of Elizabeth's awakening and to have learned how He restores us by His living water when we would wilt without Him.

Life often comes at us with TNT force, leaving us emotionally tentative and spiritually bewildered. Our circumstances often don't seem fair and certainly don't appear to be normal.

My quest for normalcy has brought me to the understanding that our commonality is in our abnormality. The good news is that that's okay. We are unique, which beats normal any day. In fact, we are so amazingly designed that God supervised the placement of our inner workings and registered our existence even before we were held for the first time. Then He who formed us takes His involvement a step further and uses our circumstances in our best interests. That leaves us free to embrace the fact that normal . . . is just a setting on your dryer.

Under His Wings

and other places of refuge

PATSY CLAIRMONT

Guideposts ®

CARMEL • NEW YORK 10512

This Guideposts edition is published by special arrangement with Focus on the
Family Publishing.

Editors: Janet Kobobel
        Larry K. Weeden
Cover design: Jeff Stoddard

Printed in the United States of America

Thank You, Lord, for making room for those who scamper under Your wings . . . just in time.

In memory of:

My dad,
Smith W. McEuen
1912-1979

My brother,
Donald C. McEuen
1936-1975

My godson,
Jeffrey D. Porter
1967-1994

Contents

Acknowledgments

Picture an unmade bed. That's what my manuscript looked like when I was working on it. All the components were there, but it wasn't very inviting. Janet Kobobel shook the sheets, fluffed the pillows, and smoothed out the spread, helping to transform this book into a more hospitable and comforting environment. Janet, you are a joy as a co-worker and have made the position of editor a term of endearment.

Mary Lou Schneemann, how grateful I am that you continue to offer your trained computer brain! Thanks for giving your expertise with patience and grace.

Sandra Fraley, what a gift you have been! I appreciate your hours of searching out permissions in the midst of your own challenging schedule.

I have surely been blessed with a plethora of friends. Eleanor Barzler, your sagacity and friendship are inspiring. Thanks also to Carol Porter, Ginny Lukei, Jan Frank, Lauren Heff, Lana Bateman, Debbie Wirwille, Danya Voigt, Lisa Harper, and Nancy and David Berrens. You all, in your own creative ways, cheer me on.

Mickey Mangun, Mary Hermes, and Jessica Shaver, thank you for sharing your tender and telling song and poems. Don Frank, I admire your gentle heart. Thank you for revealing it to us from your journal.

Thanks to my Focus family for believing in me.

Special thanks to Al Janssen, who listens to me with interest and responds with sensitivity and good humor. Larry Weeden, thank you for your tender touch-ups. Nancy Wallace, I appreciate your enthusiastic response to my efforts. Thanks also to Bev Rykerd, who is such fun to work with even when I'm not.

Mom, I continue to be indebted to you for your prayer coverage on my behalf.

Marty and Jason, I know I can no longer tuck you under my wings, but I pray you will both always take refuge under His wings.

Les, for the 32 years we've been married, you have, more times than I can count, extended to me your protection, comfort, and love. Your confidence in me has often been the impetus the Lord has used to keep me going. I am deeply moved by your servant's heart toward Him and me. I love you.

Chapter 1

Seeking Sanctuary

My friend Ann Downing has a singing style that causes my toes to tap and my heart to dance. Her voice is full of celebration. Included in Ann's repertoire are knee-slappin' songs as well as tear-dabbin' ones. One selection she often includes in her country performances (my tear-dabbin' favorite) is "The Long and Winding Road," by Mickey Mangun. My favorite line in that song is,

> *"I know I must be traveling right*
> *because I remember*
> *passing Calvary."*

For years I stumbled around emotionally, hiding in
different places. Feeling overwhelmed by even the dailiness of life, I tried to find comfort and safety in the shelter
of family members, friends, and activities. I drifted in a
world full of panic—serious, unrelenting panic that held
me hostage in my home for several years.

> *". . . my strength completely drained,*
> *I guess my face marks the pain,*
> *my back is bent from the strain."*

I retreated into my house to evade people and pressures; I longed for a safe place. Yet I couldn't escape my
inner anxiety. I would wake up tense. Days felt more like
weeks, and nights were full of fear. I slept too much. I ate
too much. I talked too much. I was into unhealthy swings
of muchness.

Then I remembered passing Calvary. That reminder
helped me eventually to give up my shaky shelters that I
might seek refuge in a much more secure place—under
God's wings. Since then I have learned that we hide
because we hurt, and we hurt because we don't understand how to heal. That's part of what this book is about,
uncovering the places we hide and discovering how we
can be healed. Healed from what? Healed from the
wounds caused by anger, neglect, lies, and other forms of
personal injury that we all struggle with to some degree.

> *"I covered many miles behind me,*
> *miles of sun and rain,*
> *and miles of smiles and pain."*

Today I am no longer housebound, I'm airborne. I travel throughout the country offering encouragement to others who are struggling emotionally. I meet folks who just need someone to validate what they're feeling. Some are stuck in unforgiveness and need help to pull free. Most are not as severely damaged as I was, but others are in even greater emotional dilemmas. I am not a professional (except in being a cracked pot), but I have learned and am learning insights regarding emotional unsteadiness, how we become frail, and how we can become stronger and more balanced.

> *"Up ahead I see a sign*
> *that points me*
> *straight ahead*
> *to victory."*

Travel with me down the winding road to emotional well-being. It's a road similar to the one the Israelites walked on their way to the promised land, which means we may uncover some giants, a plague or two, and a few pits. But we will also climb mountains, munch manna, and, with His help, gain some life-changing views.

> *"I really can't turn back,*
> *some may be using my tracks."*

This won't be a quick trip, so you may want to bring your luggage. Fill the suitcase with your honesty, some vulnerability, and a lot of tenacity.

> *"There are some times when*

the rocks hurt my feet
my body burns from the sweat
and the heat."

We will have the opportunity along the way to laugh, cry, grieve, and celebrate as we examine and adjust our reactions to life and people.

"Although it's dusty and old
for years it's borne
the traveler's load
and one day this road
will turn to gold."

Most importantly, we will respond to truth by putting one foot in front of the other as we move closer to the Savior and experience what it means to take sanctuary under His wings.

PART 1

HIDING

 *Hiders*

 *Hideouts*

 *Hidden Agendas*

Chapter 2

Hiders

Adam and Eve ducked behind the tattletale tree when they sinned, and we've been playing hide-and-seek ever since.

The tattletale couple later gave birth to a temper-tantrum son. Cain, however, unlike his parents, didn't blame. No, his was a more deadly game—killing his brother. Cain hid his murderous deed behind a lie and lost everything he loved most. Then, like his parents, he received an eviction notice. He was sent away from the harvest of the land and the fullness of God's presence.

Cain knew what was expected of him, but . . . Cain

wasn't able. He wasn't willing to relinquish his rights and submit to the ways of God, so he hid.

Truth be known, any one of our names could appear as a Peekaboo Profile, for we all have tried to cover up, cloud over, or camouflage our footprints at one time or another.

The fall of man brought with it shame, which has made hiding in the shadows easier than walking in the light. Ask Cain. Or David. Or Jonah or Elijah . . . or Judas!

Check out Jonah, the Joppa Jogger. Jonah chose napping in the basement of a boat over trumpeting truth to Nineveh and ended up bait on his own hook.

And look at Elijah, who hid out in a stone fortress. He didn't stand fast; he *ran* fast and ended up caving in.

King David didn't cave in; he *craved* in. His desires for the bathing beauty next door infected his royal judgment, and instead of marching off to battle, he sashayed with his neighbor into his bedroom. And like Bathsheba's bubble soap, David ended up in hot water.

Sheltering in his lover's arms set up King David to become one of Cain's Commandos. To disguise his lack of integrity, David, too, bumped off his "brother."

Whether in a garden, a gangway, a grotto, or a game with a gal, from the beginning God's people have played the fugitive as they ran from one hiding place to another. And today, when we dart off in the wrong direction, we, too, feel the hot breath of the enemy on our collars. For it is in the dark crannies that Ol' Beelzebub carries out his revolt.

But there is One who sees our game-playing exhaustion and longs for us to know His rest. He understands our desire for a hiding place. He woos us to His soothing side— even when it's Him we've foolishly been hiding from—so that we might find the refuge we so desperately need.

The way to His holy habitat is a path of light. That can be a problem if our eyes have become acclimated to the shadows of game playing. We will tend to pull back from the first painful light of illumination. But just as we adjusted to the deception, so we can choose to adapt to the light and thereby move closer to the Truth.

Let's begin by looking at a few profiles from *Who's Who of Peekaboo* to gain some insights on hiding.

———

Moses was plunged into his first game of peekaboo with his sister, Miriam. To save his life, his mom tucked Moses into a basket and then slipped him into the Nile. Miriam peeked at Moses from her hiding place, as her little brother's bassinet bobbed between the bulrushes. Baby Moses didn't like this game of peekaboo and bellowed his protest.

At that moment, Pharaoh's daughter, who was doing her morning aerobics on the riverbank, spotted the covered container. Upon lifting the lid, the Egyptian princess found the little basket case and wanted him for her own. She decided to raise her newfound water baby in the palace as a prince.

Funny thing, Moses didn't prize princeship any better than he liked peekaboo. And in an adult moment of childish fury, he took up bushwhacking when he bumped off an Egyptian to protect his Hebrew brothers. Evidently Moses thought hiding had worked for him once, so he would try it again. He then stashed the Egyptian's body under the shifting sand.

Well, the sand didn't shift, but Moses' favor did. When Grandpappy Pharaoh found out about Moses' dastardly deed, he dropped Moses from his will and sent out a posse to finish him off.

Moses was too big to hide in the reeds, so he set off on his steed across the searing sands and eventually ended up at the burning bush.

Barefoot and now bashful, Moses had given up bushwhacking and taken up benchwarming. Instead of finding warmth in the fire of the Lord, Moses wrapped up in a blanket of cozy excuses. Seems the Lord had a plan for this ex-basket case/bushwhacker that didn't appeal to Moses. Talk about a job placement nightmare! Moses just couldn't find his niche. But he did think his brother, Aaron, could handle this Dale Carnegie opportunity to be God's spokesman to Pharaoh. And that's how Moses advised the Lord.

I guess Moses had become so used to tending sheep that he forgot he was one. Instead of listening to the Shepherd, Moses stood on his warm bench and covered himself with his protests.

Hmm, isn't that where Moses started off his life . . . protesting? What a whiner!

So then how did Moses end up such a winner? Certainly not by being a basket case, a bushwhacker, or a benchwarmer. Those were all temporary, ineffective human efforts to find shelter. No, Moses moved into the winner's circle when he became a bondsman. He offered himself as human collateral for God's people.

Somewhere on the path to the promised land, this prophet gave up his childish cover-ups and took up righteous refuging. Moses didn't run away and hide, but instead, when things got tough, he offered his life as a sacrifice (in place of the Hebrew hellions).

The Lord responded and placed Moses in the cleft of a rock and sheltered him under His hand. The Lord hid Moses from His glory (which would have killed him) and exposed him to His goodness (which instead filled him). The change in Moses was so startling that he became a literal beacon in his neighborhood. By popular demand, he had to veil his face as it continued to reflect his holy Hiding Place—which scared the daylights out of his shady followers.

Here was a job hopper who went from thinking he couldn't converse with men to talking "face to face" with God. Wow, that gives me hope!

Of course, it's not as though Moses walked from that time forward in all the light he had. (But then, who does?) At one point, he refuged in his rights instead of the Lord's might when he found himself between a rock (the Lord) and a hard place (the people). Instead of speaking up, he literally struck out by hitting the rock and then taking credit for the water that sprang from it.

Yet his life did end with a mountaintop experience. Concealed from the view of the people, God showed

Moses, atop Mount Nebo, what none of them had seen—
the promised land. After 120 years of hiding in one way or
another, Moses died . . . and God hid his body.

Moses went from being hidden at birth by his earthly
mother to being hidden at death by his heavenly Father.

"Since then, no prophet has risen in Israel like Moses,
whom the LORD knew face to face" (Deut. 34:10, NIV).

Moses' theme song could have been "Na, na, na, can't
find me!" But then I, too, could have sung it without missing a beat. I can't begin to tell you how many times I've felt
like a basket case and wanted to hide. Often I behaved out
of the emotions of an abandoned child. I referred to myself
as "deeply sensitive." The truth is I wore my feelings on my
fingertips and then cried like a baby if you touched them.
Talk about a whiner! Not only did I whine well (Mom
always said that if you're going to do something, do it
well), but I also could have given Moses some pointers on
pouting—that is, if I wasn't too busy shouting.

Now, I have never bumped off anyone like our bushwhacking friend, but if words were bullets, I'd hate to
count the bodies I'd have left strewn in the path of my life.
You see, shooting off one's mouth wounds those around
us. Misdirected anger always leaves victims. When I finally
learned to shut up and sit down, I got so comfortable I
didn't want to get up again. As a benchwarmer, I sat down
so hard and for so long that I became a trenchwarmer. It
was difficult for me to change after I became entrenched in
my misery. Not that I liked my pain, but the price of
change was great, and I wasn't sure I could pay it. Besides,
my instability had already cost me so much that I felt too

low on funds to afford a new lease on life.

So you see, Moses' responses are not antiquated but are applicable to any of us who have ever felt deserted, misunderstood, or too inadequate to be used by God. His story gives me hope, because Moses wasn't an overnight wonder. He stumbled and grumbled just as I did—and still do at times. Yet eventually he found his way to the mountaintop and, more importantly, into the sheltering presence of the Lord.

In time, Moses gave up "Na, na, na," and I believe he learned to sing a new song:

"Rock of Ages cleft for me,
let me hide myself in Thee."

Thanks, Moses, for helping us to see that we have a choice about where we hide and that our hiding place will determine the quality and dignity of our life's song.

It's hard to sing, even the blues, when your future looks black. Color Hagar's emotions black and blue from the hard knocks life dealt her. How did this bruised young woman finally find refuge for her son and herself that ended the abuse and gave them a promising future?

I wonder if the name *Hagar* means "wrung out and hung up to dry"? Sarai must have thought so, for she not only twisted Hagar's emotions into knots with her tyranny, but she also sent Hagar scurrying into the desert to dry out . . . or up. This gal Hagar knew what it was like to be abused, intimidated, rejected, and deserted. No wonder she took up hiding.

Hagar was an Egyptian girl selected to be Sarai's hand-maiden. Now, she didn't volunteer for the job or answer a want ad. Nor was she directed to it by a career counselor. No, we are talking about a decree. But for Hagar, it felt more like "degree" when Sarai turned up the heat of her anger and tried to turn Hagar's future into desert dust.

Not once but twice, Sarai sent Hagar hot-footing it across the sands looking for an oasis. The first time, Hagar wanted a place to hide where her hormonal boss wouldn't find her and erupt again. And who could blame her?

Of course, the handmaiden hadn't helped things when she had snubbed her boss because she was preg-nant and Sarai wasn't. Sarai's response reminds me of the old margarine commercials in which Mother Nature proclaims, "It's not nice to fool Mother Nature!" And in one whisk of her wand, she wipes out half the forest. Hagar wished she had sought refuge in a forest—at least there she could have taken shelter under a shady tree.

Instead, she found herself weeping at a desert spring. Her tears, I'm sure, were intermingled with anguish at the rage of Sarai, as well as with personal regret for being spite-ful. In that lonely moment, an angel appeared and instructed Hagar to swallow her pride (talk about indiges-tion), give up her hiding place (talk about vulnerability), and return to her old job (talk about boring).

No doubt motivated by the angel's prediction of a

promising future for her coming child, Hagar returned to Sarai's encampment. After the birth of her son, she must have maintained a low profile, because we don't hear about her again for some time. Perhaps she sheltered in the angel's promise.

Years passed, and Sarai's life changed. She received a new name, Sarah, and she gave birth to a son at the age of 90. (Talk about a change-of-life baby!) The child certainly did change Sarah's life, but not her disposition. For when Hagar's son, Ishmael, was caught teasing Sarah's son, Isaac, she had Hagar and Ishmael both booted out of the camp—forever.

I wonder if, when Hagar gave birth to Abraham's first child, she believed that she and her son would be physically and financially set for life, that they had found the perfect refuge. What a jolt, then, to have her child's father hand her some bread, a skin of water, and full responsibility for the rearing of their son. Abraham placed the provisions on her shoulders and evicted her. I'll bet the bread felt like lead as Hagar realized she was carrying her son's full inheritance—with no hope of child support.

Again Hagar ended up in the desert. Was she looking for the angel? Maybe not; after all, she had to doubt his prophetic credentials at that point. Yet a part of her wanted to believe that since God had met her in the desert once, perhaps He would again. When their prisoner's portion of bread and water was used up, this single mom and her child began to give up. The blistering sun had left them parched and pleading. Hagar hid her face from her dehydrated son. She could not bear to watch him die.

What happened next? Sure enough, the angel returned. (I wonder if angels always inhabit difficult terrain?) After a short exchange, God opened Hagar's eyes. The dust of disillusionment had blinded her, causing her to miss God's provision, which was in her midst all along . . . a desert well.

Well, well, well, what looked like the end was actually a new beginning for Hagar and Ishmael. Evidently Hagar found the wilderness an ideal place to seek refuge, because she and Ishmael set up housekeeping in Paran. His nomadic lifestyle as an archer suited his feisty character. And Mama Hagar fulfilled her dream when she returned home to Egypt and selected a wife for her son from her own people.

Who could have guessed that such hardship would become a highway in the wilderness? Never again would Hagar have to run away, hide away, or be thrown away at the whim of Sarah.

When Janice married Jim, she never suspected her lot in life would look a lot like Hagar's. Instead, Janice knew her marriage was forever. Both Jim's and Janice's parents had weathered matrimonial difficulties, and they strongly supported their children's marriage. Besides, the newlyweds were deeply in love.

Jim's parents, as a wedding gift, presented them with a key to a mortgage-free home. And Jim had landed a high position in a firm that put them in a financially secure place. So unlike most young couples, they didn't have to deal with a tight budget. They found their pressure-free relationship a safe place to refuge.

After the birth of their daughter, Tina, however, Janice noticed changes in Jim. At first he seemed preoccupied, then he distanced himself emotionally, and in time he became antagonistic.

Janice wondered if Jim was upset by the weight she'd kept on after Tina's birth. So she joined a morning aerobics class, hoping the toning of her body would improve the tone of her marriage. Then she thought maybe Jim wasn't ready to share her with the baby. So Janice's mom kept Tina overnight once a week to provide them with their own time.

But it seemed the more Janice tried, the more hateful Jim acted. Then one evening, he told her to get out of his house. Hurt and confused, she wrapped up the baby and drove around the block. After an hour of tears and feeling as though she had been sent out into the desert, she decided to go home and plead with Jim to tell her what she had done to make him so angry. But Jim refused to even let her in.

Not wanting anyone to know she had been thrown out of her home, Janice rented a motel room and waited for the lonely night to end. When she was sure Jim had left for work the next morning, she went home—only to find he had changed all the locks.

Janice returned to her parents' home. In the ensuing weeks, Jim gave the house back to his parents, quit his job, and left the country.

Grief-stricken and broke, Janice wandered in the

wilderness of despair. Feelings of failure and betrayal pushed her into hiding from others. Following in the sandalprints of Hagar, Janice fell under the weight of her own heart and wept. She cried for her fatherless child, she cried for her own humiliation, and she cried over the bleak future. Finally, at her parents' insistence, she agreed to talk with a counselor.

Janice still says that her counselor was an "angel" from the Lord. Unlike Hagar's angel, Janice's was human; but like Hagar's messenger, Janice's brought her comfort, hope, and light. She helped Janice to come out of unhealthy hiding and seek refuge in the Lord, and she opened Janice's eyes to see her circumstances more clearly. The counselor encouraged Janice to let go of what she couldn't change and to find, like Hagar, her own "well." Jim's choices didn't have to determine the quality and outcome of her future.

Janice didn't have a corner on hiding. For Jim not only fled the country to dodge his family responsibilities, but he also took along a secret handmaiden he had met at work.

Life often isn't fair. Ask the Hagars in this world who experience intimidation, rejection, abandonment, and the pangs of raising a child alone. I tried to look up *fair* in my concordance, and it just wasn't there.

Fair means "proper." It's a word that's mixed with human adjustments to try to satisfy all who are involved. When we try to serve equal portions of dessert at a birthday party or try to treat the Ishmaels and Isaacs in our lives equally, we want to be fair. But more often than not, we mismeasure.

Good news, however: God is just, which beats fair in the long run, hands up. *Just* means "righteous." It's a word that is pure and established on unchanging truth and ultimately serves our highest interest. *Ultimately* is a key word, because *just* is like a missing puzzle piece. We often search to fill the empty space, but when the hidden piece "ultimately" is found and set in place, the picture makes sense.

Ask Janice. Not that her way has always made sense to her, nor has it been easy, but her trust has been strengthened in the Just One who sees her even in the wilderness. And she knows that His justice frees her from hiding in the shadows of her losses so she can walk in the light—even when her throat is parched and her heart is broken.

———◆———

Our next hider probably wouldn't have thought *broken* was a strong enough word to describe her condition. She might have suggested *shattered.* A woman left barren by loss, she eventually returned to the Harvester of hurting hearts.

Elimelech ("Elim") and Naomi had a decision to make. Times were tough, food was in short supply and diminishing rapidly, and the future in Bethlehem looked dismal. Elim and Naomi had two sons, Mahlon and Chilion, for whom they were concerned. After looking at the troubled economy and the community's limited provisions, Elim decided to shelter his family from the famine by moving to Moab.

I personally have never known hunger or been threatened by it, but my husband, Les, and I have known slim times. Our pantry has been full, but our pockets have been empty. We have suffered financial famine that left us searching for a way out. Les and I carefully evaluated our options so we could improve the quality of our lives as well as that of our sons.

I wonder if Elim and Naomi made a list of the positives and negatives for remaining in Bethlehem . . . or living in Moab. They may have created the first list, but I have my doubts about how well they thought through life with the Moabites. Of course, things like budgets, diets, and reasons to move always look more manageable on paper.

Les and I have moved 27 times in our 32 (and counting) years of marriage. Before each move, we weighed the impact on our children. I have no doubt that Elim and Naomi's desires for their family were as strong as ours, but, like us, they failed to see the full outcome of their decisions.

If you asked our firstborn what was the most difficult part of his growing-up years, Marty would tell you it was changing schools so often. Even though we stayed in the same community, he attended seven different schools, which he found not only difficult, but also painful.

If we could interview Mahlon or Chilion about their move, what do you think they might say was the hardest struggle for them? Perhaps that they were not only the new kids on the block, but that they also looked, talked, and behaved differently from the neighbors. Or that others were trying to convert them into followers of one of Moab's many gods. Then again, maybe Mahlon and Chilion thought their new surroundings were exciting and expanding—which, if true, actually presented a whole crop of other problems, ones that had the potential of breaking a mom and dad's heart.

Elimelech's name means "My God is king." If names are consistent with character, isn't it perplexing that Elim took refuge in the enemy's camp? The people of Moab came out of the incestuous relationship between drunken Lot and his scheming daughters. The Moabites had a history of idolatry and often warred against Israel. That seems to me like two strong reasons, especially when your name means "My God is king," to avoid Moab.

Following this line on names, how is it that "My God is king" and his wife, "pleasantness," raised two weak sons, Mahlon ("invalid") and Chilion ("pining")? Of course, who's to say? Those young men may have been physically handicapped, although it would seem their names referred to their personal character rather than their physical condition. Yet it's a medical fact that sustained emotional pain will cause physical disruptions.

It almost appears as though Elimelech and Naomi chose physical comforts over spiritual welfare for their sons. (Could that have been why they were weak?) Perhaps Elim thought his own strong faith would provide a fortress for his sons to hide in from the temptations that surrounded them. And maybe he *was* a protection for them. Of course, he probably had not planned on dying while in Moab, but he did. And that's one of the problems with having a human refuge: Sometimes that person leaves.

My husband's father was a powerful parental figure in mostly negative ways. In fact, he was Moab in britches. He was an abusive alcoholic who warred against everyone. He did provide definite boundaries for his six children, which in some ways protected them from young, foolish choices. But, like Elim, he had not counted on his own premature death. Les was left reeling emotionally. Viewing his dad's death as a license to live it up, Les let rowdy behavior cause him all kinds of problems.

Scripture records Elim's death in Ruth 1:3 and his sons' weddings to Moabite women in verse 4. Do you think Mahlon and Chilion's dad forbade them from making that choice while he was alive? And once he had died, Mrs. Pleasantness gave in to their desires? Just a thought.

As a mom of two sons, I confess I enjoy pleasing them and seeing them happy. And at times I, too, have been guilty of indulging some wishes that weren't in Marty and Jason's best interests—like loaning them money I knew I wouldn't get back, allowing them to stay up later than they should, or sheltering them from their father's displeasure when they needed to face his wrath. Yes, I guess I could understand if Naomi wavered when she should have stood fast . . . and I have learned, as Naomi may have, the error of indulgence.

Pining is defined as "to wither away from longing or grief." I wonder if Chilion's pining sprang up from the death of his dad. To lose a strong parental figure is not only jolting, but also emotionally disconcerting. Maybe the weighty loss of homeland and father was more than Chilion could bear. Perhaps he, like Les, was left reeling.

We don't know how much time elapsed between Elimelech's death and his sons' marriages, but within ten years after their dad died, so did Mahlon and Chilion.

Poor Naomi suffered tremendous loss in the land where they had sought safety. Elim and Naomi had intended to sojourn for a season and return to Bethlehem when the economy improved. But the seasons swirled by, and still they stayed.

Intentions. How many good ones I've had! "This will work," I surmise from my human calculations, only to learn later my prediction was myopic. I've always thought it would be great if we could Reebok down to the drugstore and purchase some spiritual Murine. A few drops in each eye and—presto!—20/20 insight and foresight.

The Scottish poet Robert Burns put it this way:

"The best laid schemes o' mice and men
Gang aft a-gley."

Bobby-boy reminds us that no matter how well we plan, life is brimming over with the "unexpecteds."

The unexpected battered Naomi's heart again and again. She was so bent over with grief that all her pleasantness spilled out. And when she rose up from the third gravesite, having buried her husband and both sons, her bruised heart filled with bitterness.

Feet weighted with dread, Naomi trudged toward Moab's closest exit and beyond to Bethlehem. No star appeared over a stable to guide her home. Besides, her heart was too heavy to look up. She didn't even see the loving intentions of her daughters-in-law as they pursued her. Instead Naomi, wrapped tightly in her shroud of depression, tried to send them away.

Like Naomi, I sojourned in depression for many years. This nook of darkness gave me a place to hole up—which I desperately needed—but it also robbed me of what would enable me to clearly see myself and others . . . light. My brooding spirit alienated me from people. Likewise, Naomi, blinded by her pain, could see no future for herself or anyone associated with her.

When my 38-year-old brother died following a car accident, my pain came like great waves that threatened to drown me. At high tide, my friend Rose read me a psalm over the roar of my grief. The Spirit of God encircled me with one of the verses like a life preserver: "I would have despaired unless I had believed that I would see the goodness of the LORD in the land of the living" (Ps. 27:13).

Despairing Naomi, now accompanied by her daughter-in-law Ruth, made the journey home. Ruth tried to encircle Naomi with her promise of lifelong care, but this bereft mother and wife could hear only her own agonized heart. As Naomi embraced the unfairness of her losses, her pain turned to bitter blame.

Naomi's complaints about how the Almighty had afflicted her diminished as she experienced His benevolent care for her as a widow. Naomi had come home to the friendship of His people and home to the Redeemer of her heart. Even though she returned with resentment, He met her where she was, and then He helped her move to a better emotional place. As she pulled out of her pain and became part of the provision for Ruth, Naomi's bitterness seemed to fade gradually.

There's always a price to pay when we seek refuge in the camp of the enemy. The good news is that a Redeemer waits for us to return and take refuge in Him.

How tender of the Father to woo Naomi's barren life home at harvesttime. And what a harvest it was! Food for her table and fruit for her lap. For from the fruit of Ruth's womb came a grandchild to fill Naomi's aching arms and to mend her broken dreams. I believe adopted Grandma Naomi encircled this child in the shelter of her care and whispered to him of the Lord's goodness in the land of the living. And to think she cradled to her softened heart the grandfather of King David and an heir to the very throne of God!

You may not see these hide-and-seek stories exactly as I do, but I think you'll agree that Moses, Hagar, and Naomi show us what a human tendency it is to dash away from difficulties and dart behind less-than-honorable shelters.

I personally have always found it easier to peek at other peoples' lives and see what they did wrong than to check a mirror and capture my own inconsistent reflection. The fascinating thing about the Word of God is that we start off learning about Bible characters and end up with a view from His looking glass of *our* character . . . and some of us don't like what we see. We begin to realize that Moses, Hagar, and Naomi are not distant kin but actually our kissing cousins with hideout routines like ours. And I wonder if they're not part of the great cloud of witnesses who are cheering us on and longing for us to learn from their mistakes and triumphs. If we could hear them, what might they say?

I think Moses might call down to us to leave our man-made tents in the valley and come up higher so we, too, can gain a holier perspective and catch a glimpse of the promised land.

Hagar's encouragement, as she serves us a cool cup of refreshment from her well, would be that we don't have to hide from a wilderness experience. In fact, the driest, most deserted times of our lives can cause us to thirst for the Living Water and discover the well that never runs dry.

Naomi's compassionate hand might soothe our troubled brows as she helps us keep in mind the only One who can shelter the grief-stricken heart and fill our empty lives with meaning.

We are reminded by our three fellow journeyers that while it is not wrong to hide, *where* we hide can help us . . . or hurt us.

Many of my hiding places have been constructed of popular, readily available materials. They fit right into our materialistic, narcissistic, hedonistic society. That means I want too much too often, think of myself more frequently than I should, and often act as though I have the right to be constantly entertained by life. This approach leaves me self-seeking, self-centered, and self-absorbed.

Yuck! Like too much sugar, an overdose of self is sickening. Let's see if we can pinpoint a few self-indulgent havens you may be sharing with me.

Chapter 3

Hideouts

Correct me if I'm wrong, but are there not strip malls on every corner throughout the United States of America? Actually, I know there are, because I've been in them. At times, malls have been my hiding place. When I haven't wanted to deal with real life, I've gone off to pretend all is well and that a new bauble will fill the unconscious ache within.

Shopping is not wrong in and of itself. It's when I use it to try to escape painful emotions, difficult relationships, or personal responsibilities that I get in the most trouble. One thing about seeking sanctuary in a mall is I have lots of addictive company. Somehow, seeing others laden down with their own packages eases my guilt.

Once I stayed out of the malls for a whole month . . . and gained ten pounds. When I set aside my packages, I then made a beeline for the pantry. I guess my theory was that if I couldn't buy off my problems, I'd bury them under a barrage of groceries. Of course, then I had to go back to the mall to buy bigger clothes.

When I wasn't shopping or eating, I was sleeping. Like a lethargic ostrich with his head stuck in a hole in the ground, I jumped in bed and covered my head, trying to escape my cluttered emotions.

Some days I would head for the mall, have lunch with a friend, and then go home and take a nap. That's a hider's home run! But when you have to face real life, you discover you actually struck out.

All my hiding places are inadequate, but each offers a quick fix. For the moment it takes my mind off my pain, my relationships that need attention, or responsibilities that feel overwhelming. But long term, my hiding places complicate my issues.

Shopping, eating, and sleeping are obvious places one might go to hide. But let's look at some of the more covert crannies, the private patterns that even we don't always realize we are sheltering in.

In the 19 years I've been raising Jason, I have asked this question a bajillion times: "Jason, why didn't you clean up your room?"

The following are just a few of his bajillion responses:

"I got in too late."

"I lay down for a minute and fell asleep."

"It didn't look dirty to me."

"I like it this way."

"My friends were coming over, and we'd just mess it up again."

"I'm waiting for Jim to get here so he can help me."

"Oh, did you mean this week?"

Every mom has heard an avalanche of excuses rumble forth from the mouths of her offspring regarding why certain tasks remain undone. And as the kids try to do a snow job on us, we are busy shoveling through their reasons, looking for the truth.

Often we find at the bottom of the pile procrastination, laziness, rebellion, fear, a need for control, a misunderstanding of what's expected, or an unwillingness to pay the price. On careful examination, we realize their faulty excuses sound familiar. That's why you often hear a parent reply, "Nice try, kids, but it won't work. I tried that on my parents, too." In fact, some of us become so adept at using excuses that we carry this hiding place into our adult lives.

I met Jody at a retreat in New York. After I finished my opening message on attitudes, she pulled me aside to confess her struggle with her mother-in-law. I asked Jody what her mother-in-law did that upset her the most. Without hesitation, she rattled off a list of offenses worthy of life imprisonment without hope of parole. I asked why she didn't make some changes in their relationship so she wouldn't feel violated. From Jody's lips tumbled an avalanche of rehearsed excuses that kept her frozen out of more meaningful relating.

As inappropriate as her in-laws' behavior was, Jody's lack of initiative to do all she knew she could didn't help her or them. No matter what solutions I suggested, Jody had a reason they wouldn't work.

Her heart had frozen over toward her in-laws. That meant her husband often got the cold shoulder, and at times her children would suffer from cold snaps.

When she finally decided to leave her icy habitat of excuses, Jody had to shovel her way through forgiveness and dig new tunnels of communication. It was exhausting work, because offenses had piled up for many winters.

Jody realizes today that she waited so long to make changes in her family relationships that the way out seemed overwhelming, and she wasn't sure she wanted to work that hard. Besides, sheltering in excuses was easier and less intimidating than confronting and forgiving. But as she made an effort and saw progress, the remaining ice crystals on her heart melted.

This is not to suggest that her in-laws still don't try to hurl snowballs at Jody. (She changed; they didn't.) But now she knows how to duck and not participate in their cold war.

Jason and Jody's tendencies to hide behind excuses are as old as Eden and as current as Congress. Remember

Moses' job opportunity as the Lord's spokesperson? When Moses cleared his throat, it wasn't a speech that came out but a list of excuses.

Or ask Aaron. You know, Moses' brother. When he was confronted concerning the golden calf the Israelites were worshiping, Aaron said, "I threw it [gold] into the fire, and out came this calf" (Exod. 32:24). Oh, moo-ve over, Aaron; my kids could have been more creative than that.

Even courageous Queen Esther did a hesitation step behind a castle wall of excuses when Mordecai compelled her to plead for their people to the king. Seems the king wasn't too thrilled with uninvited guests and had a habit of bumping them off. (I've wanted to bump off a few myself, but it hasn't worked well for me. Instead I just cook for my guests, and funny thing . . . they leave.)

We may hide behind excuses, but ultimately, excuses eradicate personal growth.

Steven made people laugh even when they didn't want to. It wasn't that he always saw the best in a situation, but he did have a way of finding the humorous or the ridiculous. He was an outrageous sort of fellow. He wore comical hats, mismatched socks, and outlandish trousers. Steven was an unending vaudeville routine.

Real life banged hard on Steven's door when he lost his job, but he just laughed it off. A new position didn't come in time to save his home, but Steven proclaimed, "Easy come, easy go." Then a battering ram hit when his wife died, and it knocked the sense of humor right out of him.

It was a scary time for Steven. He had hid behind his humor to keep from feeling. Without that hiding place, he was exposed to a lifetime of emotions he had stuffed under his endless stream of jokes.

When Steven stopped laughing, his neglected emotions demanded attention. Anger, fear, jealousy, and other feelings crowded his awareness. This time, instead of denying their existence by laughing them away, he learned to identify his inner reactions.

Steven practiced saying how he felt in a support group and talked with others about how to handle his emotions. He embraced the importance of speaking the truth in love about how he felt.

As he gave himself permission to feel and learned how to express his feelings appropriately, Steven began to heal. Naming his feelings was the first step in getting a grip on reality. It started him on a healthy journey of self-discovery that eventually led to recovery. His emotional restoration didn't eliminate his sense of humor—it balanced it.

Most of us don't use hand buzzers or exploding cigars, but we have been guilty of laughing about something that not only wasn't funny, but also wounded us or someone else. We usually chuckle to cover our pain or embarrassment. Our face says "funny" while our heart says "ouch."

Humor acts like a gate—it makes us appear friendly while preventing accessibility, lest when others enter they see our deep sense of inadequacy. We have all heard rotund people make fun of their size when the truth is they'd give anything to lose weight. Or petite people who tell short jokes while the lifts on their shoes make a grandiose statement of their own. Self-debasing humor is often an attempt to beat others to the punch, giving us a sense of control over our own shortcomings.

I have always looked older than my age. When I was young, it was great. But guess what? I'm not that young anymore, and it's not great to hear others guess that I'm ten to 15 years older than I am. I found myself doing elderly jokes about my ancient appearance before people could hurt my feelings.

"I spent five hours at the beauty parlor today . . . and that was just for an estimate," I'd quip à la Phyllis Diller.

Then I realized how dishonest that was. I was pretending it didn't bother me when it did. To lie about my feelings was to lock myself in a closet of taunting mirrors. So I started to tell my audiences what a sensitive issue my older appearance was for me. My confession didn't stop all the insensitive comments, but it helped me to become more honest. As I stepped from behind the gate of my unhealthy humor, I began to heal. That left me less likely to be devastated the next time someone wondered if I was Methuselah's mother. I learned that when our humor is forced, it's not healthy.

Hurling humor like hand grenades is a popular sport today. We think it's acceptable to pull the pin on our anger as long as we toss it in a casing of humor. The problem is it's still explosive, and someone ends up hurt. And as the victims of our gibing pick shrapnel out of their self-esteem, we accuse them of not having a sense of humor. The truth is, we haven't been willing to face our TNT personality, which has left us combustible comedians with machine-gun mouths.

How many times have you heard or said, "I was only kidding"? If we have to defend our humor regularly, chances are we're not as funny as we may think. When our defense mechanisms go up, our hearing ability goes down. We become so busy building a wall to hide behind that we block out the legitimate protests of others.

Next time you think you've told a "funny," look around to see if anyone else is laughing. Grimaces don't count. If our humor turns out to be a solo act, we need to give it up before our comedy turns into a tragedy. For when we lose the respect of someone we care about, it is a tragedy.

A good humor rule is, if it hurts someone, it isn't funny. Again, if it hurts someone—anyone—it isn't funny. I have had to apologize more than once to individuals for using convenient humor, at their expense, to win the favor of others. Just because people are laughing doesn't mean what we said or did was appropriate or loving.

The enemy didn't give us our sense of humor, but he does work at perverting it. And we assist in the distortion when we use humor as a hideout from tender, honest relationships.

A healthy sense of humor is a precious gift given to promote good news, good health, and goodwill.

Maybe shopping, eating, sleeping, procrastinating, or

guffawing aren't the places you hide in. We are a creative group, and therefore lots of other options are out there. Your hiding place is wherever you run when the first inkling of feeling hurt crops up. And chances are it's a self-indulgent spot rather than a self-revealing one, which is why God is beckoning you to come out of hiding, into the light, and to slip under His comforting wings.

Chapter 4

Hidden Agendas

When Julie received the call from Andrea, she was delighted. They hadn't spoken for many months because of a misunderstanding. Julie was heartbroken over the rift, because she and Andrea had been close friends, or so she had thought. But when weeks turned into months and still Andrea hadn't talked to Julie, she began to give up on their reconciliation.

When Andrea did call, she sounded a little distant, but Julie didn't mind; she was just pleased to hear Andrea's voice. Andrea asked Julie to meet her for lunch, suggesting a restaurant on the other side of town. That surprised Julie a little, but she quickly put that thought aside and hurried to get ready.

During the drive, Julie began to reminisce. She laughed aloud several times as she thought of fun memories she and Andrea had shared. By the time she pulled into the restaurant parking area, she was singing.

She almost skipped into the lobby and quickly scanned the booths looking for her friend. Andrea leaned from her booth and waved to her. When Julie reached the table, she was startled to find a third party present. She tried not to look disappointed, but Julie wasn't prepared to share this time, especially with Lyndie.

Lyndie was a newcomer in their community and at their church. She seemed outgoing enough, but she had a haughty air that troubled Julie. Andrea and Lyndie, though, had hit it off. Julie was surprised since Andrea had never cared for uppity people before.

Feeling awkward, Julie forced a smile and slid into the booth. They exchanged a short round of pleasantries, placed their orders, and then sat in silence. Andrea's voice broke through the strained air. "You're probably wondering why I asked you to lunch," she said.

Julie looked at the two gals and realized this was a setup. These women knew exactly why they were there; it was Julie who was in the dark. She had fallen victim to their hidden agenda.

Andrea then proceeded to let Julie know all the things she had done over the years that had hurt Andrea. Julie was stunned and embarrassed. *Why would Andrea do this,* she wondered, *especially with Lyndie present?* Andrea spewed her vengeance on her former friend until the waitress reappeared with their lunches. Julie excused herself and went to the restroom, where she hid in a stall.

Nauseated and shaky, she tried to get a grip on herself. Finally, she scribbled a note saying she had to leave, slipped it to their waitress, and headed for the shelter of her car. After fumbling with her keys, she put the car in reverse and backed into the curb. She then burst into tears and sobbed all the way home.

Later, Julie replayed the day in her troubled mind. She felt so betrayed. She had no doubt that she had made mistakes in their friendship, but the lunch had turned into a barbecue, and guess who was on the spit? Julie decided the reason they had chosen a restaurant on Lyndie's side of town was to give the tag team an emotional advantage. Ganging up and then catching Julie off guard seemed to give Andrea the leverage she wanted.

Julie wasn't sure she could ever forgive Andrea. She certainly never wanted to see Lyndie again. Pictures of Lyndie's nodding head, arched eyebrows, and sneering gaze kept returning to taunt Julie and cut deeper into her wounded heart.

We have all been hurt by someone. And no doubt we have all hurt others. But that pain is deepened by deception and hidden agendas.

Andrea and Lyndie had carefully planned this "visit." Andrea had talked through what she wanted to say about Julie to Lyndie. And Lyndie had lavished her approval, support, and even assistance on Andrea to sharpen her strategy.

Julie's experience reminds us that deception is a lie shrouded in secrecy, while a hidden agenda is a controlling scheme, a distorted plan, a treacherous tactic. Deception plus hidden agenda—hmm, this is beginning to reek like an ancient foe—you know, the one with the pitchfork, Satan.

Sometimes I need to be reminded of Satan's deceptions and hidden agendas, not only because they hurt me—even more deeply than Julie was hurt—but also because I soon forget his long-term commitment to my destruction. Understanding that Satan is the author of hidden agendas, that his language is lies, and that his motive is our demise prepares us for his attacks.

This enemy seldom shows up in his flashy red suit with his stubby little horns gleaming in the sunlight, announcing his plan to bump us off. Instead he camouflages himself and appeals to our longings and lusts.

Satan wants us to hide in inappropriate places, for he knows it will increase our dissatisfaction with ourselves, others, and life in general. We then become disillusioned and candidates for despair. That's all part of his hidden agenda.

Strategist that he is, he doesn't limit himself to corrupting our hearts toward our friends. He also lures us into his shadowy hideaways through seduction, and sometimes an observer can spot his techniques much more readily than Satan's prey can.

When the handsome young man stopped at my airplane seat row, I couldn't help but notice the bouquet of wrapped roses he placed gently in the overhead bin. He sat down and extended a warm smile in my direction. By the time we were airborne, we had begun to chat. He told me the flowers were for his expectant wife, who would be waiting for him when we landed. They had been separated, and he had decided to be reconciled with her. Seems he had gone on a business trip and just never returned.

I said I thought his decision to go home was an honorable choice and that it was wonderful he would be with his wife for the birth of their first child.

He asked if I was traveling for business or pleasure. I told him my business *is* a pleasure. I explained that I speak to women regarding their emotions from a Christian perspective. I then expected him to lose interest. Instead, however, he seemed eager to hear more. He asked me one question after another about the Lord and the Bible. He seemed to be a man tottering between two worlds, undecided about which way he would go.

Then it happened. Ms. Beelzebub herself came slinking down the aisle. Actually, she was an attractive gal, but she was certainly older than my seatmate. She stopped at our row, leaned down, and softly purred into his face, "I wish I had someone to talk to." She tilted her head, flashed her extended eyelashes, and then gave new meaning to the word *turbulence* as she swished her way to the restrooms in the back.

The young man almost suffered whiplash when he

twirled around to see where Miss Hospitality was going. He continued to talk to me, casually now, as he kept one eye glued on the aisle.

Soon she wiggled back and announced her availability to him with a promising nod. Within moments, he excused himself from our visit and galloped to her row. I noticed they bought some drinks from the flight attendants and were soon drowning in each other's company. With heads together, their laughter sporadically filled the cabin. My heart filled with sadness.

Just before landing, the young man returned to his seat and avoided my glance. Then he said, as if to no one in particular, "I'm sorry we couldn't finish our talk."

"We could have," I responded kindly. He didn't answer.

When we landed, I deplaned ahead of him. After greeting Les, I pulled him to one side to observe the man's homecoming.

I spotted a pretty pregnant girl watching on tiptoes as passengers disembarked. I figured she was the one waiting for her runaway husband to return to her. Then he appeared. The young woman rushed into his arms.

The seductress walked past the couple and then turned toward them. The foolish fellow drew his wife into his shoulder, and while her teary face was buried in his shirt, close to his heart, he waved behind her to his departing "friend." The temptress smiled coyly and waved what apparently was his business card, as if to remind him she would be in touch.

Talk about seduction and hidden agendas! This flirty female had truly played the devil's advocate, and the young man had taken the bait hook, line, and, well, you get the picture.

———◦·•◦·———

Actually, fishing is a good way to understand Satan's hidden agenda for us. I come from a long line of fishermen, the kind who won't let you move around in the boat lest you disturb the fish. Some of my kin have been known to sit in a rickety rowboat 24 hours at a stint. They sit and watch for activity in and on the water. When the action is right, they cast out, hoping to snag a whopper. When the fish takes the bait, he's reeled in and soon becomes dinner.

In much the same way, Satan slips his rowboat into the waters of our lives. Then he waits for our moments of weakness, watches for our unmet needs, and lurks in the murky, unsettled issues of our lives. He carefully checks his tackle box and selects just the right bait. When he thinks the time is ideal, he casts his line and waits for as long as necessary for us to take the bait. Then he reels us in with hopes of having us for dinner, and not as his guests. Unlike the fishermen I've known who return the small fish to the water, Satan never throws any back. In fact, he seems to favor the little ones.

Part of his lying agenda is to lure our children into his pond. He knows that if he can reel them in when they're young, he will hold a hidden advantage to use against them when they're older.

If snagging us when we're young doesn't work, he waits for misfortune or affliction to befall us and then tries to lure us into his cove to take shelter from the hardships of life. The water there is diseased, and in his polluted pool we become stagnant. We stop growing, we lose our vitality, and we begin to die. Meanwhile, Hook sits in his dinghy and guffaws.

———————

Samson was a man who loved living on the brink of danger. Of course, he eventually fell over the edge . . . straight edge, that is.

Satan sharpened his strategy to fit the weakness of Samson and his beautician friend, Delilah. Cunning creep that he is, he used a woman's coquettish ways to seduce the big boy. Then Satan dangled a bag of jingly coins to entice Samson's girlfriend. The devil knew their susceptibility.

When I tell you Satan runs a clip joint, I'm not kidding. Samson went in looking like Sylvester Stallone and came out sporting a Telly Savalas coiffure. Motivated by money, Samson's mistress gave him more than a crew cut—it was a shrew cut!

Satan's hidden agenda was to use Delilah to shorten not only Samson's locks, but also his life span. Seduction was Samson's hot button that the enemy pushed, and the result was a reduction when Samson's muscles turned to mush.

Samson gave away his hair-itage to a hidden agenda

and suffered with a blinding rage. When his captors brought him into their celebration to make light of him, he had his own agenda. Appearing to need a pillar to lean on, he became a smashing success when he literally brought down the house with his farewell performance.

This Bible story is a portrayal of betrayal. It shows us the ways of Satan, that wily weasel, and how he lures us by our lusts into dishonesty with ourselves as well as others.

Hidden agendas are tricky plots. Some are hair-raising, some are heartrending, but all are destructive.

As if this picture of Mr. Deception isn't distressing enough, add to it his ability to ensnare us with lies. "Liar, liar, pants on fire" is an accurate description of Beelzebub, old hot britches himself, with his incantations of incriminations.

"What's the matter, dummy, can't you do anything right?"

"No one really loves you!"

"You're so ugly!"

"Stupid!"

"Is this the best you can do?"

"God doesn't love you."

Those are just a few of the ugly utterances he whispers and sometimes shouts at us. As we learn how to detect his lies and schemes (by knowing the truth), we protect ourselves from his hidden agenda.

Josie knew, at four years old, that she should not

touch the pretty vase on the coffee table, but this day the sunlight caught the patterned glass and set it aglow, making it irresistible. She just wanted to hold the sparkling treasure for a moment. When she turned to set it back in place, she heard her mother's footsteps and hurried to move away. The vase wobbled and then tipped to the side and toppled to the hardwood floor.

Josie's mom stepped into the room just as her heirloom shattered. Before Josie could speak, her mom grabbed her by the shoulders and shook her repeatedly, yelling, "You bad little girl! You bad little girl!" When her mom let her go, Josie ran to her room and hid under the bed.

In the meantime, Mom had pulled herself together and felt terrible about her strong reaction and cruel words. She pulled Josie out from under the bed and held her close. "Josie, I'm so sorry. Please forgive me," she said. Then she wiped away Josie's tears. But she was unable to wipe away the indictment.

Josie was relieved her mom wasn't angry anymore, but her mommy's words kept playing in her head as she fell asleep: "You bad little girl!"

The enemy had waited for a vulnerable moment. He placed the scene in his fishing box with plans to "tackle" Josie by casting her mother's line again and again throughout Josie's life, for he knew her susceptibility to it.

As an adult, Josie found that even the least failure on her part filled her with shame. In talking this through and pinpointing the still-painful vase memory, she realized she needed to forgive her mom for responding unkindly. She also needed to forgive herself, not for being inquisitive but for being disobedient. After that, whenever the enemy taunted her with "You bad little girl," she was free not to be drawn into his cove.

Because Josie had initially taken the bait, Satan had then fed her other lures from his assortment of lies. She would need time to sort through her beliefs about herself and untangle his twisted lines. Josie believed she was bad and had acted out of that conviction. Her poor choices included unwise relationships, which also needed to be examined and corrected.

Andrea's unforgiveness, the young husband's unfaithful nature, Samson's unyielding spirit, and a child's unshielded heart were the ponds that Satan found to dangle his crooked hook in. When each of those people bit, he snagged them with betrayal, seduction, and condemnation, all results befitting his hidden agenda.

But Josie found there is One who came to make the crooked straight and to bring light even to the corners of a child's wounded heart. When she stepped from the shadows of the cove, she found safety and acceptance in His harbor. She learned of His heavenly agenda and His plans for her.

" 'For I know the plans that I have for you,' declares the LORD, 'plans for welfare and not for calamity to give you a future and a hope' " (Jer. 29:11).

PART 2

HURTING

- 🪶 *Hurters*
- 🪶 *Hostages*
- 🪶 *Hostilities*
- 🪶 *Hindrances*

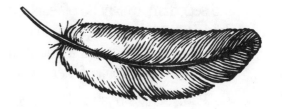

Chapter 5

Hurters

Stacy still remembers the day she reached into the cereal box to find the toy prize for her children and instead extracted a live mouse. Not only did she throw the box a country mile, but she also began to throw everything else within reach. She had had it.

Nothing had gone right for a month. Her youngest had chipped his tooth, her oldest had flunked his finals, her husband had been laid off from his job, and now a lousy mouse was chomping on the Cheerios.

Her kids didn't know what to think when cans, cups, and bowls all became airborne. This was their mellow mom? As the Windex bottle ricocheted off the TV and knocked the lamp off the end table, the kids headed for higher ground.

The shattering of the lamp stopped Stacy's stampede and set off an avalanche of tears. She cried so hard that the children risked coming back into the kitchen to see if they could comfort their distraught mom. Their efforts were to no avail, and soon all of them were in tears.

Paul, Stacy's husband, returned from the store to find shards of glass, dented cans, and a sobbing family. He was stunned. After he pieced together the story, he carried his depleted wife into their bedroom and tucked her in bed. Then he swept up the debris, assured the children all would be fine, and went in and sat on the edge of the bed to comfort his wife.

Even though this was out of character for Stacy, Paul was certain a good night's rest would put things in perspective and get Stacy back in sync. After several sullen, lethargic, tear-stained weeks, however, he realized they might need outside assistance.

Counseling helped Stacy and her family to understand that the mouse was the proverbial straw and the shattered lamp was a picture of Stacy's emotions—painful emotions she had carefully tucked under her easygoing ways. In much the same way that Paul had restored order to the kitchen, Stacy, in time, set things in place emotionally.

Pain comes in packages of all sizes. There's the pain in the neck that comes from having younger siblings (even when we really do love them). Some jobs are a pain, not to mention certain bosses. Yet to be without work adds its own emotional pressure. There's the pain that pierces our heart when we lose someone we love or the pain like Stacy's that can accumulate for some time and eventually becomes too much to bear. Whatever size the package, none of us escapes life without her share of pain. The question is not so much do we hurt, but what do we do with our pain?

Working through the hurting section of this book will be like emptying an overstuffed closet or sweeping an unkempt room. It will be a hard task, but the results will be worth the effort.

We'll begin by looking in the next chapter at how it feels to be a hostage to our pain. In the following chapter, we'll take a peek at how we become controlled by our hostilities. And in the last chapter of this section, we'll examine why we get tripped up by other hindrances. Most importantly, at least to those who are hurting, we will consider the way out of our emotional eruptions.

Chapter 6

Hostages

Joseph's brothers thought they had pulled a fast one when they ditched their younger sibling and then sold him into slavery.

I think the jealousy between them started with Joe's new coat. It left his brothers seeing colors—shades of green and raging red. Things escalated when Joe told his family about his dreams of superiority, which set off more rivalry and led to their hostility and trickery.

Joe's dreams of sheaves turned into real-life shoves when his kin pushed him first into a pit and then for a pittance sent him to Potiphar's home, where he eventually landed in the pen.

He was actually doing quite well working for Potiphar, the Egyptian captain of Pharaoh's bodyguard. The problem was Potiphar's wife, who thought she should be guarding Joe's body. Contention soon turned to detention when Joe was stripped of his position (not to mention other necessary items) and sent to prison.

Here was a young man who understood what it is to be a hostage of other people's hostilities. How painful for Joseph to realize his own brothers wanted to eradicate him from their family line. How difficult it must have been to have his boss's wife pawing him, demanding what he wasn't willing to give—his integrity as well as his virginity. How dreadful to serve out a prison sentence when he hadn't done anything wrong. Everyone else had decided Joseph's future, which seemed to leave him a victim of their vices.

Have you ever had to go somewhere you didn't want to, to spend time with someone you didn't like? What a strain! Now add to the picture the pain of finding out once you arrive that your host doesn't plan on letting you leave ... ever! His strategy is to eliminate your freedom and work out his wicked intentions toward you. You are trapped in your misery and his mastery. You have become his hostage.

That's how Joseph must have felt. And that's how it feels to be a victim of a painful past, a powerful person, or panic attacks—there is no way out, and you will never leave this nightmare.

A panic attack holds us hostage through fear. It's an assault on the body often generated by our fragile emotions. Panic leaves us confused and vulnerable to the enemy as he hisses lies in our direction. His plan is to keep us hostage by fanning our fear.

In my attempts to describe a panic attack, the word *flush* comes to mind. Not flush as in embarrassed but flush as in toilet. A panic is like repeated flushes, not of water but of terror. This terror surges through your entire body.

Imagine your heart banging against your chest while your mind stampedes wildly. Then a quaking in your hands drops suddenly to your knees, leaving you weakened. Someone then backs onto your chest with a Mack truck, while another person shovels sand into your lungs. Sustain those feelings for a few minutes and you have your basic panic attack. If you haven't had one, I don't recommend it. It isn't a comfy spot to hide out emotionally.

My first panic followed an argument with my husband, Les. It hadn't even been a big fight. But when he turned to walk away, somebody flushed. I couldn't breathe. Les rushed me to the hospital, where I was given a shot of Demeral that knocked me out. My bewildered husband took me home, and I slept off the attack. When I awoke, I felt emotionally dazed and physically drained.

I remembered in the emergency room overhearing two nurses laugh because I had this spell following an argument with my spouse. Their laughter drenched me in shame. I didn't understand what had happened to me, and I certainly couldn't find any humor in it. I was sure the physical surge of panic was an impending sign of death, and my frenzied emotions seemed to support that theory.

Following this episode, I went to my family doctor, and he increased my tranquilizers. That led me to believe the panic was all my fault and that the laughing ladies understood the joke was on me. Now I wasn't sure what was going to happen first—would I lose my mind or die? Death seemed safer, even though I very much wanted to live.

I remember thinking I must be allergic to my anger since the panic attack followed an argument. So I buried my anger deep within, and what came up in anger's place was unreasonable fear. Instead of easing my problem of panic, the fear fed it.

My circle of life was drastically altered as the panic flushing continued. At first, I blamed places and people for triggering this reaction rather than understanding the turbulence originated from within me and my ineffective ways of dealing with hurt.

In time, I narrowed my existence to the four walls of my home. I spent the next two years trying to pump up the wherewithal to get back into the flow of life. But Fear has friends, and they were crowding in. Fear hides out with Guilt, and Guilt shares his campfire with Anger. Unexpressed Anger then sends her cohort Depression to pay a visit, and Depression drags his in-law Despair everywhere he goes. So my place was filling up fast, and, like company who overstay their visit, my "guests" were becoming unbearable.

I had gone from not wanting to leave home to not wanting to get out of bed. My circle of reference was shrinking. I wished I could have a disease—not a painful or dangerous one, but one that would make my cloistered behavior legitimate to the outside world and allow me to continue refuging in my room. That way I could retain a shred of dignity, and yet nothing would be expected of me by others.

One day it came to me that my life was threateningly restrictive and so dominated by the fear of fear that if I didn't get help, I wasn't going to make it. I felt as if I were going under for the third time.

I once heard Jan Ream, author and counselor, say, "Until our pain level gets high enough, we probably won't change." Notice she didn't say we couldn't change without a high pain level, but she said we probably won't. I've found her insight to be accurate. When my emotional pain level shot up and stayed there, I was willing to do whatever it took to change.

And change I did. Later in the chapter, I'll delineate some of the steps I took. But for now, the important point for you to hear is that mine has not been a microwave cure—one zap and I was well. It has been an ongoing recovery and the hardest work I have ever done.

If you are a panic-attack sufferer, you will need to roll up your sleeves and commit to the task of your own well-being. Others can offer advice, comfort, and medication, which can all be helpful. But until you take an active role in your own restoration, dramatic change will be unlikely.

I wanted the Lord to heal me in my sleep so I could rise up righteous in the morning. Instead, He has been teaching me I need to be involved and responsive in the healing journey.

Healing is a risk because to be healed, we must trust. Those of us suffering emotionally have a broken trust factor that makes healing difficult. We'll consider that factor in the next chapter, but first let's talk about survival skills. How can we manage the dailiness of life in the midst of panic flushes?

A question I have been asked over and over is "How did you deal with the panic?" Panic is like a circle. A panic attack has a beginning and must come full circle once it begins. The size of the cycle depends on our response to the feelings of panic. If we fan the flame of fear, our circle enlarges, increasing the intensity of our emotions and the duration of the cycle.

The following are a few of the favorite lines the tempter spews in our direction during a panic to increase the severity of our attack:

"This is the worst panic you have ever had."

"You are going to lose control."

"You are losing your mind."

"You are going to die."

"You will never get well."

Lies, lies, lies! But how can we know they're lies? Let's test them.

"This is the worst panic." Whatever we are feeling at the moment seems the most intense we've ever experienced, because we are closest to it. This is the worst headache; this is the best movie; this is the most scrumptious dinner; this is the brattiest child; and so on. When we tell ourselves this panic is just another cycle of discomfort, we help to neutralize its momentum.

"You are going to lose control." When we buy into the lie that we must be in control to be safe, we increase the panic's ability to hold us hostage. Most of life is uncontrollable (weather, unforeseen circumstances, people's responses, taxes, etc.), and yet generally speaking, we remain safe.

"You will lose your mind." This lie tells us our panic is caused by a weakened mind. Instead, panic is fueled by our fragile emotions, which feed the mind inaccurate information. Sometimes the mind has been fed wrong information from the outside, and then it conveys the misinformation to our emotions, which overreact. We are not going to lose our minds; we just need to change them.

"You are going to die." Have you? I rest my case.

"You will never be well." Each time we experience a panic attack, our tendency is to negate any growth we have had. If we have an attack after going for a while without one, we think it's a sign we are right back to square one, which is usually not true at all.

Once I learned to defuse the lies, I began to make progress. First, I changed my thoughts during a panic cycle. That's not easy! It feels like trying to ignore a screaming child who is seated beside you on an airplane. But with effort and practice, you can learn to block out the bad information by a repeated act of your will and focus on things that help you to settle down.

I would tell myself, *You have been through this before, and you will make it through this time.* I would insist that my muscles relax as a way to reduce tension and be an active participant in my own get-well program. At first, like a rebellious child, my muscles resisted my command, but as I persisted, they obeyed.

Learning how to implement your own healing strategy will lessen the panic attacks' frequency and intensity. At times you will suffer setbacks, and a more insistent panic will sneak up on you. Remember the enemy likes sick surprises. Don't indulge his lies or his tricks, but draw on your resources

Call upon the Lord. (Remember who's in control.)

Calm your body. (Relax.)

Collect your thoughts. (Renew your mind.)

Carry on quietly. (Restore your schedule.)

Those of us who have been or are being held hostage by panic are people given to extremes. Finding balance will not be easy for us, but it is possible. For instance, if you talk too much (and you know if you do), develop listening skills.

If you make yourself and everyone else nervous by your anxious rushing about, take ten-minute quiet breaks to slow yourself down. Your body and mind will contest this discipline at first and thank you for it later.

If you are a couch potato, set realistic activity goals for yourself each day. Note the word *realistic*, because with our extremism, we will tend to either overwhelm ourselves and feel defeated or trade in our "couch potatoness" to become busybodies.

When we hide our insecurities behind gabbing, gallivanting, or other emotional indulgences, we impede our progress and coddle our weaknesses. A true retreat is when we find emotional relief. That happens when we disarm the terrorists who hold us hostage. Panic can be conquered by implementing a new strategy, facing our fears, and resolving our inner disharmony one issue at a time.

Joseph had plenty of reason to panic as he found himself rejected and neglected by family and strangers. As he moved from the bottom of a pit to being a pawed slave to long-term accommodations in the penitentiary, he was accumulating a painful past of prodigious proportions.

His life raises the question, "What else could go wrong?" It reminds me of the guy who was recovering in the hospital from the flu. On his way back to bed one morning, he stepped into his bedpan and slid into the hall, crashing into the medicine cart, which dispensed drugs in all directions. The fellow broke his big toe in the melee. A bevy of nurses found their attempts to help him back into bed humorous, and as they giggled, he slid through their hands onto the floor, hitting his funny bone. He grimaced and rolled over onto the foot of one of the nurses, causing her to lose her balance and sprain her ankle. At that point, I'm sure he suspected life was out to get him.

Joseph might have echoed the sentiment. Woven throughout the tapestry of his life were the threads of misunderstanding and isolation—with his brothers, his father, his "employer," and his employer's wife.

Few of us have experienced such extended separation from our families coupled with the added dilemma of incarceration (although I've known fleeting moments when sending my kids to the Big House seemed easier than keeping them at my house). During Joseph's internment, I wonder if memories were not his most regular visitors, memories that tumbled through his cell like circus clowns. The teasing voices of his brothers sneering and jeering at the show-off dreams of his youth may have reverberated off his cell walls. The dreams, which were God-given, probably seemed more like empty vapors in his restrictive world.

Mingled with his brothers' voices, Joseph may have heard his own voice full of regret—haunting regrets of how, in the past, he had flaunted his preferential robe in the faces of his rejected and jealous siblings. Sadness that he sometimes chose to strut his colors like a peacock's feathers, encouraging the boys to pluck his luck. At times, Joseph's cell probably seemed crowded with the intense temptation to blame himself and others for his painful past.

Even though he avoided embitterment, we also note his pent-up pain being released when his brothers were brought back into his life years later. Joseph shed tears that seemed to evoke a storehouse of emotions: joy, anger, grief, and love.

Joseph is not alone. We, too, feel that panic and past pain seem to be in cahoots when it comes to holding us hostage. Sometimes yesterday carries a loaded six-gun and seems to use our tangled emotions for target practice. When it hits dead center, Regret yells, "Bulls-eye!" That's why we need to ask the Lord to protect us with His Spirit when we "visit" our younger years—an exercise we must undertake to begin the healing process.

Without God's protection, we might remember incorrectly and add to our compost pile, or we might remember so clearly that we embrace our right to live in rage. The Holy Spirit is the one who will lead and guide us into all truth, which brings the liberty of resolution. Also, we need a support system (a wise friend, a competent counselor) to help us hear what we are feeling, to hold us accountable to change, and to initially validate us as we grow.

When Ginger first phoned me, she said she suffered debilitating headaches whenever she knew she would have to see her mother. It was obvious her mom-stuff had been stuffed too long as far as her body was concerned. I asked if she had someone she could talk to and pray with regarding her feelings. She said her pastor's wife, Carlie, was a friend whom she trusted and respected, so I encouraged Ginger to meet with her once a week for a while.

The results were painfully wonderful. Each week, Ginger would write letters about the abuse she suffered at the hands of her mom. When she met with Carlie, she would read the letters and then talk about what had happened to her as a child. Sometimes Ginger cried, and so did Carlie. At times, Ginger felt and expressed her contempt for her mom. Eventually Ginger released her right to stay angry, and her body and emotions responded by releasing her head as their hostage.

Ginger and her mom will probably never be best friends, but Ginger now enjoys short visits with her without suffering physical repercussions or emotional roadblocks.

A principle I learned from Lewis Smedes in his book *Forgive and Forget* is that forgiving others doesn't make them right, but it sets us free.

Joseph must have had a full-time job forgiving all his offenders, because the "big" people in his life came on like the Gestapo. His brothers even formed a posse and held him hostage. Instead of lynching him, though, they sold him into slavery, clinching the deal with a bag of coins. (I know kids who would gladly donate their siblings to slavery!)

Young Joseph found his "new life" threatened by his boss's powerful wife. Seems she suffered from attention deficit, and she thought Joseph should be her personal tutor. He resisted, she insisted, and he ended up "enlisted."

She persuaded her husband that Joseph was a jerk, and Potiphar used his influence to have him deposited in the local slammer.

While others determined his outer surroundings, however, they did not have the power to dictate Joseph's inner responses. He stated clearly to his brothers at their reunion, "God sent me before you to preserve life" (Gen. 45:5).

What an awesome reply from a man who had his path diverted because of his siblings' hateful hearts! He suffered deeply at the hands of insensitive people who used their strength to abuse and misuse him. He had evidently wrestled through the injustices of life with the Almighty and realized God was all-mighty and able to use even the treachery of others for his good. Somehow, embracing God's providence in spite of the bullies in this world frees us from allowing their powerful ploys to take us captive.

Joseph's life is an example of how panic and our past are joined in their hostage-taking efforts by powerful people. When we allow strong people to back us into a corner, we become their prisoners. (Joseph chose a physical prison over the emotional jail Potiphar's wife offered him. It's better to be locked in a cell than to drink from another's well.)

Sometimes we feel we must submit to controlling people or risk their rejection. Gratefully, Joseph took that risk and ran for higher ground (and a robe). For some of us, though, controllers have a stranglehold on our emotions, and we haven't figured out how to shake free of their suffocating grasp because we desperately want their approval.

Tom felt nauseated as he stepped from his car and headed toward his house. His temples were pounding so loudly that it was difficult for him to listen to his own thoughts. He felt as if he were nine and had to tell his dad he had flunked a spelling test. Instead, he was 49 and had to tell his dad that he would have to move into his own place.

Tom's dad had come to visit a year prior and had just never left. Now Tom couldn't put it off any longer. The pressure on his wife and children, not to mention Tom's bleeding ulcer, was forcing him to speak up. But it's hard to talk to a tank. A retired army officer, Tom's dad was used to giving orders, not taking them.

Tom tried to clear the fear from his throat. Then, sounding far more confident than he felt, he blurted out the eviction notice. He then steeled himself for the fallout. His dad moved briskly about the room but said little.

In the following days, Tom's house was filled with his dad's stony silence. But Tom felt good about his decision, because he had done what he knew needed to be done. An inner settledness helped him to endure the loss of his dad's approval.

After a week, Tom's dad asked if he would look at an apartment he had found. Tom, relieved his dad had heard him and taken him seriously, was glad to assist.

Changing the direction of an unhealthy relationship is extremely intimidating, because change usually brings confrontation. The "c" word is a scary one for hostages.

But once change and confrontation are resolved (as much as we are able), we feel a deep satisfaction and a healthy sense of self.

Any way you look at it, whether our hostage-taker is panic, our past, or a powerful person, being a hostage is a hellish experience. The enemy would lock us up and keep us there. But our Liberator came to set us free. That doesn't mean we won't experience a myriad of feelings including fear, sorrow, misunderstanding, and intimidation. But we don't have to allow them to keep us hostage. We can learn from Joseph.

The panic Joseph surely felt as a lad being rejected and neglected by family and strangers must have left him shaken. Add the panic to the powerful people and his painful past, and his story gives us an up-close-and-personal look at someone who overcame his worst nightmares to live out his highest dreams.

Chapter 7

Hostilities

"Thar she blows!" I felt like a Mobyette (a female whale spotter) as I stood atop a craggy point and saw my first whale spout. What a kick!

My friend Linda and I were at a seaside park in Monterey, California, while the whales were migrating. We were perched, binoculars in hand, on a high rock, looking out at the Pacific Ocean. The park guide had told us to watch for the spouts. I had no sooner approached the point when I spotted what appeared to be a geyser, followed by a two-pronged tail that waved in the sunlight and then disappeared into the ocean depths. Once I saw

71

four whales spout simultaneously. They lined up like a train, surfaced, and then all blew their tops together.

Actually, that has happened at my house. But instead of whales, it was males. My husband and two grown sons have all lined up and spewed about something. Okay, okay, so I was in the pack— oops, I mean pod (family of whales)—too. All right, the males were the ones shouting, "Thar she blows!" and I was the one spouting. Satisfied? But my pod has spewed a few times, too. So there.

In some ways, Les and I are like two peas in a pod. We both have a lot of dynamics, which is the nicest way I can think of to say we are gifted spouters. We have had to learn appropriate ways to express our anger rather than surfacing just long enough to blow our tops and then diving back out of sight.

We blamed each other's anger on our nationalities until we discovered every other couple does, too. Les referred to my stump-jumpin' fury as being a direct result of my ridge-runnin' Southern heritage. I called him a French dip that had been dunked one too many times, leaving his temper too hot to handle.

As long as we were blaming, we weren't changing, and our unresolved conflict grew in intensity. When we risked change in our relationship, we found we had hidden other important and often more accurate feelings behind our anger. At times we felt misunderstood, inadequate, embarrassed, or hurt, yet we responded temperamentally. We also learned that some of our legitimate anger was being taken out on the wrong person.

It was a relief to learn that being angry was not always a sin. Les and I discovered anger wasn't wrong unless we used it to get our way, to dodge responsibility, to annihilate someone's worth, to intimidate others, or to cover up other valid emotions. We had been guilty of all of those at times.

Scripture warns us, "Do not let the sun go down on your anger" (Eph. 4:26). But I confess I have sometimes taken a bath in wrath. I've soaked in it, lathered up with it, and then splashed around in it. I've lingered in it for days, months, and even years. The result is not unlike sitting in a tub too long—we shrivel up.

We see the signs of a world drenched in wrath. Rape, murder, and other abuse issues are rampant and usually the result of rage on the rampage. How did we become such a volatile society? We are like a global time bomb; can't you hear us ticking?

I'll admit I don't have all the answers. (Don't tell my husband.) In fact, I don't even have all the questions. But as a sporadic spouter, I am learning about my own anger and how to handle it more appropriately. I'm not saying I always do it right. Sometimes I still blow it, or should I say blow up. But like vintage wine (nonalcoholic, of course), I don't pop my cork as easily now.

———

Probably one of the clearest understandings of my misplaced anger came years after my agoraphobia. Long ago, I read a book (don't ask me the title; I can't remember it) that captured me with one paragraph. It told of a young child who lived in a house that had only one window. One day, someone threw rocks at the window, damaging the child's viewing place. This caused the child's perspective to be distorted and a variety of harmful emotions, including deep-seated anger, to take root.

From this concept, I, with my artistic flair, have developed stick-figure drawings to help others who are struggling with anxiety, anger, and so on. The house represents our lives, and the window represents our only place to view the outside world.

When we want to see out, we go to our window.

From the window, we view other people, and in our limited, childish ability, we make decisions about how they relate to us. (A child's world revolves around himself or herself. Come to think of it, so do a lot of adults'.)

When we wonder about God, we go to our viewing place, look up, and try to understand how He relates to us and we to Him.

One day, a great big person (or persons) comes into our lives and throws rocks at our window. The big person could be male or female, a parent, an older sibling, a neighbor, a teacher, a relative, or someone else.

The rocks represent physical, emotional, or sexual abuse, deprivation—or all the above.

The dictionary defines *abuse* as "to use wrongly or improperly, misuse. To hurt or injure by maltreatment. To assail with contemptuous, coarse, or insulting words: revile."

Deprivation is described as "the act of depriving (to take something away from)."

When a rock, a combination of rocks, or all the rocks hit our window, they affect our ability to see clearly. Now when we look at people, we see them as they appear to be through the damage that has occurred to us, and we feel anger.

When we look up toward God, we see Him as He appears to be through the distortion that has occurred, and we feel anger toward Him for not protecting us.

When we want to know if we have any worth or value, we go to our window to capture our reflection. What we see is a broken image. We then tend to buy into the lie that we have no worth or value.

When the big people who came into our lives were not looking to God for what they needed, they didn't know how to give to us what we needed. When we went to them for direction, protection, and correction and instead were violated in some way, it taught us at a deep level, *It is not safe to trust. If we trust, we will get hurt.*

Now, not only do we have a broken perspective, but we also have a shattered ability to trust. I've found that when I can't trust, I must be in control to feel safe. But people and circumstances are unpredictable, which creates a constant threat to my security, adding to my feelings of hostility.

As an adult, I responded to my shattered window by watching my universe become a small world, which is not to be confused with Disneyland's adorable ride. Mine was more like Pirates of the Caribbean, full of tension, tyrants, and terror. I found myself held captive in my home, harassed by Hostility's family: Fear, Guilt, and Depression. It took time, but I eventually left the cove and found refuge in a safe harbor.

When Terri first called me from Phoenix, she suffered from panic and depression. She was on medication for both but continued to struggle. She hoped I could fax her a solution. I understood her desire for a quick fix. I, too, had wanted *the* pill, *the* program, or *the* person to rescue me.

I explained to Terri that I had some answers, but that they weren't easy or fun. I told her what I said earlier in this book: Getting healthy emotionally is the hardest work I've ever done . . . but also the most worthwhile. I challenged her to pull on her sweats and her Reeboks, because healing is an ongoing journey. Along the way she would find hope, joy, laughter, and even some value in her struggles. Of course, she also risked the likelihood of running into some fears, failures, and hostilities.

In response, Terri told me that when she was a little girl, her father was a strict disciplinarian. Even though she breezed right over that part of her story, a flag went up in my mind.

"If you were naughty as a little girl, what might your father do to correct you?" I interrupted.

"Well, many times he would take me in the bathroom and stick my face in the toilet," she reported without emotion.

Aghast, I told her as calmly as I could that her father's behavior was abusive.

Perplexed and agitated by my response, she said, "No, you don't understand. I was a very difficult child."

"No, you don't understand, Terri," I said. "You have assumed responsibility for your dad's harsh behavior. There is nothing a child could do that would justify that type of inhumane treatment."

Terri found that hard to receive and even more difficult to believe.

When the rock of her father's hostile behavior struck Terri's window, she wasn't prepared emotionally, physically, or spiritually to handle it. To survive, she did what you and I do when we're not equipped for life's hardships—she hid.

Terri took refuge in the rigid shelter of perfectionism. She thought, *If only I could do better, act better, be better, then maybe, just maybe, someone would love me. But I must never let anyone into my hiding place lest that person find out what I'm really like and not love me just as my dad doesn't.*

Terri was not wrong to hide. Hiding helped her to survive. But the childhood hiding place she selected complicated her life as an adult. I believe that, because of children's immaturity and the lies of the enemy ("Your abuser's behavior is all your fault!"), children often choose hiding places that isolate them or set them up for more violation.

Often people who hide behind perfectionism appear to be untouchables. We see them as snobbish, condescending, and sometimes hostile. The truth is they have deep-seated anger and can't risk additional rejection. I call them the "white picket fence folks."

A picket fence looks inviting and hospitable. We are drawn to the perfectionist with her painted pickets in a tidy row. But as we approach her, we run into some problems. The fence has no gate; there is no point of entry. Also, the fence is much higher than it seemed from a distance. On close inspection, the pickets appear threateningly jagged, like an angry sneer.

We back away, confused and disappointed. The

perfectionist breathes a lonely sigh of relief. She believes we would have been far more disappointed had we found out how imperfect she really is. The perfectionist, with her unvented hostility, has driven each picket in like a stake. For her the stakes are high, because exposure throws her back into the painful emotions she felt as a victim. Rather than risk feeling her sadness, which is intense because it has penetrated so deeply into her soul, she lives in emotional isolation.

I met Carolyn at a ladies' luncheon in Seattle. She was the last one in line, and she had waited for an hour to talk to me. She greeted me and then said, "I don't really have anything to say except hello."

It didn't seem likely anyone would wait an hour just to "hello" me. I began to converse with Carolyn and noticed how articulate and attractive she was. When I pressed her on why she had waited so long to chat with me, she insisted all was well. She said good night and told me she would see me the following day at my workshop.

That night, I dreamed that Carolyn was hiding inside a beautiful house protected by a gateless fence. The fence not only kept me and others out, but it also held her captive.

After the workshop, I told Carolyn about the dream. Without hesitation, she said heatedly, "I put a gate in once, only to share my heart with a friend and then be devastated by her rejection." Her rigid posture, tense jaw, and trembling hands betrayed her inner pain and hostility.

"Carolyn, it's a risk to trust," I agreed. "People will fail us. But isolation is not the answer. Insulation is. One of the ways we can insulate ourselves, or have healthy boundaries, is to choose people to talk with who have come far enough in their own emotional recovery that they will not be shocked or offended by our past."

An idea crossed my mind and I added, "Carolyn, let's be friends."

"Sounds too scary," she responded honestly.

"How about putting in a gate and letting me sit on your front porch? We'll be porch pals," I suggested.

"How do we do that?" she asked with guarded interest.

"We will correspond, and as you feel safe, you can tell me about your life."

That was seven years ago. Carolyn and I gradually graduated from porch pals to parlor pals and now forever friends. Both of us are able to talk freely with the other. Carolyn eventually revealed her secret of sexual abuse. When she saw I was not going to reject her and that I genuinely cared, our friendship deepened.

Carolyn's method of dealing with her past was to fence herself in with her secrets. Her pain was other-inflicted, but her isolation was self-inflicted as she eliminated the gate and sharpened the pickets.

To have ripped the fence down would have been the opposite extreme, leaving her open to anyone and everyone. Boundaries are necessary for healthy relationships.

There could even be times when removing the gate and putting in pickets is necessary to protect yourself from an aggressive intruder.

But once the fence is erected, it staves off friend and foe alike. It isolates us from relationships and from emotions like joy, peace, and a sense of well-being. The anger Carolyn held inside had become a fierce companion. It caused her bouts of depression, self-consciousness, and occasional misdirected outbursts of rage. The thunderbolts of her biting criticism, directed at herself, had punctured holes in her self-esteem.

Carolyn and Terri needed to vent their feelings (with a trusted friend, support group, or counselor) about the ones who misused them and to work through steps of forgiveness (journaling, prayer, and confrontation). But they also needed to give up their "kiddie klub house" of perfectionism that prevented them from having honest relationships as adults. Their pretending and hostility had left them lonely and exhausted.

Les and I came into our marriage with anger issues, and then we kept lighting each other's fires. When we weren't setting off each other's old issues, we were adding new kindling. We couldn't get too close to each other lest we get scorched. It wasn't until we sought the safety and warmth of the Lord's love that we learned ways to douse our own flames.

We discovered the Lord is not taken aback by our

hostilities but instead takes us back . . . to Calvary. There He suffered the impact of a cruel and torturous cross. He knows about rock throwers, abuse, and pain—and the anger such treatment causes. On the cross, He paid the price for our hostilities and provided the way for our freedom.

When we enter the sacred sanctuary of His company, we find He nudges us toward new steps of growth and healing. First, He encourages us to see our rock throwers for who they are (fallible human beings) so that we might conclude those chapters of our lives. Then He moves us to current events as He requires us to take responsibility for our self-protective behavior. That behavior separates us from what we need to do—stop sheltering behind our control mechanisms, the blame game, and our hostilities.

But it's scary to dismantle our hideouts. I'm thankful that He understands our hesitation and insecurity. The Lord doesn't ask us to give up our hiding places without offering us a permanent place of refuge . . . under His wings.

Sometimes, as we walk through our issues, we find out we're furious with God (though we seldom admit it) because He didn't prevent painful events in our lives. A poem by Jessica Shaver was placed in my hand several years ago, and I have carried it in my Bible ever since to read aloud at retreats. Jessica conveys honestly her need to make peace with God in this poem titled "I Told God I Was Angry":

> *I told God I was angry;*
> *I thought He'd be surprised.*

I thought I'd kept hostility
quite cleverly disguised.

I told the Lord I hate Him;
I told Him that I hurt.
I told Him that He isn't fair;
He's treated me like dirt.

I told God I was angry,
but I'm the one surprised.
"What I've known all along," He said,
"you've finally realized.

"At last you have admitted
what's really in your heart:
Dishonesty, not anger,
was keeping us apart.

"Even when you hate Me,
I don't stop loving you.
Before you can receive that love,
you must confess what's true.

"In telling me the anger
you genuinely feel,
it loses power over you
permitting you to heal."

I told God I was sorry,
and He's forgiven me.
The truth that I was angry
had finally set me free.

When we express and confess our hostility toward the Lord, it brings down any barriers we've placed between us and the only One who can give us relief, comfort, counsel, acceptance, and the joy of intimacy.

Chapter 8

Hindrances

After years of hearing about Weight Watchers, my turn came to do more than watch my weight balloon. The winter had been especially cold, and thinking I was a walrus, I had put on extra layers of fat to see me through till the thaw. But the snow had melted, and my added coverage had not. In fact, it hung like water-filled saddle-bags from my midsection. I was starting to waddle, which got on my nerves. It takes so much longer to get anywhere when you slosh from side to side.

When I arrived at my first Weight Watchers meeting, I knew I was in trouble. The other attendees were weighing in. I don't do scales. I don't want to know what I weigh. I don't have to know how much to know I'm too much. My splitting pant seams, my "awesome"-sized panty hose, and my hubby's giggles when I donned my nightie were all the clues I needed. Of course, the fact that my nightie could serve as an awning for our front porch didn't help. Actually, I bought it gigantic because in comparison it made me feel small, which is all part of the strategy when you're in denial. Don't change yourself; instead, change your underwear (which my mother told me I should do anyway).

At any rate, I'm sure I have the record for the shortest stint in that organization's history. One look at the scale (have you seen the size of that puppy?) and I was history. I went right to the candy factory to celebrate my ability, even under pressure, to retain not only my unnecessary weight, but also my weighty denial.

Hindrances are things that tend to trip us up. Remember the little boy at school who was constantly sticking his leg into the aisle in hopes he would send someone tumbling? He was a hindrance.

Hindrances can be small and impersonal like lost car keys, or they can be bigger and more personal like my extra weight. Hindrances can also be barricade-size, creating a constant obstacle course in our lives. One of the taller hurdles we will have to scale (there's that word again) to be healed is denial. Of course, having to high jump our defensiveness is no easy matter, either. And watch out for the quicksand of the double bind: You can be up to your elbows before you know it.

Let's lace up our high-tops and climb those hindrances so we can truly run the race.

———◆———

Defensiveness is a roadblock to becoming emotionally healed. I know; it has certainly held me back.

A number of years ago, I joined a troop of friends to attend a convention in Chicago. For fun, one of our friends handed out round, shiny dots that we were to press onto our hands. This circle supposedly would change colors according to how healthy we were. We giggled as all the spots changed from black to sea blue to vibrant green . . . that is, except for mine. Mine remained midnight black.

One friend, in her desire to help me out, held my hand to warm my circle and give me some color. Within moments we looked down, and all the color had drained out of her dot, leaving it dingy gray. She released my hand to examine her fading dot, and before our eyes it returned to a beautiful blue-green.

We laughed at my lack of color and my ability to be a drain. Then one friend looked at me and said, "All kidding aside, Patsy, I see how you struggle with your health, and I think my nutritionist could help you."

"I've been to plenty of doctors," I shot back defensively. "Their cures are worse than my ills." Anger and embarrassment surged through me. But even the flow of hot emotions didn't change the bleak beacon on my hand.

My friend, not put off by my displeasure, pursued her

train of thought. "When I first went to this doctor, my energy level was low, and she helped me with a diet and vitamins. Why don't you give her a try?"

All heads turned in my direction. I felt uneasy and misunderstood. I had tried plenty of routes to health throughout the years without any lasting results. I had finally decided it was just my lot in life to be a sickee, an anemic-looking, wimpy whiner. My friends were all healthy gals who I felt couldn't grasp my dilemma. They had never walked a mile in my orthopedic moccasins. I took a breath and muttered something about not being able to afford a nutritionist even if I had wanted one.

In frustration, my friend said, "Patsy, I have always found you to be teachable until we get on the topic of your health. Then you shut down and move away from any possible resolution. It's almost as if you've closed the door on hope and resigned yourself to never being well."

Hot tears stung the corners of my eyes. Trying to hold myself together, I accused my buddies of not understanding. They dropped the topic, but I retained my anger. In fact, I held onto it tightly. The first chance I had, I rushed to my room to escape the company of my friends and release my pent-up feelings.

I burst into my room and into tears. I stomped around and talked aloud to the Lord about my accusers. Then I picked up my Bible and dropped to my knees next to the bed. Through the tears over my unjust treatment, I looked down at my open Bible. Like a neon sign, these words lit up: "Sing a new song" (Ps. 144:9).

I dabbed at my tears to clear my vision and looked again. "Sing a new song." The words broke through my wall of denial and defensiveness, causing me to consider my friend's insight. I realized I had closed the door on hope.

"Sing a new song."

"But how, Lord?" I asked aloud. "I don't even hum well."

An idea came to me, and I took the hotel notepaper and wrote an apology to my friend for my angry resistance. Then I asked for her doctor's telephone number.

That was 11 years ago at the time of this writing. Today, thanks to Dr. Starr's compassionate manner and wise insights, I'm humming along, doing better than I ever thought possible.

Defensiveness and denial are like twin boulders that create walls. My rock-hard resistance initially prevented me from being able to hear, much less embrace, the truth. Ever try to listen through a rock?

At various times in our lives, we either throw rocks, carry them, or both. The heavy hindrances of defensiveness and denial keep our inner conflict weighed down and covered over so that even we do not recognize our own emotional disharmony. Some of us go through life singing "I did it my way" while feeling picked on, misunderstood, and in an ongoing struggle for control.

Truth, on the other hand, can cause those self-centered behaviors to crumble, leaving room for change.

I remember visiting with a woman named Trish who said she didn't like people who needed credit for everything they did. She referred to a cousin who kept fishing for praise after helping her with a dinner. I could hardly believe my ears. I had never met anyone who needed more applause than Trish. She seemed to require constant standing ovations, which honestly get tiring to hand out. I wasn't surprised she liked being patted on the back; I know I do. But I was amazed Trish was not aware of her exhausting demand on others to keep her pumped up.

Some wise guy once said that if we hate a quality in someone else, it usually means that quality is within us, but we haven't "owned" it yet.

A friend recently mentioned that I'm an intense person. That took me by surprise, because I had never thought of myself that way. I could feel myself resisting her evaluation. I tightened up and uncomfortably slid down in my chair.

When we become tense and uneasy, someone has probably struck a nerve. My response signaled I was about to roll out my boulders to hide behind. Instead, however, I risked thinking through her description and realized *intense* is an accurate word for me. I am intensely happy or intensely sad, and sometimes I'm intensely intense.

Since owning that insight, I can now spot times (lots of them!) when I'm too intense, and I have made an effort to lighten up. Now I think of myself as being on a hot-air-balloon ride. When the balloon starts to fall from intense undercurrents, I drop a few sandbags to lighten my basket and regain some altitude.

Not that I've ever really been in a flying balloon. I don't do altitude. It gives me attitudes. Especially when all that separates me from a free-fall is a basket, a sheet, and a torch. Sounds more like the components for a picnic and a barbecue, which I prefer to do in a park on the grass. To get me airborne, you'll need something with engines, metal, wheels . . . and a long stairwell on rollers that never leaves the ground. The closest I ever got to a hot-air experience was while embracing a bouquet of balloons at the circus. Oops, am I being too intense? Back to my original point . . .

We are unable to recognize the truth about ourselves when we're crouched behind denial and defensiveness. While we're hiding, we feel temporarily safe, but we lose touch with the information we need to change and grow. We can't fix what we haven't faced.

Another hindrance to personal progress is the double bind, a no-win situation characterized by confusion, contradiction, and control. In the bind, we are trapped by two contradictory requests that leave us no way to win. We're perplexed and begin to doubt our ability to reason. We feel too threatened to challenge our crazy-making captor and therefore remain under his control.

Because we moved a lot when I was a child, I had

many friends. I met Donna when I was 14. Donna lived on the next street, and we often ran back and forth to each other's homes. Her dad nicknamed her Tubby because of her generous size. He was always teasing her about her weight, slapping her on the rear when he walked by her, and verbally goading her to go on a diet.

When mealtime came, however, I would watch confused as he loaded Donna's dish with mountainous piles of potatoes and oversized portions of food. Then he wouldn't allow her to leave the table until she cleaned her plate. Many times Donna would plead with him not to make her eat so much because she wasn't hungry. But he enforced his full-plate rule, always adding to her plate, especially starches. After dinner, he would start the tubby talk again.

Donna was in a double bind. She not only couldn't win, but the control he used and the confusion he stirred also kept her strapped into his sick system.

When Jill's husband insisted she find a job to help with the household expenses, she didn't hesitate. With her background in teaching, she was able to work at a Christian school. Halfway into the school year, her husband began to complain that her job was interfering with his comfort. He wanted her more available to him. Every night after teaching all day, she listened to him object to her absence.

Jill felt emotionally worn out by his complaints and gave her notice at the school. After she had been at home for several months, however, her husband resumed his old recital of how she needed to help financially.

Jill was in a double bind.

When we get caught in such a dilemma, we often feel we have a case of the "crazies." To get out of that suffocating cycle, we must pinpoint the bind we're in and then set new boundaries that open up our options so it's possible to come to a resolution.

For instance, if Jill stayed home, she needed her husband to agree to stop his accusation that she wasn't doing her part. If she went back to work, he needed to agree to take greater responsibility for his own comfort and not whine about her lack of availability. He could have it one way or the other, but not both. No more double binds.

We are responsible for our own sanity. We must not blame others for our "crazies" when it's in our control to make healthy changes. We hinder our own progress when we knowingly take part in a double bind.

___

In the movie *The Mission*, a man kills his beloved brother in a fit of rage. Afterward, he is overwhelmed by remorse and guilt and decides to punish himself for his unspeakable deed.

He is then given an opportunity to serve others who are less fortunate than himself. But to reach these remote people, he must scale a treacherous mountain. To chastise himself for his past sin, he ties a huge bag of weighted debris on his back with heavy cords before he starts the climb.

As you watch the strain and the pain this man bears with every step of his climb, you want to release him from the unnecessary encumbrance of the debris. For it not only holds him back and slows him down, but it also threatens his very existence. Finally, after a number of harrowing slips, with bloodied head, raw hands, and arms gouged by the rocks, he falls into an exhausted heap on the top of the mountain ledge.

A native appears and stands over the man's rock-beaten body. Suddenly the native lifts his spear as if to plunge it through the still form. Your heart wrenches because you know what it has cost the man to get there, and now for him to die seems so grievous. But instead of piercing his body, the native cuts through the cords that bind him, freeing him from his heavy hindrances.

Amazingly, as the man looks up at the native and sees what he has done, he accepts his gift of freedom.

Well, fellow rock climbers, what are you backpacking up and down the craggy mountain of life? Boulders of denial or defensiveness? The jagged rocks of a double bind? Are you tired of holding up your defenses? Are you feeling encumbered by the emotional games of others? There is One who longs to set us free. Christ has already paid the price, but we must be willing to set aside the hindrances that so easily beset us (see Heb. 12:1).

HEALING

Chapter 9

Hikers

In this section, I'm merely one wayfarer prompting another to begin the healing process, and for you who already have, to take the next important step. Like all trips, when we can't see around the bend, the long and winding road seems endless. At such points in the path, I find it helpful for someone to extend a hand and cheer me on.

The following chapters are not a shortcut to healing, as much as I wish I could offer one. (I took a shortcut to a friend's house once. I arrived . . . three hours late.) I am convinced that to shortcut this healing journey is to short-change our chances of becoming truly Christlike.

As a foretaste of our upcoming journey, let's travel down the New Testament highway to observe Christ as He encountered the hurting. The first thing I notice with relief is that our Physician took time for those afflicted. Second, He often used touch to transmit compassion (the bent woman, the leper, the man with dropsy). And finally, He always spoke the truth. When we listen to His conversations, we hear Him convey truth through both tough and tender talk. The tough words pierced the conscience and exposed the content of the heart. The tender words penetrated pain and produced peace. He seemed to always have the right word and the right tone for each person.

Have you ever met a hothead? I stayed in a hotel recently in which a high-school singing group was also housed. One of the chaperones evidently had been pushed past his sanity point and began to rant and rave at two of the students in the lobby. He yelled inappropriate comments at one girl and included defamatory statements about her mother. His voice level continued to rise in an obvious attempt to humiliate her publicly. He felt those young people had shown a lack of regard for others and had displayed bad attitudes. This was a definite case of the pot calling the kettle black.

Christ also met His share of hotheads—not only the arrogant, mouthy Pharisees, but also a few patients who were out of control. Yet He had a right response for each. For instance, there was the Looney-Tunes fellow who skipped naked as a jaybird through the tombstones at a local cemetery (see Luke 8:26-27). That guy needed a Physician to help him get his head on right.

Imagine debarking from a boat and being met by a graveside demoniac in his birthday suit. Sounds like material for a very bad dream to me. This boneyard romper was given to seizures of rage until his visit with Christ. Jesus' tough talk transformed the desperate man into a dressed man, one who was clothed in his mind as well as his body. Now, instead of wanting to run madly, he sat quietly at the feet of His Savior.

You can imagine the demand Jesus was in when word spread there was a competent doctor in town. It was not unusual for Him to be pressed by crowds as the well-wishers, the curious, and the needy pursued Him. Such was the day when, in the midst of the throngs, a slender hand sought out the hem of His garment (see Luke 8:44). Immediately, Christ asked who had touched Him. His followers were amazed at His question when it was obvious many had been in physical contact with their Master. But Jesus knew something the others didn't—except for the woman with the slender hand. She knew what had happened: She had been healed, and she began to tremble.

She knelt before Him and told Him what He already knew—her story. Christ gently affirmed her faith and proclaimed her well. That woman with her unclean illness knew she should not have been in the crowds, much less touch anyone. But she couldn't help herself. She, like many of us, had suffered for so long, and the local yokels had only added to her pain and humiliation. Her healing that day came from a compassionate Christ and had more to do with the issue of her heart than the issue of her blood.

Christ spoke tough words of rebuke to the demoniac, and He spoke tender words of affirmation to the diseased woman. He saw their need for a sound mind and a simple faith—and that is what this section is all about. In chapter 10, we'll talk about our need to have a sound mind so we can get a head start on the challenging path before us. In chapter 11, we'll consider our need to be heart smart and take some important steps of obedience. In chapter 12, we'll be reminded that there are some things we can't do, change, or understand, and that those are His parts to take care of.

Jairus learned about His part when, after entreating Jesus to come and heal his only daughter, he received word she had died (see Luke 8:41). How despondent that father must have felt! All hope must have drained from him as he realized it was too late. But Jesus said to Jairus, "Only believe" (Luke 8:50).

When we have done all we humanly know to do, we have no choice but to wait on God. The rock-hard place of believing without seeing holds the potential for great growth in our lives.

As we spend time with the Lord to get our thoughts straight, to allow Him to touch the painful issues of our hearts, and to accept the truth that much of life is outside our control—but not His—we will begin to see measurable progress in our personal journey. Let's continue on together.

Chapter 10

Head Start

I am an eclectic collector. One of my small but joy-inspiring collections is my children's books. For wrapped up inside this oldster's body is a youngster, one who is still exhilarated by the sight of a dewdrop, a ladybug, or a bluebird.

Nestled on my bookshelves is everything from *Heidi* and *Star Mother's Youngest Child* to *Winnie the Pooh*. I love a well-told tale that wraps its story around the child in each of us and gives us a hug.

The *Secret Garden* is that kind of nurturing adventure. Filled with intrigue, sadness, discovery, and growth, this timeless story dances on the edge of our youth yet nudges us into the grown-up world.

When the children in the tale first discover the garden, it's a wondrous find. But not because of its beauty. That was covered by brambles and weeds and would take precious effort to release. The immediate joy came from finally finding what they knew existed and sharing the tangled garden with trusted friends. For the children, the garden held a secret story of tragedy (a young mother's accidental death) and the priceless key to healing (when the children are freed from physical and emotional isolation).

Emotional and relational restoration for adults is like that story in many ways. Some of us hold secrets we have carefully concealed in untended plots in our hearts. Scary secrets, shameful stories, and silent sins. We sometimes sense their prickly presence as they pierce our self-esteem and puncture our relationships.

Other times, our struggles are a mystery to us. We wonder at our lack of color, fragrance, and fruit. When we can't grasp the truth that we are caught in the brambles of our past, walled in by our self-protection and isolated by our keyless lock of resistance, we, like the hidden garden, wither.

To turn the once-lost key is a risk. But entering the untouched garden of our losses and working to untangle our emotions and relationships can release us to flourish.

Does this mean one garden excavation and we're finished? Actually, no. It means that through many weeding sessions, we become current with the Lord, ourselves, and others. After that, it's far easier to keep up with the weeds, briars, and pruning required for our ongoing growth.

In the previous chapters, we have considered the truth that when we feel threatened or overwhelmed, we hide. Often we hide because we hurt and we don't know what to do about our pain. Once we have set aside our denial (yes, I do have problems, and yes, sometimes I *am* the problem), have given up our defensiveness (yes, I am willing to hear what you're saying without fighting for what I deem to be my rights), and have stepped out of the double binds others have put us into (yes, I will take responsibility for my sanity), *then* we can change. Healing can begin. Denial, defensiveness, and double binds keep us from growing. Those powerful *d's* are places we hide when we feel unable to change or are unwilling to do so.

In this section, we enter the path of resolution. We will begin by considering our heads—the way we think— which is often the path to our hearts. We will look at the heart in the next chapter. Sometimes the Lord starts in our hearts and then works on the head. Wherever He begins, we need to respond, and responding often requires relinquishment. To relinquish is to give up, give in, and give over whatever He asks of us. That sounds scary, but it's a pivotal point to establishing a healthy mind-set. When we decide to be His, we become less resistant to the weeding and pruning and more single-minded in our focus on the path ahead. Growth comes down to this question: Are we willing to hear, learn, and change?

Many years ago, Denise was devastated when a long-time neighbor began to pursue her husband. In time, Denise was served with divorce papers. She had rushes of rage followed closely by paralyzing panic. Denise loved her husband, and she could not understand how that woman could deliberately set out to take Denise's husband, the father of their five children.

Feeling desperate, Denise went to church and knelt alone at the altar. She prayed and cried out to the Lord about the offense. Then something unexpected happened. A memory from her childhood flooded her mind. She saw herself as a young girl borrowing a dime from another girl. She immediately recognized the other girl as the neighbor who had broken up her home and shattered her heart.

Denise felt a strong urge to pay back the dime. She immediately resisted, arguing with the Lord and restating her case of personal injustice in detail. The conviction didn't lessen, however, so Denise ignored it and threw herself into her busy week.

The week weakened Denise. She felt miserable, mistreated, and maligned. She couldn't understand why the Lord was worried about one thin dime when she had been emotionally assaulted with a million-dollar offense. Finally, when she knelt to pray for His mercy and guidance again, she agreed to do what He asked of her.

Denise arrived at the woman's home and reluctantly knocked on her door. The woman answered and was stunned to see her.

Before she could change her mind, Denise blurted out, "When we were little girls, I borrowed a dime from you, and I've come to pay you back."

The woman stared as Denise extended the coin and pressed it into her hand. The baffled former neighbor watched as Denise turned and walked away.

Later, Denise told me that when she started down the steps toward her car, such joy came over her that it was all she could do not to shout. Something liberating and healing happened inside her when she relinquished her right to understand and obeyed God's seemingly outrageous request.

The other woman eventually regretted marrying Denise's former husband, and they, too, divorced. But she never apologized to Denise for her offense. Denise never understood what the dime business was all about. She did say it was the hardest money to let go of, yet it produced the greatest returns she had ever experienced. In the process of letting go of her ability to understand, she found she also loosened her grip on her hurt feelings, her wounded spirit, and her harbored resentment.

An unteachable spirit will lock us out of our own garden. What a wretched thing! Our pain (our secret garden) holds the potential for Eden (our spiritual garden), the paradise of inner liberty and longed-for intimacy. But we must be willing to uncover our hidden garden and allow the Gardener access. We don't want to be like the father in *The Secret Garden* who, because he wouldn't face his pain and loss, sealed off the very place in which he could have found solace.

After we have relinquished whatever God has asked us to, we desire solace. Solace allays the troubled and anguished mind. To be a recipient of God's clarity for my muddled mind, I seek a place of solitude.

How often do you desire to be soothed, cheered, and comforted? "Frequently" is my response. Sometimes friends offer me that type of aid, but more often than not they are busy with many things, distracted by their own needs or incapable of touching or changing my deep inner discord. But there is One who imparts solace and more, much more.

Solitude is an important prerequisite to solace. When I'm flitting, fighting, and forging through life, I don't have the presence of mind or spirit to accept the balm He offers. But when I nail down my hypersandals in a quiet place and lean in to hear His voice and then respond accordingly, I often receive cheer and comfort. Not that I always get what I want from the Lord, but He meets me at my need. It may be only one word, but a word from Him is life, and it sustains me.

I am a people person. I'm a lights, camera, action kind of gal. But I have learned to treasure and even yearn for my alone moments with Him, times when I leave the spotlight of others and sit under the searchlight of His Spirit. In those intervals, the Lord not only consoles me, but He also constrains me. For He knows I need to linger in those moments of light where I meet and retreat with Him.

There I gain a healing level of sanity, a settled sense of self, an inner reservoir of understanding, and a medicinal sense of humor.

It seems like an oxymoron to say we need to seek solitude to recover from isolation. But isolation is like desolation (a desert) to the soul, whereas solitude is like irrigation (a garden) to life. In isolation, I suffer rejection and barrenness. In solitude, I am restored by His acceptance and given the privilege of fruitfulness.

At times our thoughts, like brittle stickers, have to be dislodged when they press against our faith. It's easy in the dailiness of life to buy into the madness of the world—not to mention our bent, when left on our own, to think twisted thoughts. It's in the quiet, as we meet with the Gardener, that He pulls the brambles off our brains. This allows Sonlight in and moves us from being uninformed and misinformed to being transformed and conformed—transformed in our thinking and conformed to the image of Christ.

The Lord consoles, constrains, and at times, much to my consternation, convicts me when I spend time with Him. Not long ago, I attended a prayer seminar in which we were asked to think of our hearts as a garden and the Lord as the Gardener. Then we were to consider in prayer what the Gardener needed to tend to in our garden.

I wanted to place a garden in my thoughts that portrayed my heart. We had planted a small English garden next to our house that was crowded with such flowers as lilies, daisies, sweet williams, yarrow, and hollyhocks, so I pictured that one. I remembered its summer abundance, its sweet aroma, and the delightful array of colors it produced. I liked the thought that my heart was this bountiful garden. I wanted the Gardener to validate my choice, so I asked, "Lord, is this my heart?"

I did not hear an audible voice, but there was such a strong inner impression of "no" that I knew I had picked the wrong spot. Somewhat disappointed, I mentally moved to the front of our home, where we had put in some tidy landscaping. We had planted mostly shrubs, but some flowers were there that made it attractive though not as showy as the other locale.

"Is this my heart?" I inquired of the Gardener.

Again, "no" resounded.

Feeling confused, I remembered that the west side of our home had a scraggly line of ostrich ferns. My first thought was *Oh, no, I deserve a better spot than this.* After a few hesitant moments, I asked, "This is my garden, isn't it, Lord?"

"No" was all I heard.

I thought, *What's left?* Then I remembered a few stray tulips that had appeared at our back fence, and my mind headed in that direction. On the way to the fence, I mentally passed an old, broken shuffleboard slab. I sensed I should stop. I did, and then I heard, "This is your heart." I looked at the concrete chunks, and I began to cry.

Initially, it seemed unkind to guide me to that plot. God didn't show me what I wanted, but He gave me what I needed—a mental picture of my resistance to His cultivation. When I owned that insight, I could then change my thinking about the Gardener's tilling, hoeing, fertilizing, and other necessary tasks. Once I submitted to His gardening touches, my heart's soil began to soften. (I was also encouraged when we had the chunks of cement removed from our yard and found the unused soil underneath rich with potential.)

My life has taught me that conviction almost always precedes cultivation. If I am to be healed, I must be willing to see my true condition.

What does the garden of your heart look like? What must you allow the Gardener to do to tend it?

Another step on the way to restoration is to study the Scriptures. That helps us to develop realistic expectations about our healing journey.

The day I gave my life to Christ, I remember I had never seen the sky so blue or the grass so green. For a time, my world became Eden as I enjoyed my "beginning." I imagined that was how it would remain as I explored one garden path after another, always aware of His presence.

But before long, things began to change. I was still on the path, but at times I would trip over rocks in the trail, and I often felt alone. Eventually, I decided the Lord wanted to use the rocks as stepping-stones that would lead me up to Him. That was a comforting thought, just not an accurate one, because one day I fell into a pit. It took me a long time to crawl out of that deep place of intimidation and isolation. It took even longer to figure out how those occasional, though sometimes extended, pitfalls fit into my relationship with the Lord.

I have since learned that our journey is not an upward, angelic ascent or even a strenuous staircase to heaven. It's more accurately depicted as a trip to the promised land. And I do mean *trip*.

A WANDERING JOURNEY

We would all like to think that our spiritual growth and maturity might proceed something like this:

(a steady, smooth progress) — X

Where we are now   X

Most of us, however, do not experience our journey toward God this way. As a second choice, we would gladly settle for a Christian growth experience that would go something like this:

(plateaus of experience, marked with leaps of growth, each lifting us to a higher plateau) — X

Where we are now   X

But most of us do not experience growth like this, either. A map in the back of one of our Bibles depicts the journey of the Israelites from slavery in Egypt to the promised land something like this:

The beginning   X   X
of their journey

RED SEA

(From *How to Conduct a Spiritual Life Retreat,* by Norman Shawchuck, Rueben P. Job, and Robert G. Doherty [Nashville: The Upper Room, 1986], p.13. Used by permission.)

Check out the Israelites, the weary wayfarers who have gone before us. Thumb through the book of Exodus; it is their travel log and can help to mentally prepare us for our journey. In fact, you may want to get out your magnifying glass and examine the details of their trek. For we will have, like the Israelites, rocky roads and lengthy droughts—not to mention oversized enemies who, at times, seem to tower over our understated faith.

In tough times, I tend to wonder why my garden seems to be withering, why the weeds are growing faster than the blossoms, why the soil is depleted, and where, oh where, is the Gardener.

Having a clearer understanding of my walk with Christ protects me from unrealistic expectations, including the belief that nothing bad will touch me, and allows me to see how, in His hands, all things have value. I have to give up the belief that my life will be an Eden and embrace Exodus as a reality. Otherwise, when loss, pain, and the unexpected happen, I am left floundering with my fragile faith fed by my anemic understanding.

Exodus exposes hardships, plagues, and enemies, but it also encourages us with mountaintop perspectives, daily provisions, and His pillars of protection. Exodus reminds us that we are in transit. This life is not our home. We are sojourners (strangers with no rights of citizenship). When we understand this, we will not be caught off guard by droughts, deserts, or disasters and come to the wrong conclusions about life or the Lord. Exodus prompts us on to the promised land. One day, one glorious day, we will enter His eternal "Eden," settling our citizenship once and for all.

Meanwhile, setting aside our hidden pain, seeking solitude, realistically setting our minds on the path ahead, and searching the Scriptures are ways to protect our thought life and will give us a head start toward healing.

Chapter 11

Heart Smart

Great beads of perspiration blanketed Les's forehead as he sat gripping the arms of the chair. "What's wrong?" I asked, startled by his gray appearance and alarmed by his sweaty face.

"I'm not sure," he said haltingly.

"What are you feeling?" I knelt next to him.

"Numbness up my arm, face, and into my mouth," he reported.

That was Les's first heart attack. He had been struggling with chest pain for a couple of years, but he had been given a clean bill of health by several specialists.

What the doctors decided was no big deal was actually a life-threatening health issue.

After his heart attack, a specialist misread his heart catheterization report and prescribed medication instead of surgery. Les looked terrible and functioned minimally in the months that followed.

Before long, we realized something had to be done. At my urging, a heart surgeon checked out Les's reports and immediately scheduled open-heart surgery.

The four blocked arteries were steadily strangling Les's life away. The surgeon told me that Les would be safer when the doctors took his heart out of his body and held it in their hands than he was without surgery.

His operation was a success, but his recovery was shaky because of complications. He developed adult-onset diabetes, which added strain on his heart as well as turbulence throughout his body and emotions. In more recent times, Les has had two more heart attacks, and his bypass work has begun to block up.

Throughout this ordeal, Les has exhibited a courageous spirit, a lively sense of humor, and a noncomplaining attitude. I find that not only admirable, but also amazing.

It seems to me that some people handle pain and loss with greater dignity than others. I'm an other. If I suffer, I make sure everyone in a five-mile radius suffers with me. Les has shown me a better way.

This is not to say Les hasn't had to make painful adjustments to his dramatic health condition. In fact, he went through a period of grieving, sorrowing over his damaged health, his lost work future, and his restrictive lifestyle. Had Les not faced his loss and grieved, he would not have had the inner space for courage, humor, and fortitude. His disappointment, anger, and broken dreams would have crowded out his jovial nature and his hope for the future.

None of us gets through this life without experiencing loss—of loved ones (through distance, divorce, and death), income, reputation, home, innocence, and so on. But many of us harbor our losses and therefore our grief, leaving us little room for joy or other life-giving qualities. Our hearts become heavy and, if unattended, hard.

After I spoke on grief at a retreat, one of the participants, Mary Hermes, took a quiet walk and penned this poem:

ROCKS

It seems to me the rocks we sometimes hurl
are unshed tears that harden into stone,
then mount in jagged piles around our souls.
At last we cannot walk through them or see or feel
except the pain of pressing edge.
And then we cast them from us as we can,
praying they do not strike the ones we love.

When we don't have the strength left to throw our rocks, they become walls.

Jeanie, a pretty 18-year-old, slipped from her bed, grabbed her robe, and ran quietly through the house and out the back door. She reached a clump of trees just before her body wrenched with sickness. Finally the waves of nausea stopped, and Jeanie stole back into the house and to the safety of her room. She knew this would be the last morning she would have to worry about hiding her illness.

Ted, Jeanie's 19-year-old boyfriend, picked her up later that morning for their drive to the city. He nervously reread the hand-scrawled map several times and checked his rearview mirror more often than was necessary. The ride was quiet except for surface prattle and the loud pressure of fearful anticipation. When they arrived at the rickety house, Ted quickly ushered Jeanie inside.

A large, barrel-chested man in street clothes entered the room. He handed Ted a newspaper and pointed toward a tattered chair. He then ushered Jeanie into a kitchen, where she sat down on a wooden chair next to a table. The big man had her hike up her skirt so he could place an injection into her thigh. She was then blindfolded and guided into another room, where she lay on a table.

Jeanie heard the shuffle of feet and unfamiliar voices whispering directions to each other. The cramping began, and soon the ordeal was over. Several people left the room. Then the blindfold was removed. A woman in a floral blouse and tan skirt busily set instruments back in order.

Jeanie's eyes took a moment to adjust to the light, but eventually she found herself staring at peeling paint on the ceiling. The woman handed her a packet of pills and instructed her to take them if she experienced heavy bleeding.

"Where is the baby?" Jeanie asked, lifting her head to see.

"It's gone," the woman said dryly.

"What do you do with them?" she asked reluctantly.

"We flush it down the toilet," the woman answered as she helped Jeanie to a seated position so she could leave.

Ted assisted Jeanie to the car. Somewhere between the decaying house and their vehicle, they made an unspoken vow never to mention, even to each other, what they had done on this cold November day.

Ted and Jeanie married and went on to settle in a lovely New England village. Jeanie gave birth to two adorable daughters and a handsome son. Ted was successful beyond their dreams, affording them finery and financial security. To acquaintances, all seemed idyllic.

But Jeanie and Ted had carefully built a facade around their lives. Jeanie struggled with any kind of honest confrontation, and Ted became sexually involved with many women.

Then something happened that Ted and Jeanie could not hide or deny. Jeanie was diagnosed with AIDS as a result of infected blood received following routine surgery. After the initial shock of her impending death, Jeanie found herself longing to bring closure with her loved ones on unfinished business.

One day, Ted and Jeanie were driving to the doctor's

office when the "Focus on the Family" program came on their radio. The subject of the day: abortion. Jeanie was flooded with her own memories, and she began to pray for courage to speak of the unspeakable. Pushed by the reminder that her time was fading, she blurted out, "We need to talk."

Jeanie had been so guarded with Ted that her intensity surprised him. Out of curiosity, he asked, "Sure, honey, about what?"

The silence broken, Jeanie began to pour out her buried pain, guilt, and loss over their secret baby. Ted looked away but listened to Jeanie's request. She wanted a private memorial service for the baby—just the two of them at the family plot in the cemetery. Ted nodded his head in agreement.

Many years had passed since two panic-stricken young people sought a way out of the result of their passion. Now they stood over an empty plot. Jeanie laid a heart-shaped lace pillow with a rosebud on the ground.

Straightening up, she began to read the tribute she had written:

> *Our little innocent one,*
> *we want to say good-bye.*
> *We've missed the opportunity*
> *to hear you laugh and cry.*
>
> *Because we were so immature,*
> *we wounded you one day.*
> *But God knows we are sorry;*
> *for forgiveness we did pray.*

Tho' many years have passed,
still you linger in our hearts.
Our little, innocent one,
we'll not remain apart.

For when life's battle's won,
our God, He knows 'tis true,
as David did his son,
that we will come to you!

Jeanie and Ted embraced and, through gentle sobs, spoke words of remorse and grief to each other and to God. The barriers between them crumbled as truth and forgiveness mended their broken hearts and relationship.

They named their baby Emily and took the white, heart-shaped pillow home to represent their waiting child and remind them of God's forgiveness.

The remaining months of Jeanie's life were seasoned with deep joy even in the midst of her physical pain. She died peacefully in Ted's arms.

It took an incredible amount of courage for Ted and Jeanie to work through such a tender and tragic part of their lives. Years of unreleased tears and unspoken loss stood between them like the Great Wall of China. For 30 years, they hid on opposite sides of this seemingly insurmountable barricade. Their vigil of silence left them emotionally isolated until finally Jeanie risked the exposure of the secret. Ted and Jeanie spoke the truth to each other, sought forgiveness, and expressed their grief. The wall crumbled.

If Jeanie were alive today, I believe she would encourage us to take bold steps toward resolution. Speaking the truth in love was the turning point for them. It brought Ted and Jeanie out of their refuge of silence and placed them under the protection of God's healing wings.

Jeanie's story reminds us it's never too late to make an honorable choice.

The grieving process is much like Les's surgery. When we allow the Great Physician to examine the issues of our lives, He may need to hold our hearts in His hands. What a vulnerable position to allow someone to scrutinize us that closely and find out what makes us tick . . . and what ticks us off!

Unreleased anguish can, in time, turn to unreasonable anger. That anger, like rocks, can and will block the "arteries" (our relationships) and add to the damage in our hearts.

To become tenderhearted, insightful, and responsive to the Lord and others, we must first wade through our losses. That means a willingness to feel the effects of our loss, to examine our hearts under the tutelage of the Holy Spirit, to release tears, and to relinquish our rights to understand. In doing so, we will feel the pain, but we'll learn appropriate ways to express it. Sometimes it will be through the healing release of tears, prayer, some form of art, or words (spoken or written).

Journaling can expedite healing, because our hands are extensions of our hearts, and many times we will write what we wouldn't risk saying. It's almost as if we bypass our defense mechanisms and, in a safer form of expression, say what's really on our hearts. I don't keep a daily journal, but when I do write, I'm often surprised at what I learn.

During a particularly dark time in my life, I wrote this poem:

WINTER

Winter came early and would not depart,
Winter came early to a tender, young heart.

Frozen inside, the child would not feel,
Locked in her pain, she could not heal.

Icy responses replaced her trust;
Numbed by life's season,
her soul formed a crust.

Hardened by bitterness,
chilled with despair,
Encased in the cold with no one to care.

Icicle tears clung to her face,
Frigid reminders of her shame and disgrace.

Winter came early to a tender, young heart,
Winter came early and would not depart.

I knew I had felt sad, but until I wrote those lines, I had no idea how heavy my heart was.

I took this poem to my friend and counselor Ruth

Ann. We talked about a lot of past and current issues, and that was very helpful. Then Ruth Ann said she was looking forward to the rest of the poem. I wondered what she meant. But one day, after I had talked and walked through many of my losses, I sat down and finished the poem.

SPRING

Spring came late, late in her years,
Spring came late to thaw her tears.

The little glazed sculpture
stood frozen in place,
Till the light of the Son
dissolved her disgrace.

The icicles fell to the ground below;
Her heart, warmed with love, melted the snow.

No longer a statue in an ice-cold rhyme,
No longer a victim locked in a crime.

Spring came late to thaw her tears,
Spring came late, late in her years.

While I chose to express my emotions in a poem, Tonja's journal is filled with expressions of her artistic flair. She drew this revealing depiction of how she felt about all the unspoken secrets from her childhood:

Secrets

The following two journal entries are from a woman and a man in the first steps of personal loss. Judy was an incest victim who was working through her hurt when her father suddenly died. Initially devastated because she could never restore the relationship with her dad, she wrote:

> *He's gone . . . he's really gone. No time to say good-bye. No time to say I still love you. Why? Why didn't he call me and say he was sick in the hospital? He didn't have to be alone. No warning . . . no time to say good-bye. No last hug. How I longed for a hug that felt pure. . . .*
>
> *Now there is no hope. He is gone. The striving is over. But my heart aches for the loss of a redeemed relationship that could have been but never will be here on earth.*
>
> *Daddy, I can live with your death . . .*

I can live without your presence . . . but can I live without "the hug"?

Don struggled with pain and disappointment as he journaled before his dad's funeral:

> *Lord, you do take care of us. It's been so difficult for me, Lord, as I think of my dad. Grief just wells up inside of me from time to time. It's like a wave that comes and then leaves and then comes again.*
>
> *Lord, how special it was to see the program with my picture in it in my dad's papers. Father, he was proud of me. He just didn't know how to say it. I don't know if I'll ever get over my relationship with my dad. The tether is breaking, and I'm grieving over it. This has been hard for me. . . . It seems so insignificant to spend only two pages writing two days after my dad died. I cried for most of the day.*
>
> *Lord, am I grieving two things: the loss of my dad and the loss of never having a dad? Father, You are giving me insights as to what life is all about. Relationship is the most important thing we have or do. . . . It starts with You and works through all the things we do and people we come in contact with. I long for better relationships with my children and wife and You. It's*

hard. It doesn't come easy for me. . . .
Father, there's going to be so much
emotion tomorrow at the funeral. Help
me, Lord, to get through it.

Whether you express your feelings in a poem, a draw-
ing, or a letter, the important benefit of journaling is that it
gives you somewhere besides inside yourself to carry your
emotions. It also helps you to define your unfinished feelings.

Grieving is a process, not an address. Because we
have experienced loss doesn't mean we should set up
house with it. When we're willing to let the Lord do some
internal surgery and then work through the recovery time,
we will eventually enter the lighter and brighter season of
spring.

Les's health problems haven't gone away, but they no
longer dictate his level of joy. The same will be true of us,
for we will be aware of some losses throughout our lives.
But now the weight is His, and we are no longer emotionally immobilized and stunted. Instead, we become heartfelt
comforters able to extend heart-smart help to others.

Chapter 12

His Part

The long and winding road led Moses high atop Mount Nebo. When he reached the summit, he leaned against his staff to steady his footing and then looked at the vista spread before him. His breath caught in his throat. Stretched out as far as his eyes could see was the land of milk and honey—lush, green, fertile, and fruitful, just as Jehovah had said it would be. Moses' heart palpitated from the thrill of the view, and his eyes flooded with tears of wonder.

Hours passed before Moses stepped back and lowered his ancient body onto a stone ledge. From his seated position, his eyes once again swept across the panoramic scene

that portrayed his people's place of promise. Longing
sprung up anew in his heart that he, too, might enter the
land. He had traveled so far, so very far. But the desire was
quickly crowded out by regret. Stinging tears overflowed
his eyes and slipped down his cheeks. Moses had not
imagined what his fury could cost him.

He leaned his head against Mount Nebo's solid side,
closed his eyes, and remembered. Memories of a lifetime
moved through his mind. He thought of his mother and
how she had loved him enough to release him into the
sovereign care of Jehovah. She had done all she knew to
do for as long as she could for her baby, and then she had
had to trust God to do His part.

Moses wished his mother could see the incredible
sight of the long-awaited land. But how would he explain
why he would not be joining their people for this part of
the journey? "No," he whispered to the mountain, "it's
better she doesn't know."

Moses' mind drifted to the palace—the horrible,
wonderful palace. Years laced with separation from his
family, yet important years of being schooled. And Moses
learned far more than was taught. He saw firsthand the
habits and practices of the Egyptians, information that
would be helpful when he returned to negotiate with
Pharaoh. Moses could not have known then how
Jehovah's hand was in that palace part of his life, equip-
ping him for the journey ahead.

His thoughts shifted from the palace to Midian and the
shrub, the one aflame with the very voice of God. How
long had it been since that day? he wondered. Then, with-

out realizing it, Moses slipped out of his sandals. Even the touch of cold stone to his bare feet did not jar him out of his blazing-bush reverie. His eyes dried as if from the warmth of his thoughts. He recalled his reluctant fireside chat with the Lord, amazed at His patience with him.

Then an uneasiness stirred within Moses when he reviewed the mistakes he had made in his life. He wondered if the Lord God had written the commandments on the same material as Moses' head . . . and his heart. No, he didn't have to wonder; Moses was sure of it.

Then the miracles he had witnessed began to flood his thoughts: the pillars of cloud and fire, the wall of water, the food from heaven, the retreating enemies, the tablets, the tabernacle . . . The pictures of God's part passed before him for hours on end. Moses' heart filled with praise until he finally had to release it or burst. In an old man's quivering voice, yet with the gusto of a youth, he sang the song he had sung after crossing the Red Sea. It echoed throughout the mountain as though it pleased its Maker.

Moses stood, straightened his robes, and again drank in the view. The setting sun blanketed the land with shadows as if to put it to sleep. The tears cascaded down Moses' face, but these didn't sting. These tears were sweet like manna. A smile crossed Moses' face, and he sat down again on his high throne of stone. When he pressed his back against the "chair," he noticed how it flared out on the sides . . . like wings. His smile deepened and spread across his heart. Then God showed Moses what He had withheld from him before—His glory.

I can only imagine what it must have been like for

Moses in his last hours when he saw first the promised land and then the Promise Maker. But one thing I know: There's nothing like a mountaintop to help us gain perspective. From that vantage point, we become more aware of not only our limitations, but also His interventions.

The long and winding road led Hagar to a hot hideout, a desert spot that offered her and her son soothing sanctuary. There's something about being a "prisoner" that causes you to value more deeply your freedom. Then hard times become relative. And a desert becomes an oasis.

I think if we could talk to Hagar, she would not change one sandalprint of her path. For she not only gained a son but was also led to the well of the Living One. When Hagar had nowhere to turn and no one to listen to her, the God Who Sees saw and heard. Hagar showed her willingness to accept Him and His promises when she returned to Sarai's tent. Hagar did what she could. God did what she couldn't.

How gracious and generous of God to make Himself known to an "outsider"! Hagar's name would not have made the "Most likely to chat with Jehovah God" list. She was the wrong nationality, the wrong upbringing, and the wrong tax bracket. Yet the angel (thought to be Jehovah Himself) spoke with her. He drew her into His oasis of provision.

The long and winding road led Naomi back home. "Home"—what a wonderful word, full of comfort, acceptance, and provision! (That's why our kids keep returning.) But home for Naomi was where she dragged her broken dreams to bury them. She had already buried everyone of importance to her. All she had left were dreams that could now never be fulfilled. When your dreams die, hope becomes the pallbearer, and bitterness becomes your roommate. Ask Mara, "Bitter," the name Naomi assigned to herself as she returned home.

The long and winding road led Ruth to a harvest of hope. She gave up everything she had and ended up reaping all she would ever need.

What was it that caused Ruth to follow her mother-in-law, Naomi, to her homeland? To follow meant a departure from Ruth's place of birth and her husband's place of death—reasons that make most people feel too connected to the land to leave it. Besides, Ruth would have to say good-bye to family and friends, the ones who usually help us survive life and loss. She would leave behind comfortable traditions and known gods to pursue a life of servitude among strangers who worshiped the solitary God.

I wonder if Ruth's husband, Mahlon, had told her stories of his land and his relatives as well as his God? Perhaps that was when a longing began to form in her heart. Or maybe, as she observed the interaction of his family with each other, Ruth was aware they had something she did not. I wonder if Naomi, during better days, was such a winsome woman that Ruth desired to be like her? It could be that Ruth's first encounter with God came through the behavior of Mahlon and his family, and she could not bear to lose that spiritual touch point. Whatever the reason, the results of Ruth's choice leave us breathless.

Naomi's thoughts after the burial of her sons were like a graveyard. Her mind was full of bones without breath and her life without a future. Naomi had said her last good-byes to her husband and sons, and then, with her heart wrapped tightly in grave clothes, she headed home . . . to wait to die.

But her trip was interrupted by an outrageous request by her daughters-in-law, Orpah and Ruth. They wanted to go with Naomi. Couldn't they see she had nothing left to give them? Naomi convinced Orpah to go home, but Ruth refused to leave her. In fact, Ruth went so far as to relinquish her rights to have a future aside from total devotion to the welfare of her dear mother-in-law.

Because she was so full of death, however, Naomi's ears could not take in the words of life spoken by Ruth. They didn't penetrate her pain.

Actually, this moment in Ruth's life was probably in part a result of Naomi's prayers. For Ruth did not just devote herself to her mother-in-law that day but also to Jehovah, the God of Naomi. This was Ruth's conversion day. Yet instead of celebration, she received rejection. But Ruth had not come with her choice contingent on Naomi's ability to hear her. She had come with a mind set on her new life.

Three times Naomi instructed her to return to her own people. Ruth stood her ground. Holy ground. Naomi had no strength left to fight, and Ruth was too committed to give in or up.

The long and winding road led the two women into Bethlehem, where the city was stirred by their arrival. Naomi was honest with her old friends and confessed her emptiness and bitterness. She had gone away with her most precious possession, her family members, and had returned home without them.

Ruth's heart must have been so full of Jehovah that she had no room for offense even when Naomi said God had "brought me back empty" (Ruth 1:21). Ruth had promised to stay at Naomi's side as long as there was breath in her body, and Naomi told everyone she was "empty"? What was Ruth, chopped lox?

Perhaps Ruth realized that no one could replace Naomi's sons. She might have been aware that Naomi needed some seasons at home to heal from her grievous losses. Whatever her thoughts, Ruth continued her focused efforts to serve Naomi and did not allow a slight to become a fight.

Ruth's offer to work in the fields, a difficult and some-times dangerous job, shows her humble heart and servant's spirit. Her willingness to serve was rewarded in ways that surpassed anything she, her mother-in-law, Boaz, or you or I could have imagined. The harvest from the field produced not only barley and Boaz (a mate), but also a baby. Not only did Jehovah give Ruth a husband and an heir, but also a heritage. Not only did she give birth to a son, but she also became part of the lineage of "the Greater Son."

Naomi's heart began to heal when she saw the basket of barley, then learned of Boaz, and eventually allowed their baby to fill her empty arms. When Mara leaned over to pick up the baby (her part), her bitterness poured out. When she stood up, Naomi's pleasantness returned (God's part).

Ruth took the long, winding road away from all her former comforts, all her hiding places, and took refuge under His wings. She did her part, and He did the rest.

―――――・◦＊◦・―――――

Ruth is a picture of relinquishment. A true sojourner. A sweet-spirited servant. When she turned her back on her former ways, moved from Moab, and headed toward Bethlehem, Jehovah opened a whole new life for her.

Likewise Naomi, even in her bitterness and anger, arose and walked away from the camp of the enemy and returned to the home of her heart and her Healer. Jehovah met her in her emptiness and filled her with the produce of the field and the pleasant fruit of His Spirit.

―――――・◦＊◦・―――――

Like Moses, we have much to remember—years filled with, yes, our failures, but also God's interventions. Like Hagar, we, too, have felt imprisoned in relationships, but God has been our awaiting oasis. Like Naomi, we have suffered unspeakable losses. At times our bitterness has consumed us, and we have lost sight of God's generosity.

We are a hurting and needy people.

But are we willing to be like Ruth? Will we let go of our failures, our sorrows, and our woundedness? Are we willing to walk in His direction? Even one faltering step to begin? Have you pinpointed your hiding places? Are you willing to identify your hurting places?

To assume mental and emotional ownership of our personal pain is to take long strides toward the path of restoration. To take a step is to begin doing our part. God will respond and do His part. He will bring healing.

I don't know where the long and winding road is leading you, but I do know this: If you remember passing Calvary, you are on the right road.

Chapter 13

Finding Refuge
...at Last

We buried my friend's 26-year-old son last week. An accidental gunshot took Jeff's life. We have more questions than answers. We are offended at people who have all the answers and no experience with devastating loss.

I watched the heart-wrenching scenes as the family tried to come to grips with their tragedy. I can still hear the travailing of the mother's anguished heart. I can still see the wrenching of the father's grief-worn hands. I can still feel the distraught sobs that racked the sister's body as I held her. I can still smell the hospital and the funeral home. Memories march before my mind like soldiers, causing me to relive the agony. If it's this difficult for me, Jeff's godmother, how much more magnified it must be for his birth mother! I can't imagine.

As I watched Jeff's mom, Carol, the week after his death, I observed a miracle. I saw her move from despair to hope. From franticness to peace. From uncertainty to assurance. From needing comfort to extending it.

I witnessed a mom face her worst nightmare and refuse to run away. Instead, she ran to Him. When grief knocked the breath out of Carol, she went to the Breath Giver. I watched as the Lord placed His mantle of grace around her and then supported her with His mercy.

The grief process has just begun for Jeff's loved ones. The Lord will not remove His presence from the Porter family. But there may be moments when He will remove their awareness of His presence. That will allow them to feel the impact of their loss. For He knows it would be our tendency to hide even behind His grace to protect our fragile hearts from the harsh winds of reality. He offers us refuge, but He also promises us wholeness. Wholeness means we are fully present with ourselves and with Him. Therefore, we have to own our pain. If we don't, part of who we are we must either shut down, avoid, or deny. That would leave us estranged from ourselves and divided in our identity. Also, we would never heal in a way that would allow us to minister to others.

The God of all comfort does not seem to extend His comfort to make us comfortable. Perhaps that's because our tendency would be to become La-Z-Boy believers, content to crank back our chairs, put up our feet, and snooze through the losses of others. Instead, He offers His comfort that we might be motivated by mercy to tenderly extend kindness to the hurting.

All those who came to Bruce and Carol's house and to the funeral home brought with them two gifts. The first gift was allowing the Porters to feel pain, and the second was sharing the pain with them by their presence. Some, depending on how close they were to family members or to Jeff, would draw out more emotion than others. The closer they were, the stronger the response of pain, but also the greater was that person's ability to support and comfort.

I observed some who came to the funeral home because they could not stay away and yet were fearful to enter into the pain. They stood cautiously on the sidelines and seemed to be testing their ability to approach the family and speak. I watched as they finally risked stepping toward Jeff's loved ones. But before those mourners could speak, sobs filled their beings, and the family they came to help comforted them. The frightened visitors then quickly retreated, exhausted and shaken from the effort.

If we don't feel, weep, talk, rage, grieve, and question, we will hide and be afraid of the parts of life that deepen us. They make us not only wiser but also gentler, more compassionate, less critical, and more Christlike.

We went to dinner with Bruce and Carol after church on a Sunday. Before the meal, we joined hands, and Bruce prayed. It was tender; it was compassionate; it was insightful; it was powerful. I had never heard Bruce pray like that before. It was obvious he was embracing his pain and that God was sheltering him under His healing wings.

Our tendency is to believe we have one or the other, shelter or pain. But I believe God allows us the benefit of both. He does not remove the believer from reality but transforms the realities into righteousness for our welfare and His glory.

My 78-year-old mom came to the funeral home to offer condolences to the family. Carol leaned down to hug her, and my mom said in a voice full of empathy, "I know how you feel; I lost a son, too."

Realization spread across Carol's face as she remembered my brother's death, and with deep emotion she choked out, "Yes, yes, you know how I feel, you know how I feel." I stood by quietly as my mom and my friend held each other and wept tears of mutual understanding.

How healing it is when someone understands us! Recently I wrote a story about a friend and then read it to her. She wept. I asked her, "What are you feeling?"

She replied, "I feel understood—something I have felt so seldom in my life that it leaves me emotional."

There is someone who hears our hearts and understands even our unformed thoughts. Christ is that one. He woos us, and He waits for us to come to Him. With arms outstretched like open wings, He welcomes us. In this life we need a hiding place, and Christ offers us that—a place of comfort, a place of healing, but not a place of painlessness.

There will come a day for each of us when, like Jeff, we will reside where He presides and hiding won't be necessary, for we will be home . . . at last. Finally, we will be in a place where our tears will dry, our pain will pass, our hearts will heal, and we won't ever need to hide again—not from ourselves, not from each other, and, hallelujah, not from the One who knows us the best and loves us the most.